I0799846

IMAGES
of America

SEBAGO LAKE
WEST SHORE
STANDISH, BALDWIN, SEBAGO, AND NAPLES

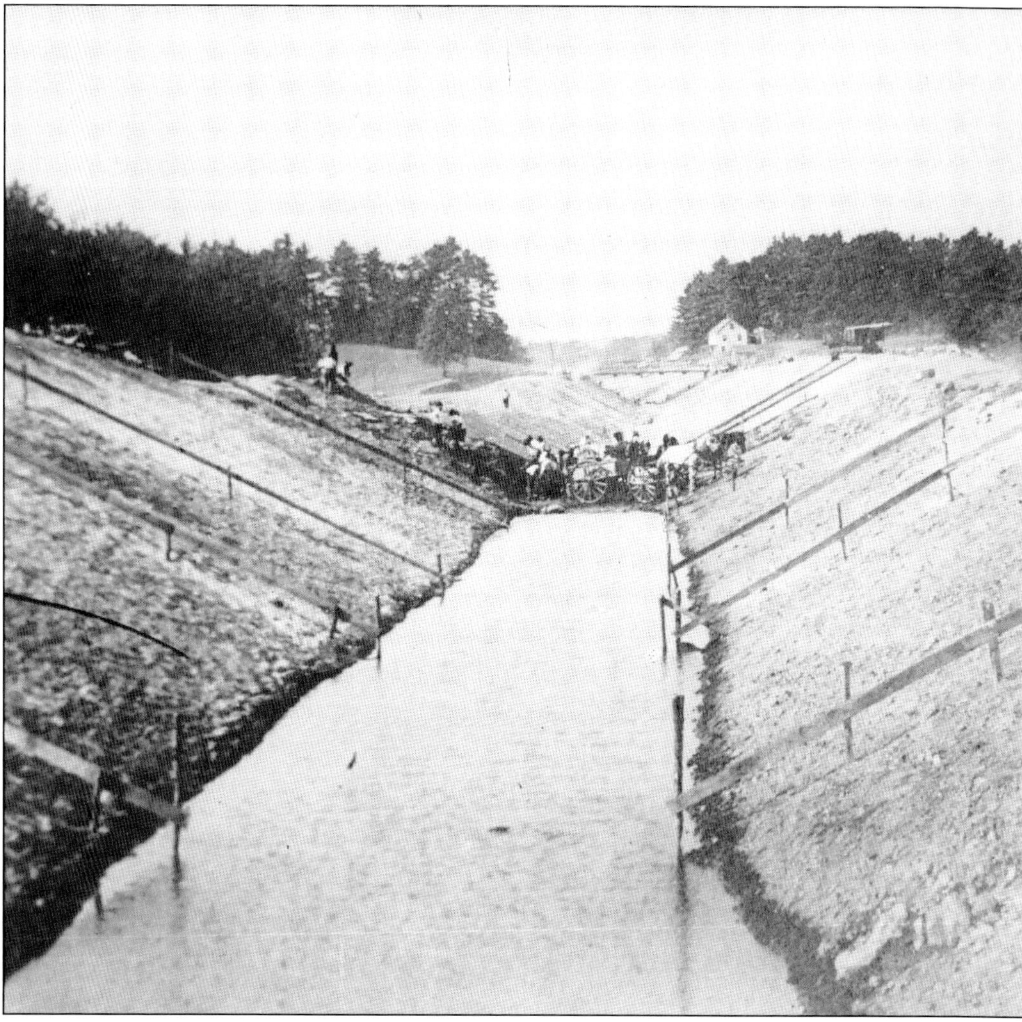

The Eel Weir Canal. In 1903, S.D. Warren of Westbrook purchased the water rights at the foot of the Sebago Lake Basin, constructed a granite dam, and then began to extensively deepen and widen the long-abandoned stretch of what had been the Cumberland & Oxford Canal as far as North Gorham where a dam and power station (still in operation) had been erected. The name was derived from the Eel Weir Lock, one of 27 locks built along the original Cumberland and Oxford Canal (1830–1870) that extended from the Sebago Lake Basin to Stroudwater in Portland. The lock was located in Standish just above the bridge, which spans the present canal on Route 35.

On the cover: Bachelder's Brook, *c.* 1908, empties into Sebago Lake between Cox's Point and the breakwater constructed by the residents of North Sebago.

IMAGES
of America

SEBAGO LAKE
WEST SHORE
STANDISH, BALDWIN, SEBAGO, AND NAPLES

Jack and Diane Barnes

ARCADIA
PUBLISHING

ISBN 978-0-7385-0156-7

Published by Arcadia Publishing
Charleston, South Carolina

Printed in the United States of America

Library of Congress Catalog Card Number: 99069058

For all general information contact Arcadia Publishing at:
Telephone 843-853-2070
Fax 843-853-0044
E-mail sales@arcadiapublishing.com
For customer service and orders:
Toll-Free 1-888-313-2665

Visit us on the Internet at www.arcadiapublishing.com

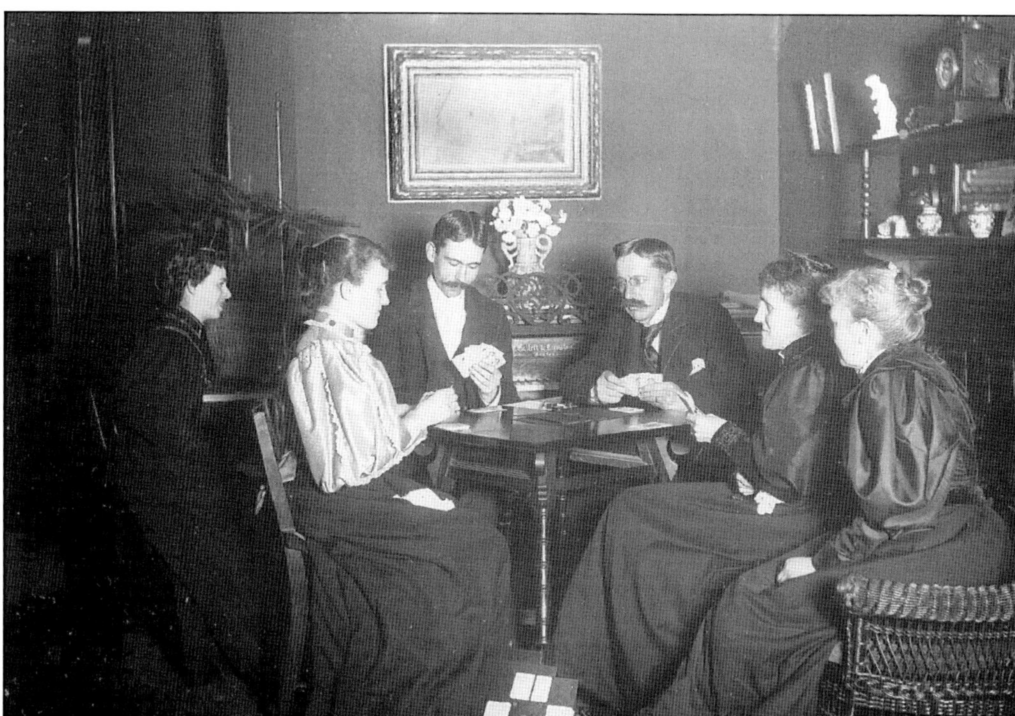

AN EVENING OF BRIDGE, C. 1890. This Victorian-attired coterie, very likely made up of summer residents, enjoys a pleasant evening of bridge in what may be the present residence of Mildred and Robert Walker on Route 35 near Sebago Lake Village in Standish.

CONTENTS

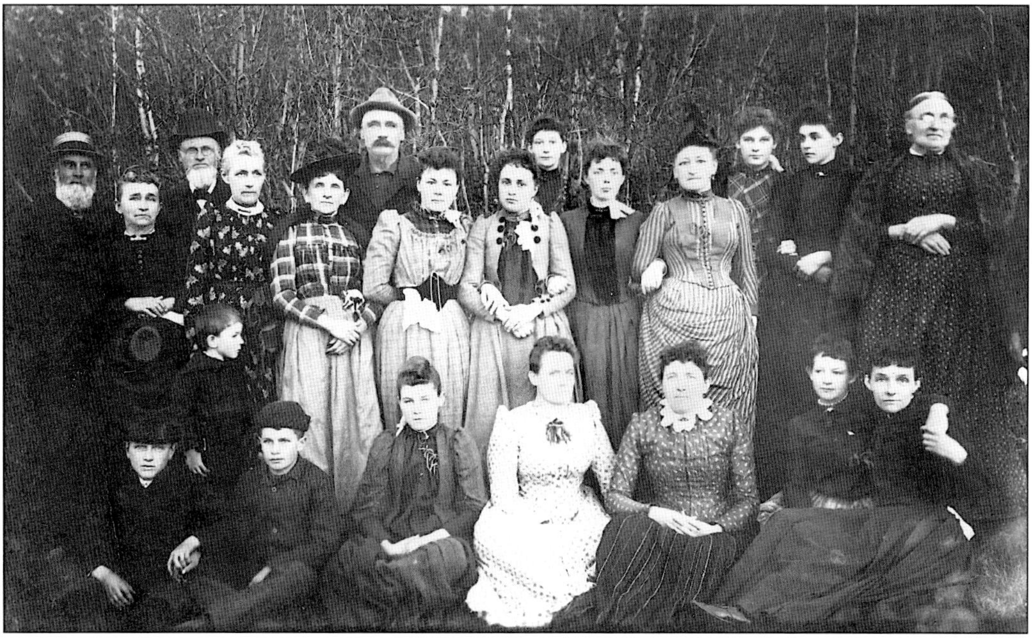

THE GATHERING, c. 1878, Gathered at New Limington (Convene) in Sebago are, from left to right, the following: (front row) Bert Gray, Henry Weed, Charles Haley, Eva Whitney, Ella Pike, Lon Richardson, Lucy Pike, and Sarah Haley; (middle row) Mrs. Robertson, Delphine Weed, Rose Gray, Berta Lombard, Cary Lombard, ? Lombard, Rachel Dyer, and unidentified; (back row) Charles Davis, Andrew Robertson, Al Gray, and Jenny Whitney.

ACKNOWLEDGMENTS

In addition to expressing our profound appreciation for the indispensable help and generosity of the Standish, Baldwin, Sebago, and Naples Historical Societies, we should like to extend our gratitude to the following individuals and companies: David Robinson, Harold Jordan, Beryl Jacobson, Ethel Hulett, Janet Logan, Jolene Webber, Myrlice Waite, David Drew, Mildred Walker, Richard Higgins, the Standish Telephone Company, Ruth Chaplin, Audrey and Edna Kenney, Paul and Vaneta Burnell, Madeline Wescott, Mary T. Watson, Clayton Locke, Ruth and Roy Wood, Harrison Wood, Lester Wood, Woods Mill, Eleanor Mitchell, Marcia McKenney, Pearl and Norman McKenney, Carolyn Brooks, Josiah Pierce, Glenn Hains, Henry Black, Shirley and Gordon Milliken, Olive Sanborn, Mabel Rounds, Etta Riley, Lauren Sanborn, Mary Flint Irwin, Leona Greene, Dot and Kenneth Douglas, John Douglas, Evelyn and Audrey Martin, Mose Russo, James Taylor, Eulalie Lewis, June Allen, Janet Anderson, Ned Allen, Alice Allen, Robie Bachelder, Betty Moriarity, Larry Nason, Ann Burns, Franklin Irish, Herbert Jones, Irene Bragdon, Harold Butler, Meryl Watson, Andrew Buck, Donald Buck, William Weeks, Wilma Irish, Robert Dingley, Nancy Hanson, Ernest Knight, the Sebago Lake Garage, Hubert Clemons, Richard Fraser, Robert McDonald, Paul Neal, Ed Pierce, Joyce Bibber, and Joel Eastman.

INTRODUCTION

Since the earliest European settlers began straggling into the wilderness area and building rude shelters, clearing land for subsistence agriculture, damming up streams, and erecting sawmills and gristmills, the four Cumberland County towns featured in this work have been closely bonded economically and, to a degree, socially and culturally, to the west shore of Maine's second largest freshwater body and one of New England's loveliest watersheds: Sebago Lake. Even before any of these four towns—Standish, Baldwin, Sebago, and Naples—were settled or incorporated, loggers ventured up the Presumpscot River to the Sebago Basin and began harvesting the colossal white pine along Sebago's primeval forested shoreline. Prime logs, many of them destined for the masts of the king's vessels, were floated and poled down to Falmouth (Portland) Harbor by the same water routes from which the loggers had arrived with their saws, axes, and oxen. And it was this water route, along with the Saco River, that provided the early intrepid settlers with arteries by which they were able to penetrate the wilderness hinterland with their families and meager livestock.

Gradually, more and more settlers arrived at the fort in Pearsontown (Standish). After Quebec had fallen to the British and the Peace of Paris was signed in 1763, ending well over a century of French and Indian wars, many of the settlers chose to continue on to Flintstown (Baldwin), and farther up the Saco River and the Pequawket Trail. Not long after Standish and Baldwin were incorporated, farmers, craftsmen, and mill owners were producing more than could be marketed locally. However, it was a slow and tortuous route by land to the waiting markets in Portland and beyond. Consequently, entrepreneurs began looking to the identical route taken by the early loggers and settlers to Sebago Lake. But since the Presumpscot River was only partially navigable, it became clear that a canal linking Portland to Sebago Lake was necessary to alleviate the transportation dilemma. So in 1821, the Cumberland & Oxford Canal was chartered. The initial plans were to provide an efficient all-water route from Portland to Waterford Flat.

By 1827, construction of the canal got under way, and it was completed and operable by 1830, four years after Sebago separated from Baldwin and four years before Naples became incorporated. In the ensuing 40 years that the canal was maintained, the 50-mile waterway from Portland to Harrison conveyed tons of produce, products, and passengers to and from the Sebago Lake area, including the four towns in this study. It was a gateway to the outside world. By 1870, the railroad out of Portland reached the shores of Sebago Lake, ending the colorful, abbreviated canal era but at the same time ushering in an exciting new era: that of the steamboat.

Excursionists and vacationers could step off the train at Sebago Lake Station, embark on an awaiting steamboat at the long wharf there, and enjoy a scenic trip up Sebago Lake via the Notch between Frye Island and the Raymond Cape. Then they would twist and turn up the sinuous Songo to either disembark at Naples at the confluence of the Chute River and the foot of Long Lake or continue the 12 miles up the elongated waterway to Harrison. By 1883, the miniature Bridgton and Saco River Railroad had reached Bridgton, and by August 1898, Harrison. Many steamboat passengers chose to disembark at Plummer's Landing in Bridgton or at Harrison and return to Portland by taking the lilliputian train to the Bridgton Junction at Hiram and transferring to the Maine Central's White Mountain Division.

The dynamic steamboat era and the ever-surging influx of summer visitors impacted the hamlets and hill farms, as well as communities along the lakeshore, such as Sebago Lake Village, East Sebago, and Naples Village, at a time beginning around 1880 when agriculture was on a rapid decline. Hill farms as well as farms near the chain of waterways converted to boardinghouses. Soon thereafter, hotels such as the magnificent Bay of Naples Hotel and the Douglas Inn in Sebago, several miles inland from the lake, were opened. Shortly thereafter, numerous boys' and girls' camps were founded on the shorelines of the lakes and ponds. Those who had not forsaken agriculture found a ready market for their produce, and a large percentage of the indigenous population found much needed employment.

With the growing popularity of the automobile, roads improved. The steamboat era ended, and a few decades later the trains stopped running. Overnight cabins and later motels replaced the boardinghouses, inns, and hotels. Today, there are fewer and fewer boys' and girls' camps, but summer cottages have mushroomed along the shores of the lakes and ponds and no longer does tourism come to an end after Labor Day. Those currently gleaning a living from the prevailing glacial soil in the four towns comprising the west shore of Sebago Lake are minuscule, and only the lumber mills in East Baldwin still hum. More than ever, though, the ineffable scenic beauty of Sebago Lake and its surrounding environs and the broad spectrum of outdoor activities that the area affords continue to attract greater numbers of visitors, thus greatly enhancing the economy. Furthermore, with an increasing number of people converting summer cottages into year-round homes and buying up and renovating what were once working farms, the four towns have become decisively cosmopolitan.

Through vignettes from old photographs accompanied by exposition and narrative, we have attempted to present a brief sketch of the early development of the four towns in this work and to depict what the west shore of Sebago Lake was like from the second half of the 19th century, before it was drastically altered during the two decades or so following the end of World War II.

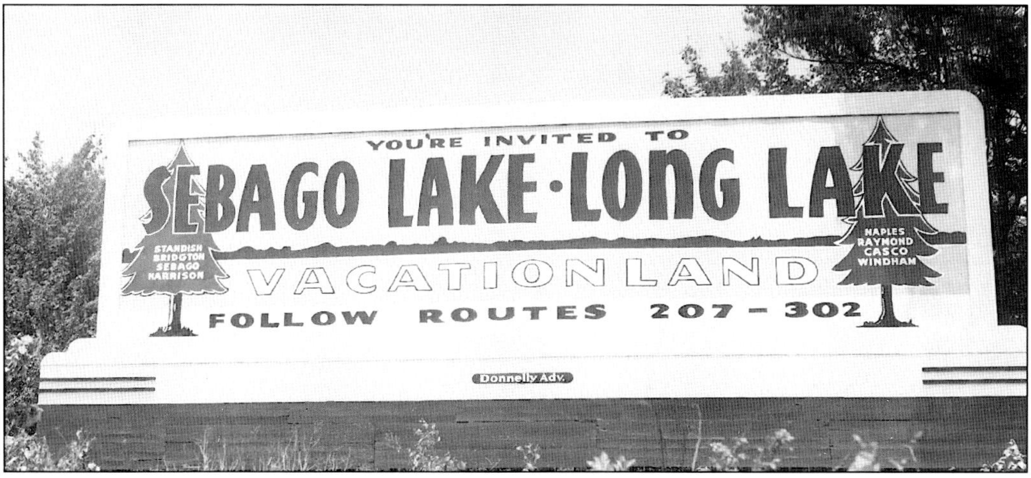

A Welcome Sign. We welcome you to beautiful Sebago Lake land and especially the West Shore.

One

STANDISH

First Settled: 1750
Incorporated: 1785
Population: 7,000
Area: 61.4 square miles
Principal Settlements: Standish Corner, Steep Falls, Sebago Lake Village, Richville

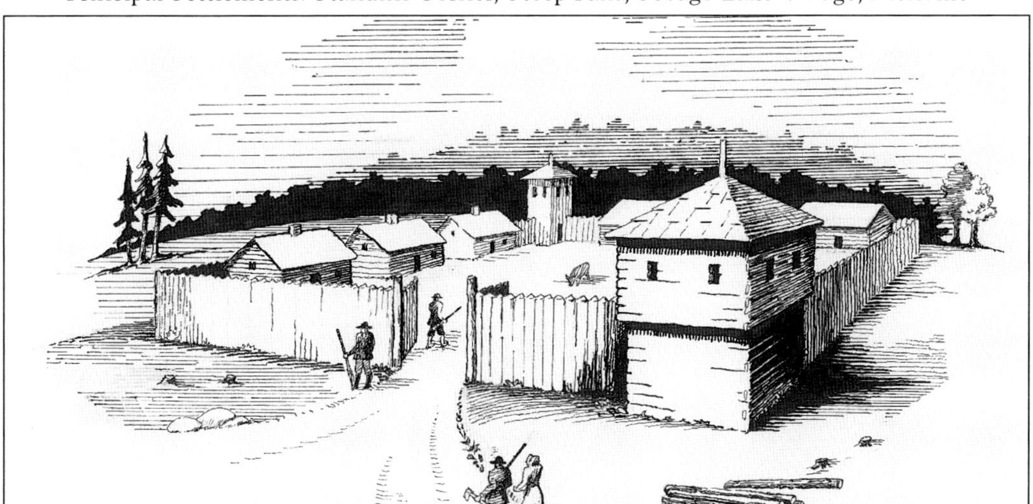

THE PEARSONTOWN FORT. The Pearsontown Fort (sketched by Richard Higgins) was erected in 1754, following a meeting held in Falmouth by Moses Pearson and other proprietors of the infant township of Pearsontown, at what is now the intersection at Standish Corner, where the old town pump used to stand. It provided the earliest intrepid settlers with protection from the threat of Indian attacks while they cleared and began tilling the land in the shadows of the blockhouse and palisades. Although it was partly destroyed by fire set by Indians before its construction was completed, there is no evidence that it was ever attacked thereafter. Without this crude fortress, it is unlikely that Standish would have been settled until after the British captured Quebec in 1759.

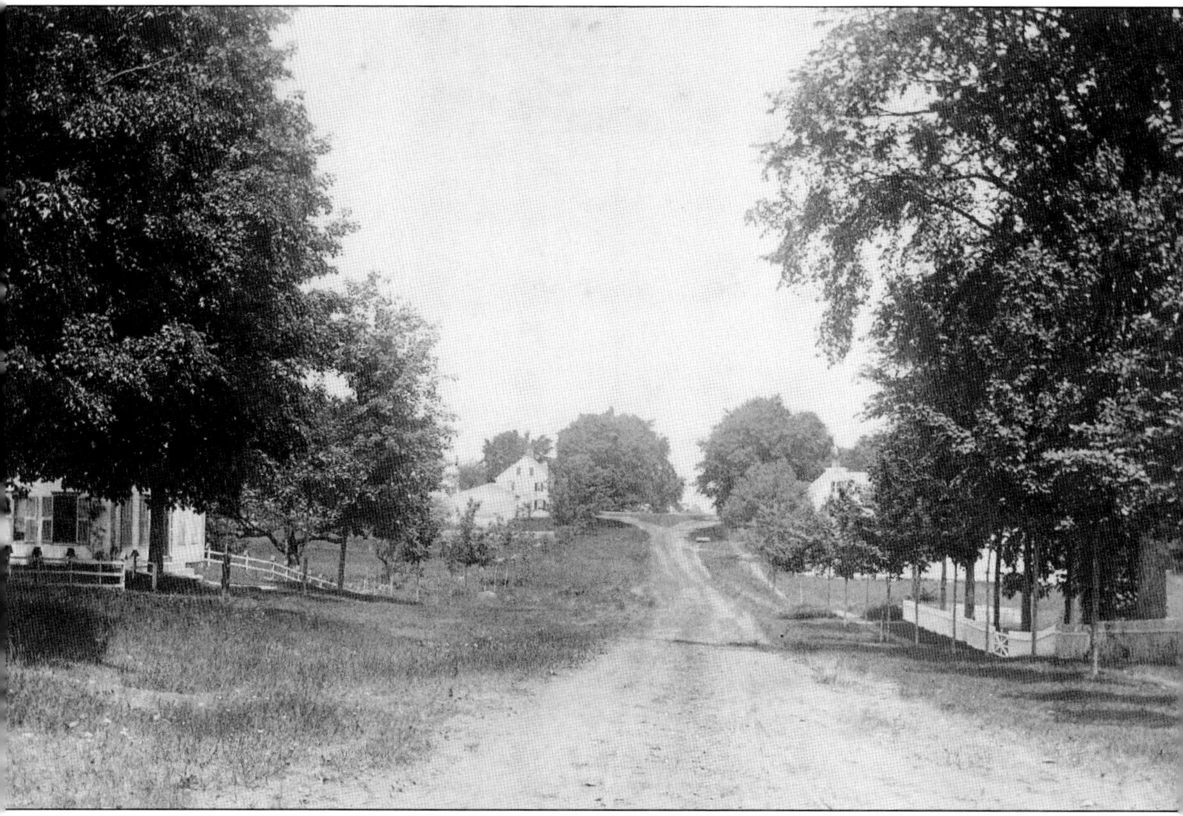

WHERE ROADS CONVERGED C. 1890. Dusty Bonny Eagle Road (now Route 35) leads down to elm-shaded Standish Corner, at the time a bustling community. The large house down at the corner on the left, opposite the location of the old fort, was built by Sam Dennett in 1793 and is now the home of Richard Higgins. The house behind the picket fence in the right foreground (now the location of the Standish Professional Building) is the Cressy homestead. Standish, located in the southwestern corner of Cumberland County, owes its existence to Capt. Moses Pearson and 39 men from Falmouth (Portland), veterans of King George's War (1744–1748), who participated in the successful capture from the French of Louisburg on Cape Breton Island in 1745, and to Captain Humphrey of Amherst, New Hampshire, who fought in a different theater. Their only hope of compensation for their valor and the hardships they endured was to petition the General Court of Massachusetts in 1749 for a grant of land located in York County in the province of Maine. The petition was granted on April 20, 1750. The proprietors were allotted approximately 39,000 acres, which included the Raymond Cape (annexed to Raymond in 1869) and Frye's (Frye) Island (which became Maine's newest town on July 5, 1998). Although originally named Hobbs and Pearsontown, the name was changed to just Pearsontown after Hobbs succumbed to smallpox at Fort William Henry on Lake George, New York, in 1757, while participating in the last of the French and Indian wars. In 1785, the name was changed to Standish in honor of the famous Capt. Miles Standish. Only two of the Falmouth proprietors, Ephraim Jones Sr. and Benjamin Mussey, actually settled in Standish. Although Moses Pearson never lived in the town originally bearing his name, he was largely instrumental in its settlement, sparing neither money nor energy. Certainly, however, much credit for setting Standish in motion goes to Ebenezar Shaw and his son Josiah, who built the first sawmill in Pearsontown in 1762. Thanks to Timothy Higgins, who built a water-powered gristmill on his farm at Oak Hill in 1792, local farmers no longer had to travel two days to the gristmill in Saccarappa (Westbrook).

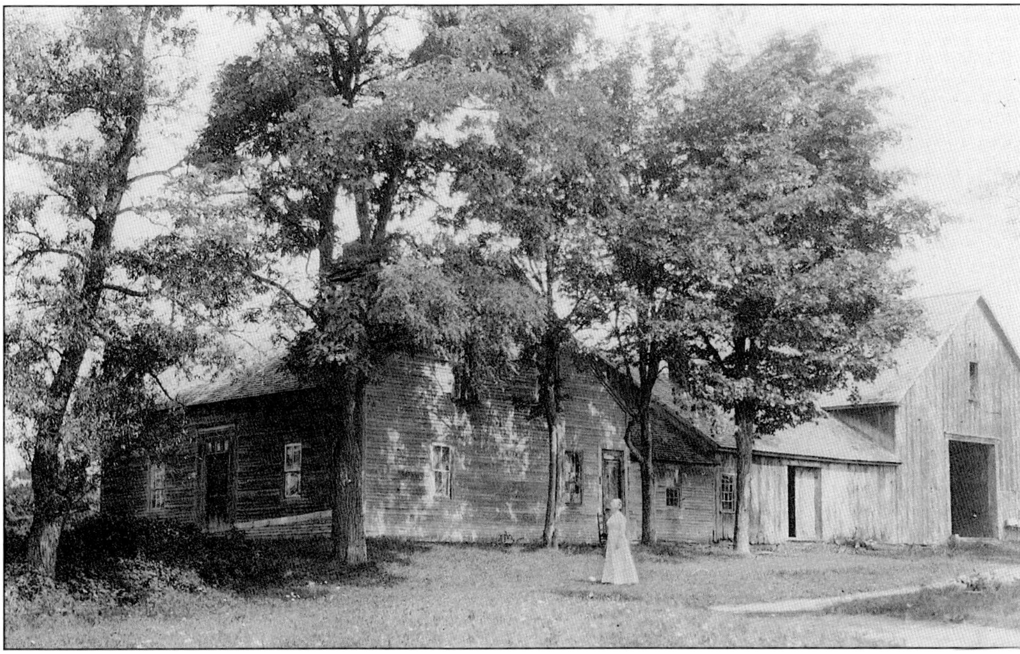

THE JOSIAH SHAW HOMESTEAD, C. 1895. The Josiah Shaw Homestead was built by the son of Ebenezar Shaw in 1774 at the corner of Route 25 and the Blake Road. It was Josiah who came from Hampton, New Hampshire, and helped his father build, in nine days, the town's first sawmill on the Shaw's Mill Road, which provided the beams and rough lumber for this and similar early dwellings.

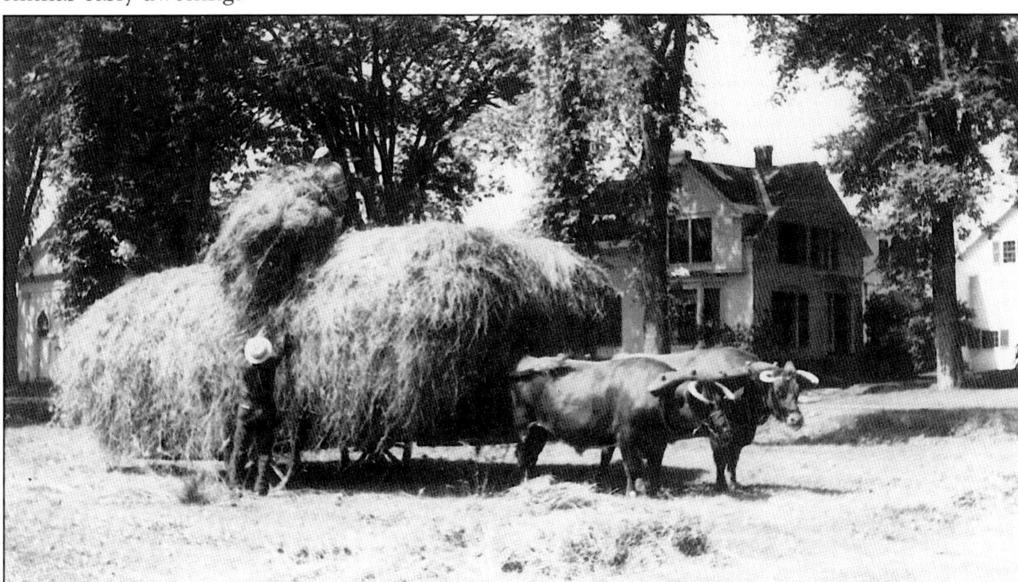

THE GATHERING, C. 1910. Herbert W. Dow and an unidentified helper display impressive skill in making a load of hay in a field between what is now Route 25 and the Oak Hill Road, which in more recent times has been replaced by an asphalt parking lot for the Standish Supermarket, now occupied by Seavey's. Many, like Dow, preferred working with oxen, as "they're calmer than a horse and less stubborn than a mule."

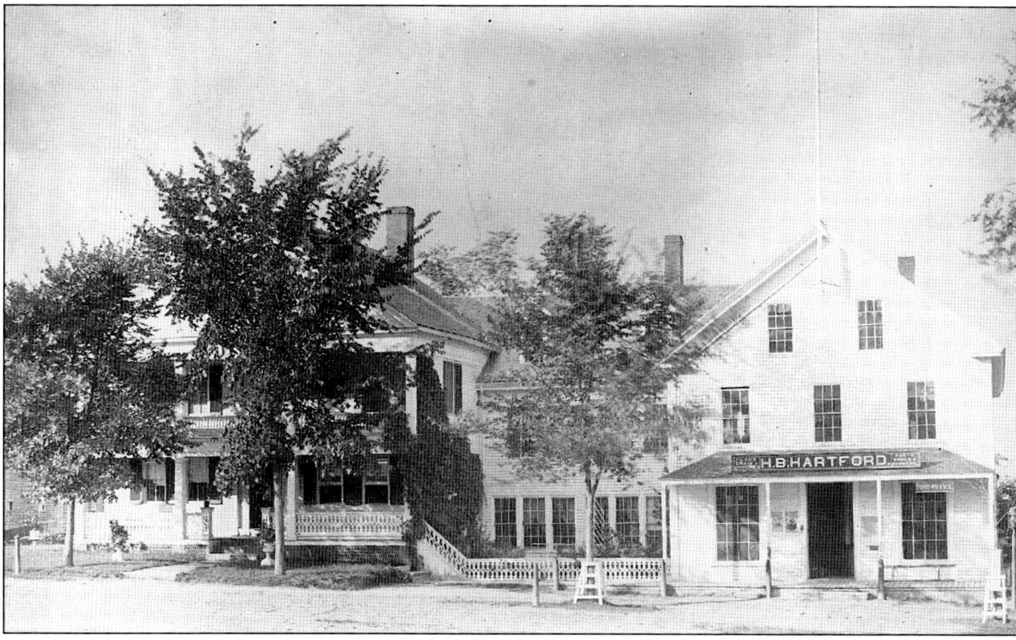

The Original Henry B. Hartford Complex, c. 1900. Henry B. Hartford lived in this magnificent Greek Revival house and operated, with Albert Butterfield, the store and post office attached at Standish Corner, where the Tavern on the Hill is now located. Hartford's son Harry ran a printing office upstairs, where the Standish Telephone Company (and later its first switchboard) was also initially located. It was originally called the Hartford Line, because in 1895 Hartford built the town's first telephone line connecting his store with his cottage on Watchic Lake.

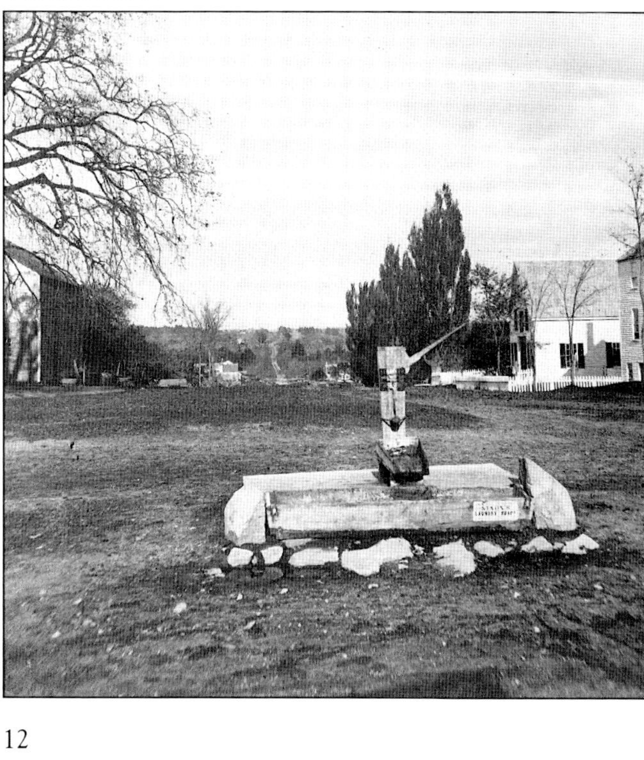

The Old Town Pump, 1879. Until shortly after the Portland & Ogdensburg Railroad was built, Standish Corner not only hummed with economic activity but also provided a vital link to towns much farther inland, all the way to Vermont. In the 19th century, it is said that the road through Standish to Portland was four lanes: the center lanes for horses and the two outer lanes for the methodical oxen. Beginning in the early 1820s, this well and pump provided cool water for travelers, teamsters, and beasts here at the crossroads, looking east. The last pump to stand here was rescued by Dick Higgins in the 1950s as new construction at the corner got under way.

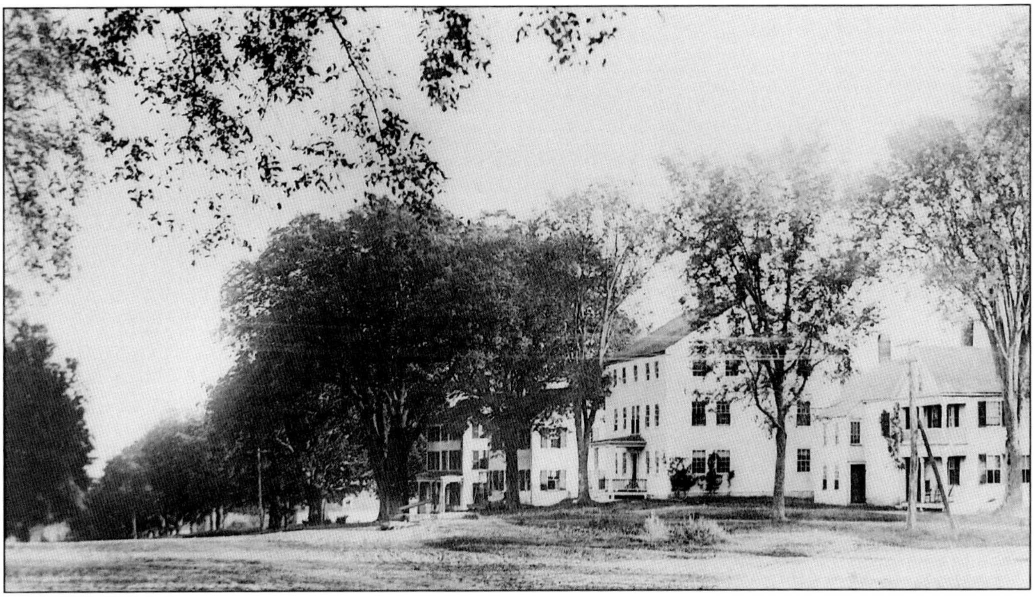

STANDISH CORNER, C. 1890. These stately homes, three of which still remain, were mute witnesses to so much history passing by their doors, especially the imposing relic of the stagecoach days: the three-and-a-half-story Tompson House and Tavern. The Tompson House was built *c.* 1801 by William Tompson, son of Rev. John Tompson, who moved to Standish in 1768 and built a parsonage (later made into an inn and tavern by Edward Tompson).

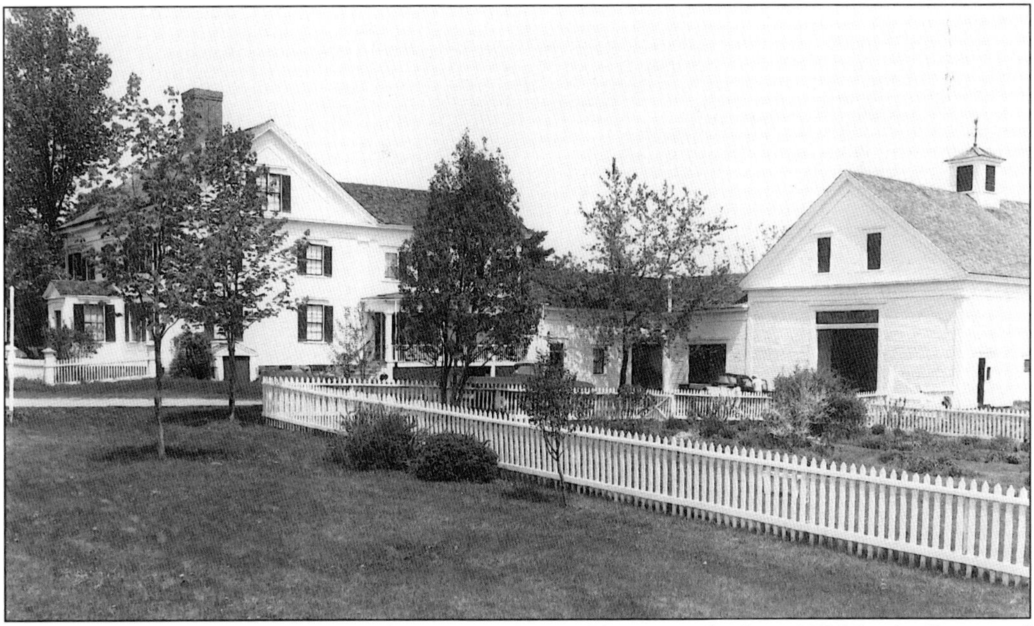

THE PARSON MARRETT HOUSE. The Parson Marrett House was built in 1789 by the Reverend Daniel Marrett, who is said to have owned the first horse cart and cookstove in town. The War of 1812 brought prosperity to Portland, where the banks in fear of a British invasion surreptitiously emptied their vaults of what was mostly gold bullion and had it trundled by six yoke of oxen out to the Marrett House for safe storage.

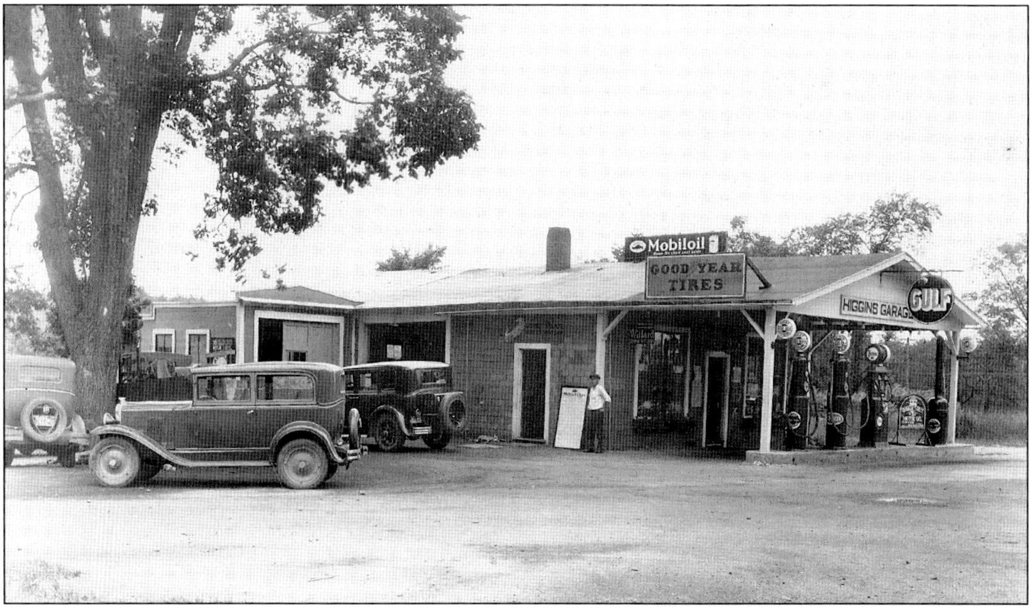

HIGGINS GARAGE, C. 1932. The automobile was in its infancy when Elmer Higgins purchased the Dennett homestead at Standish Corner in 1916 and two years later began operating a garage in his barn. In 1922, he completed this garage, located on the Ossipee Trail (Route 25). For many years it was run by his son Richard Higgins and is now owned by his grandson Robert.

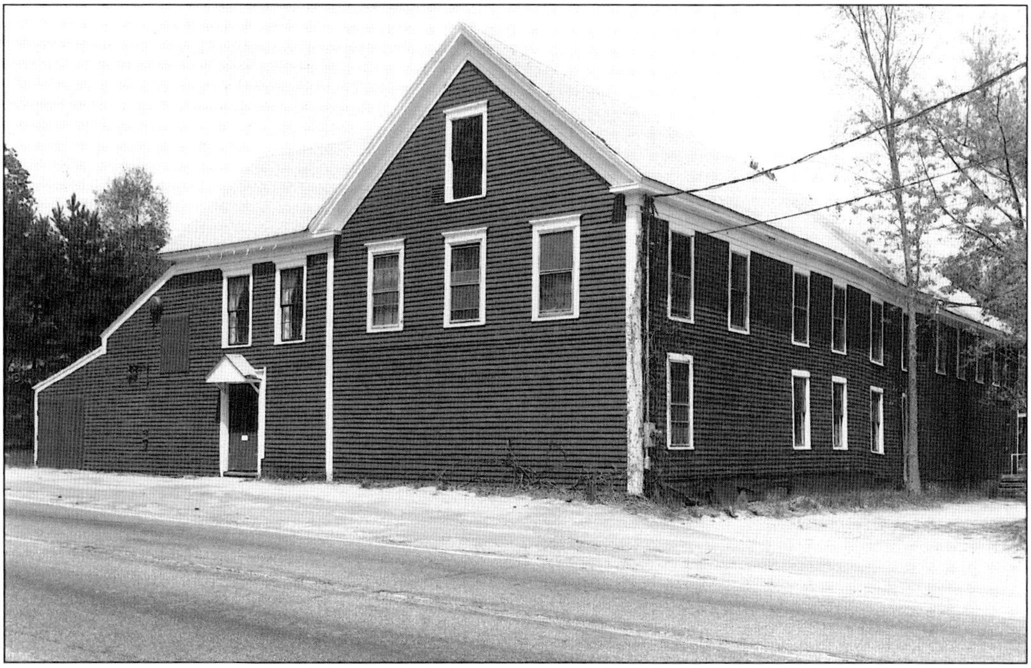

THE ORIGINAL HANOLD COMPANY, C. 1950. This company was built in the early 1920s, nearly opposite Higgins Garage, and was called Hanold's Shirtwaist Company. As the business began specializing in manufacturing sportswear for camps, schools, and retail, the name was changed to Hanold's Outfitting Company. In the 1960s, the company moved into a new building between Standish Corner and Sebago Lake. In 1996, the factory was closed.

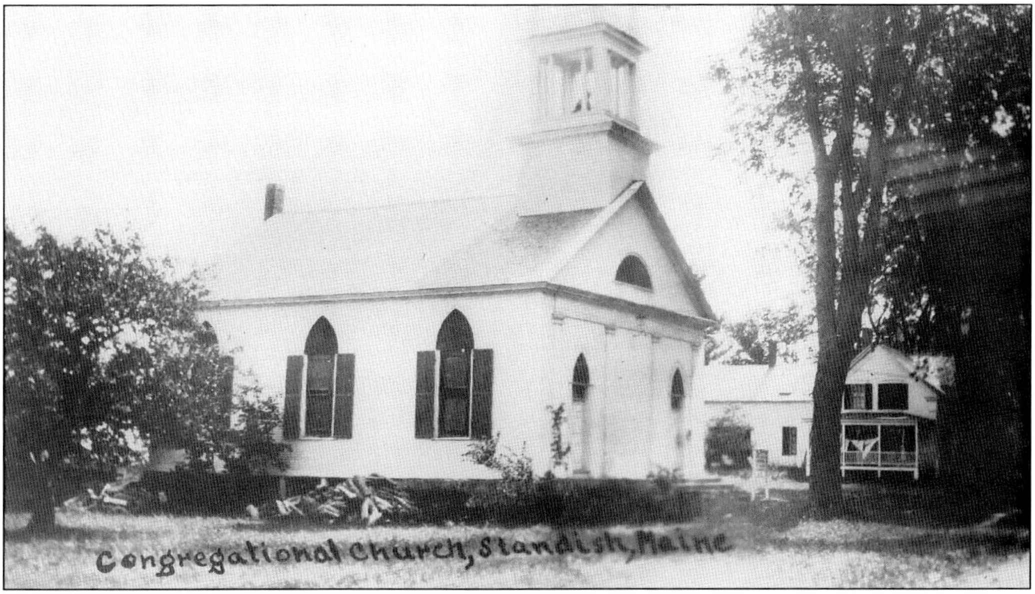

The Congregational Church. The Congregational church at Standish Corner on the Oak Hill Road was founded in 1834 by Reverend Tenney and a group who broke with the congregation at the Old Red Church, built between 1804 and 1806. Pearsontown's first minister was the Reverend John Tompson, who preached for 15 years at the first meetinghouse, said to have been built in 1766 from the timbers of the old Garrison.

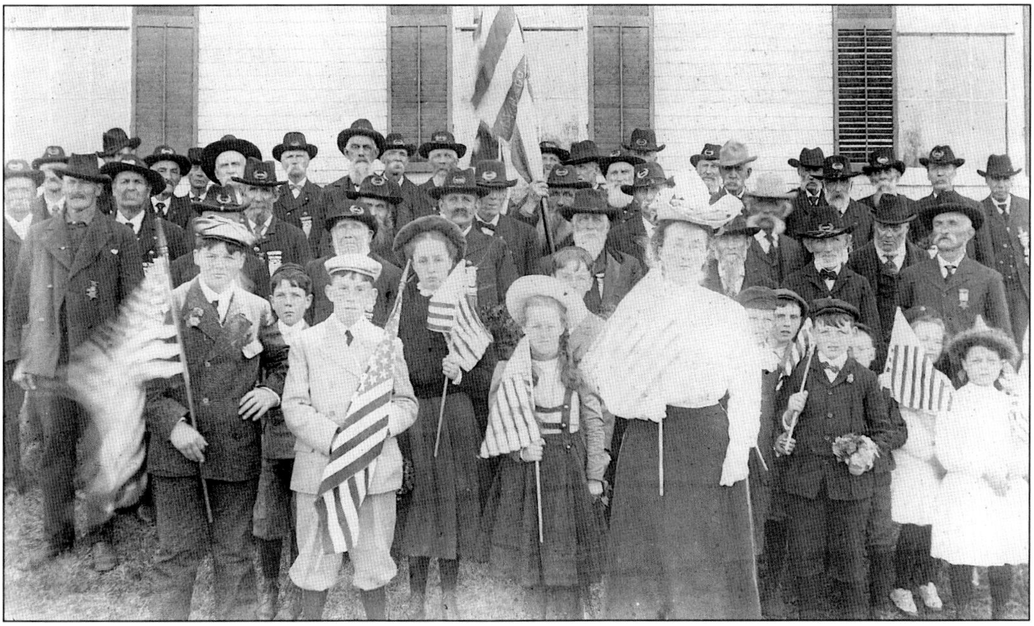

Honoring the Veterans, c. 1900. An impressive number of Civil War veterans of the Grand Army of the Republic gather at the and the C.A. Warren Post on this Memorial Day to be honored by South Standish schoolchildren and their teacher. The post is named after Charles A. Warren, who died in 1867 from wounds he received during the Battle of the Wilderness. Originally, this building was the Methodist Episcopal church located at Standish Corner, but it was moved here c. 1883.

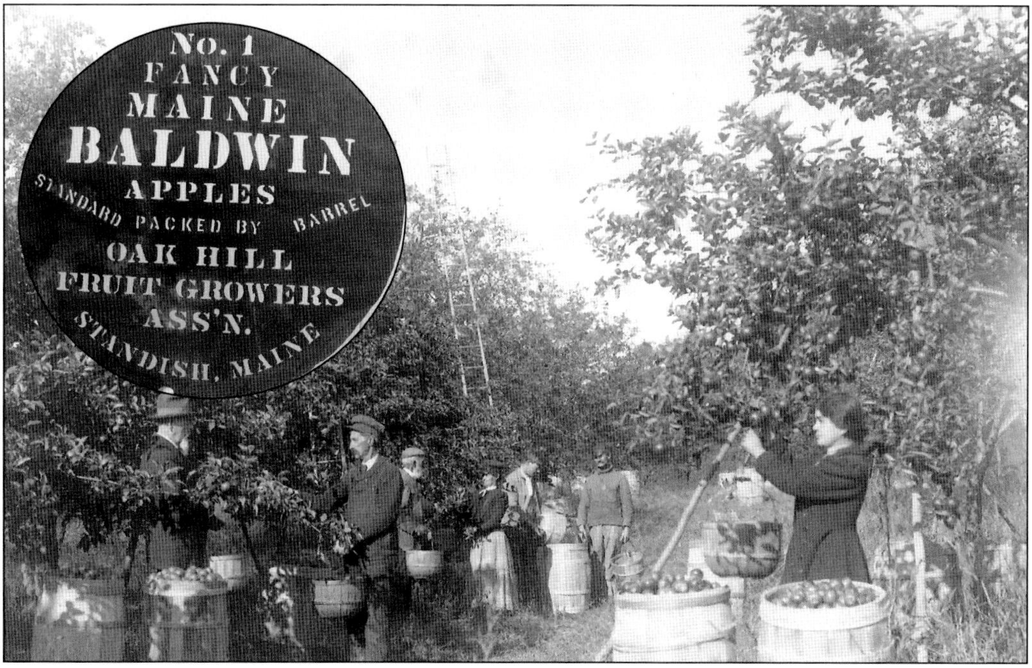

The Apple Harvest, 1907. The C.S. Phinney Orchards, located near Standish Corner on the Bonny Eagle Road (Route 35), and numerous other orchards in towns once linked to Portland by the C&O Canal, bristled with activity during the autumnal apple harvest. The barrels reflect the indispensability of the local coopers. Charles Chase, a Grand Army of the Republic veteran, is the man with the goatee.

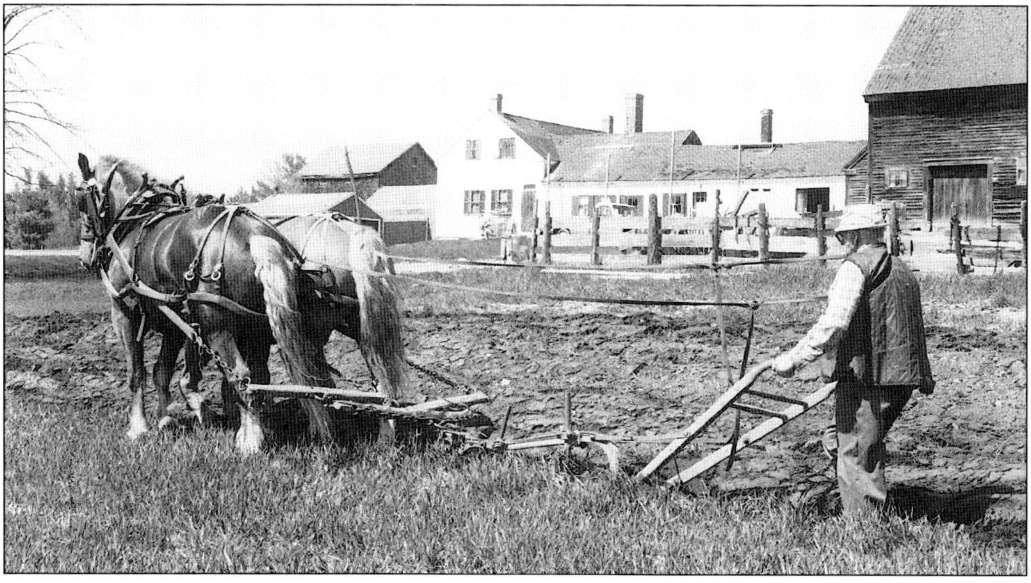

"He That Tilleth His Land Shall Be Satisfied." By the time Ralph Sturgis (born in 1911) was 3 years old, he was driving a pair of "hosses." He continued working with horses until he died in 1994. Here on his South Standish farm in his twilight years, he works in perfect unison with his team, turning over a velutinous carpet of turf, ever mindful of his grandfather's saying: "Turn over the sod and save hoe'n."

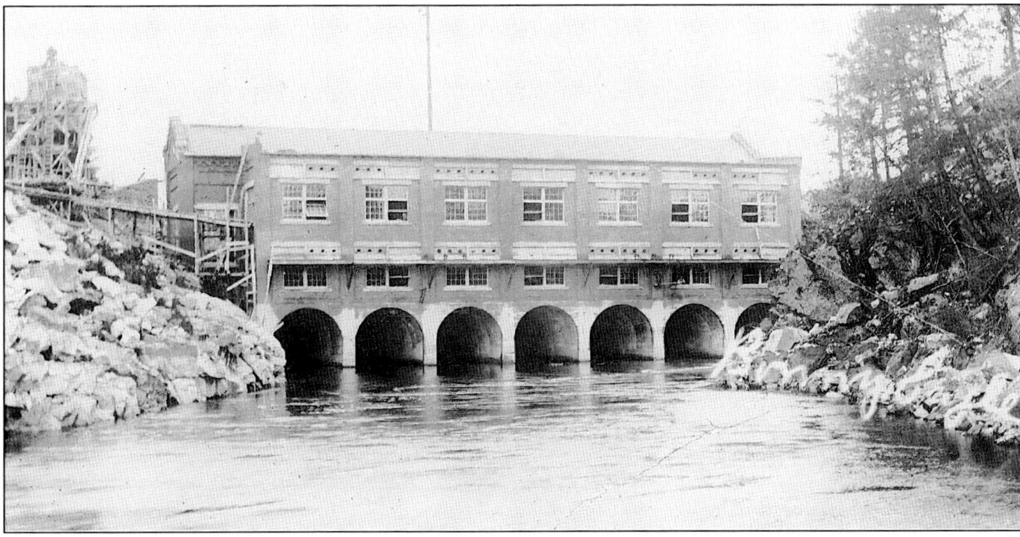

THE BONNY EAGLE POWERHOUSE, C. 1912. The Saco River first served as an artery all the way up to Pequawket (Fryeburg) and into New Hampshire, before a road was carved out of the wilderness, and later served as a vital conduit by which logs were floated down to the numerous sawmills that sprung up along its banks, all the way down to the Atlantic Ocean. The river also generated the power to turn the waterwheels and later the turbines for electricity. The Bonny Eagle Powerhouse was constructed between 1910 and 1912 at Bonny Eagle Island on the Saco.

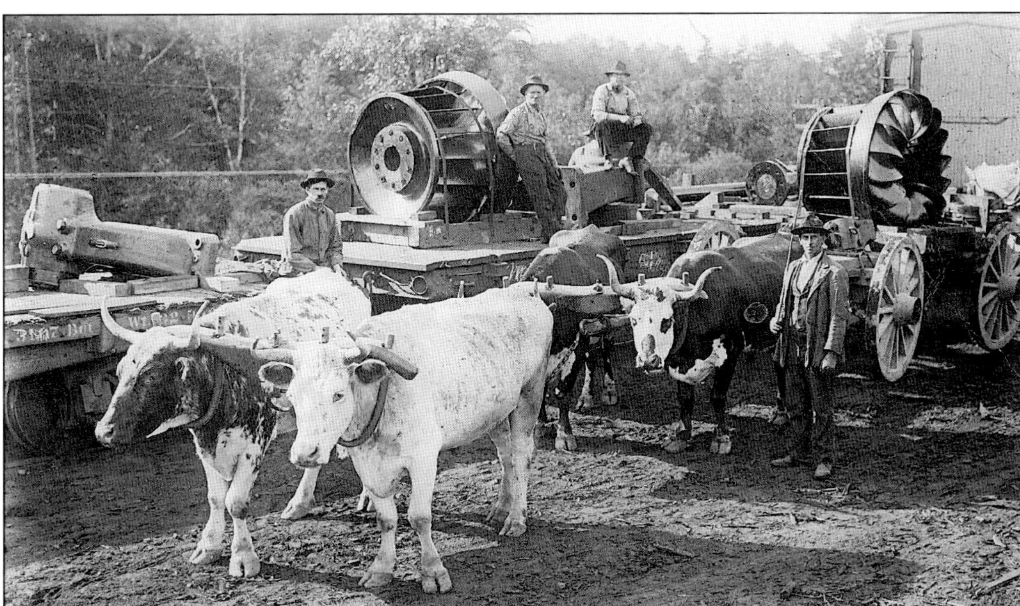

PREPARING FOR THE LONG HAUL, C. 1910. At the Buxton Depot, turbines for the powerhouse are being unloaded from a flatcar of the now defunct Sanford–Rochester Railroad onto an oxcart, which will convey them over the Mountain Road to Bonny Eagle Island.

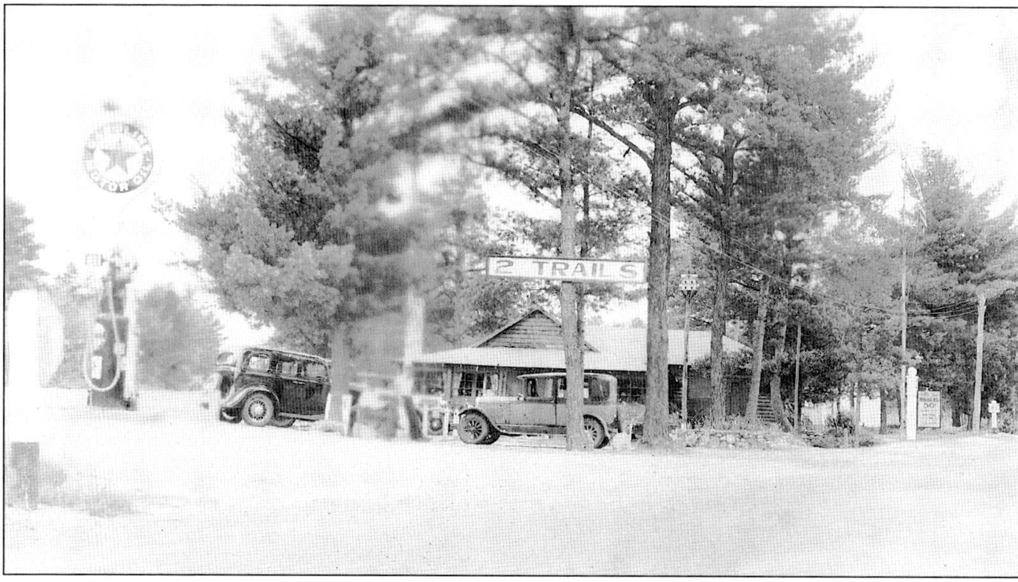

TWO TRAILS, AUGUST 4, 1936. For nearly three quarters of a century, Two Trails—where the Pequawket Trail (Route 113) branches off from the Ossipee Trail (Route 25)—has been a popular place for motorists and truckers to pause for sustenance and refreshment when passing either to or from Portland. At the time of this photograph, Two Trails was owned by the Switzers.

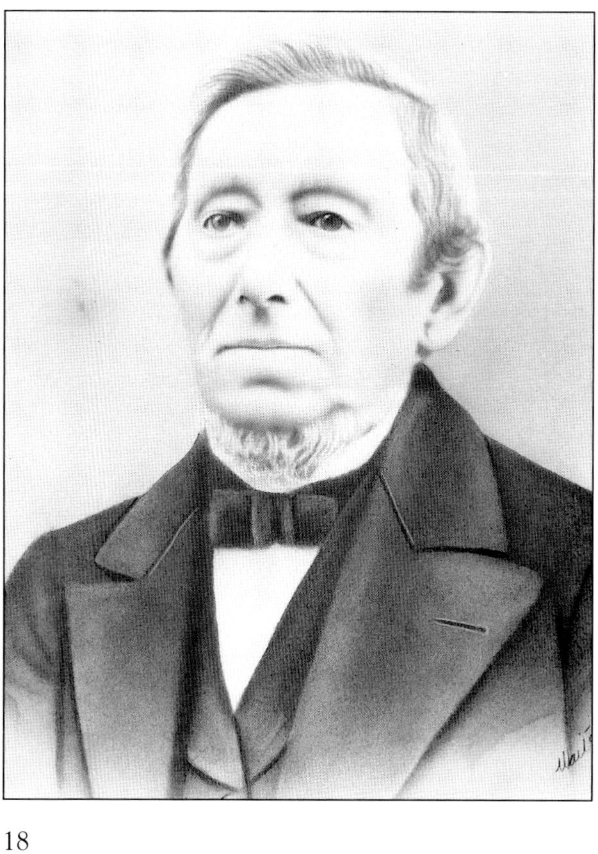

MYRICK PAINE. Myrick Paine (1769–1858) was the eldest of the three sons of Joseph Paine, who originally came from Cape Cod, moved to the Oyster River area in New Hampshire, and then to Cabbage Patch in Standish. The father purchased the land at Watchic Lake that is still referred to as the Paine Neighborhood. Later, Myrick and his two brothers, Richard and Joseph, moved out to Watchic Lake and began clearing land. Because of the substandard quality of the soil, however, they were limited to subsistence agriculture. But they were skilled coopers and carpenters, and each built his own cooper shop and made barrels, mostly for the Portland market. In 1797, Myrick Paine built the Cape at the bend in the road, which, is now owned by the Horners. Later, three other houses were constructed.

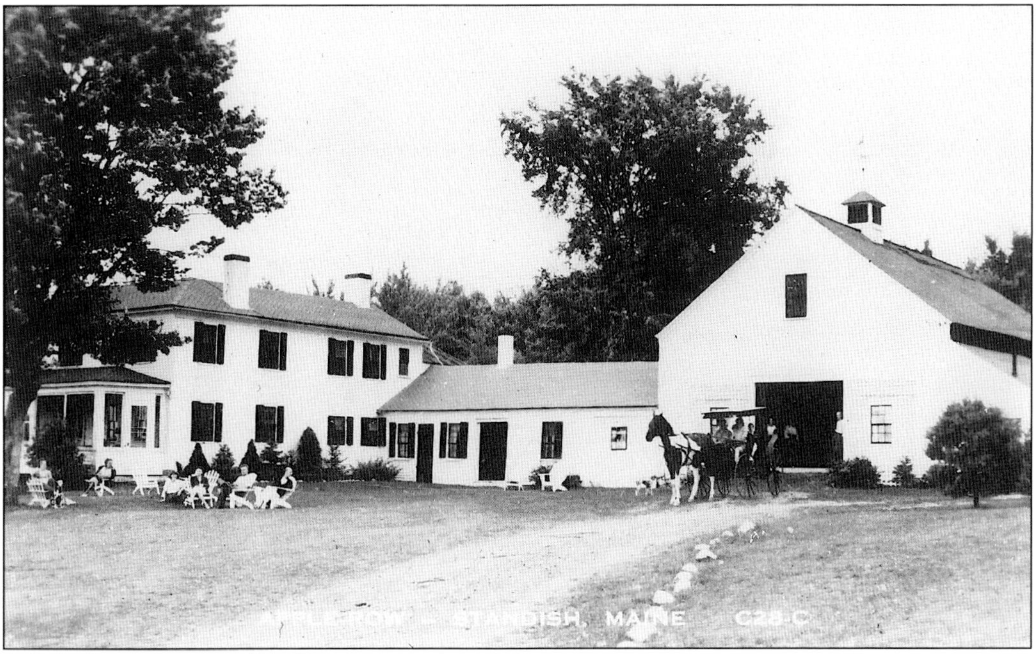

THE APPEL-ROWE FARM, C. 1950. This magnificent farmhouse constructed by the Paine brothers is an outstanding landmark on Route 113 overlooking Watchic (Pond) Lake. For many years Charles and Julia Stone owned the place and took in summer boarders. In 1938, Ruth Appel and Margaret Rowe, both educators from Massachusetts, purchased it, made significant improvements, and operated it as a resort and a riding stable.

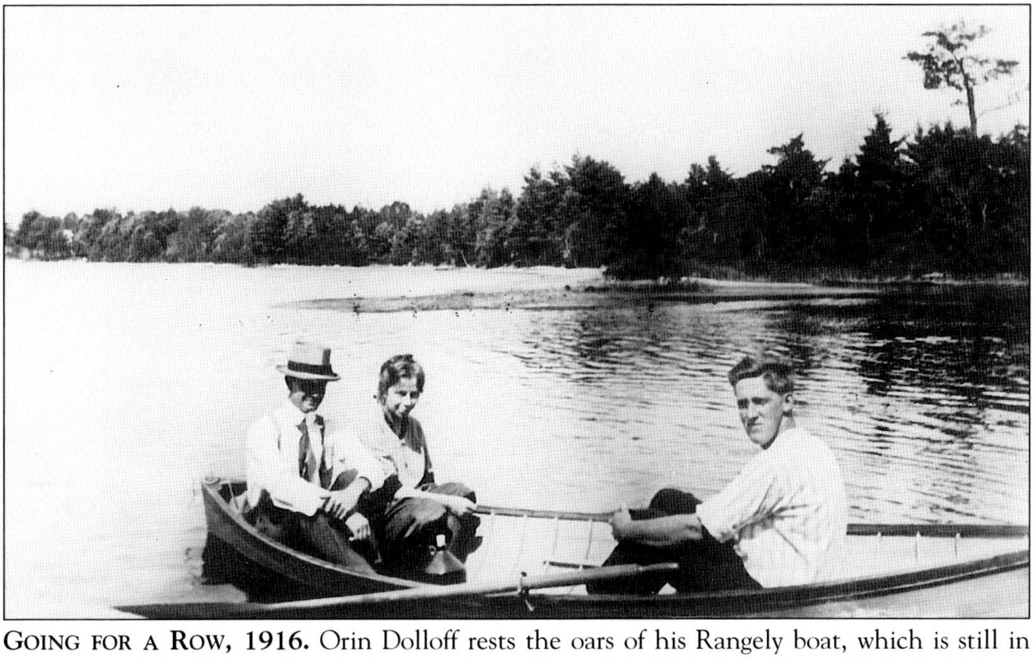

GOING FOR A ROW, 1916. Orin Dolloff rests the oars of his Rangely boat, which is still in existence, while George Beard, the principal of Standish High School, and Zelia Bridgham, Dolloff's future wife, enjoy a leisurely boat ride on the quiet waters of Watchic Lake, near the sandbar marking the entrance to Paine Brook.

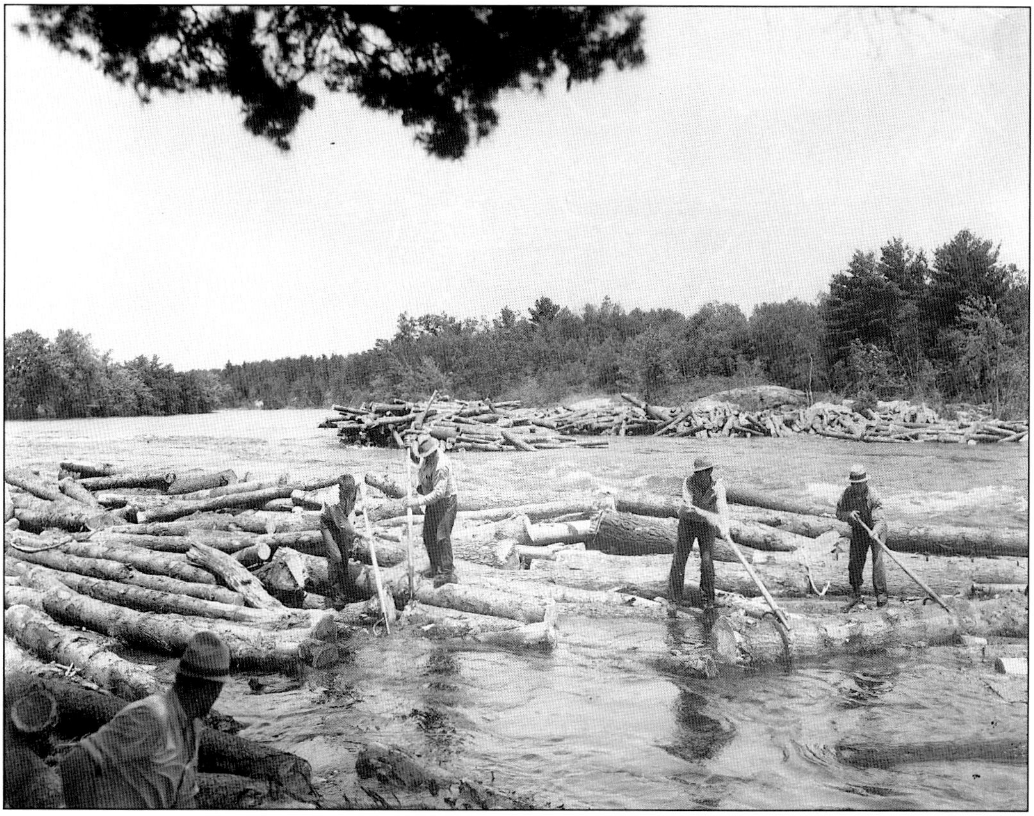

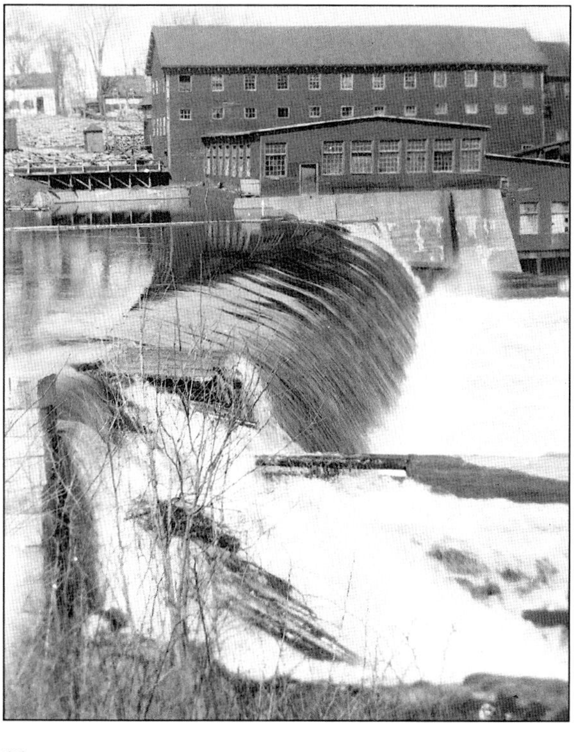

The Last Log Drive, July 1940. About as soon as the danger of Indians had ended, men ventured inland and began logging, branding, and floating the logs down the Saco River to feed the insatiable appetites of the numerous sawmills that had mushroomed along its banks. Because of economic factors rather than the environmental laws of later years, this was the last dramatic episode in which men, with their peaveys and poles, pitted their courage and skills against the swiftly flowing water of the Saco as they approached the Limington Bridge.

Steep Falls, c. 1920. The dam and falls on the Saco, which separate Limington and Standish, provided the power for this pulp mill, built by the Boston Excelsior Company *c.* 1892 on the Standish (Steep Falls) side of the river.

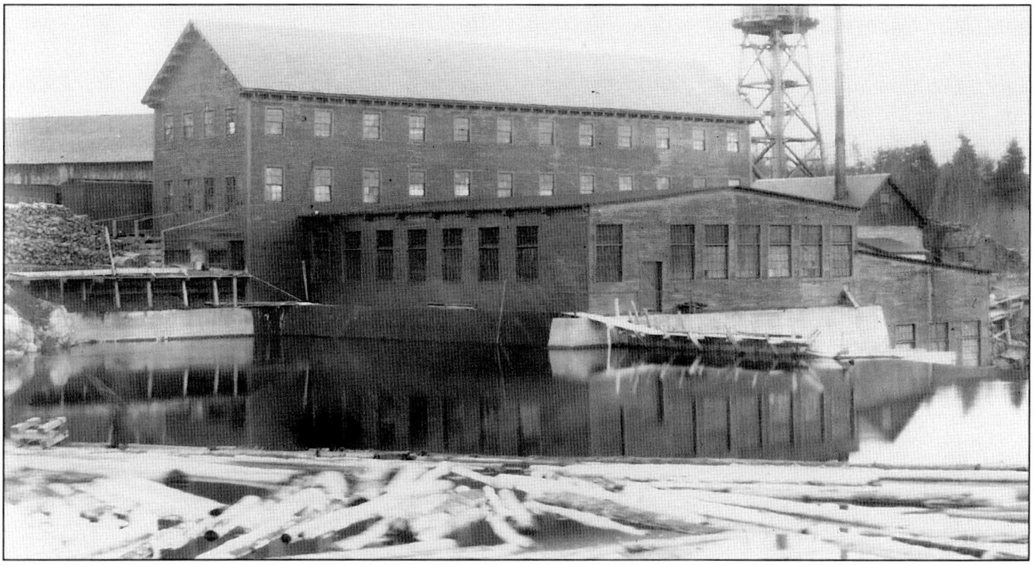

THE ANDROSCOGGAN PULP AND PAPER COMPANY, C. 1928. This mill complex built by the Boston Excelsior Company became known as the Androscoggan Pulp and Paper Company and produced pulp that was shipped by rail to South Windham to be processed into paper. Many of the logs used for pulp here at the mill were floated down the Saco River from Baldwin, Hiram, and even farther up the river. The area just above and below the falls at one time was referred to as the log landing. The mill burned in November 1935.

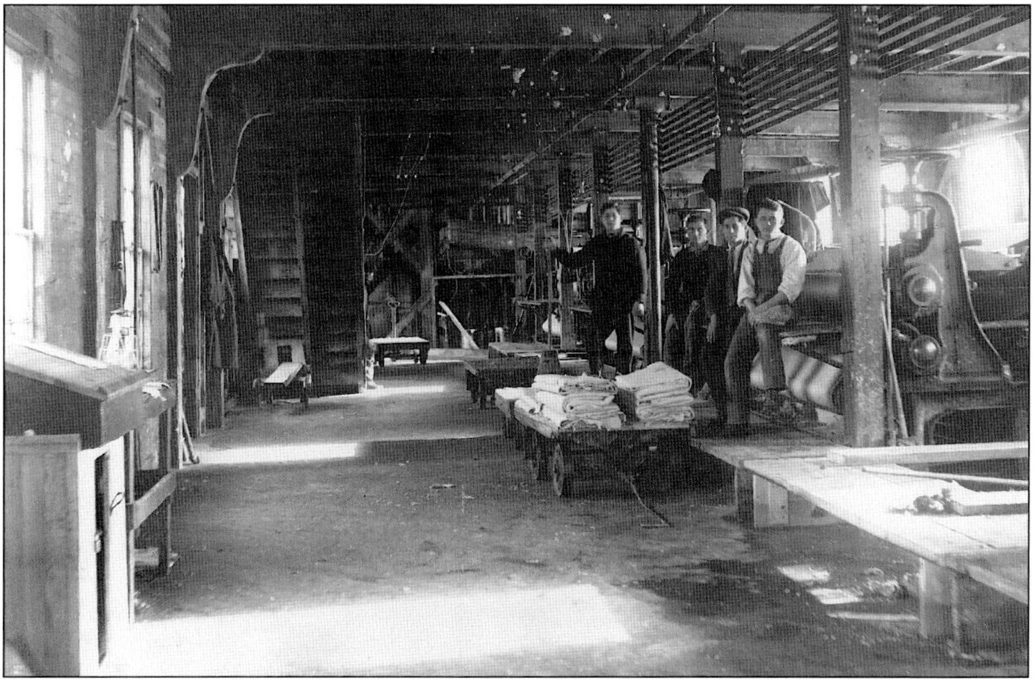

THE INNER WORKINGS, C. 1925. Four unidentified workers take a break from operating their machines (rollers and cutters) at the Androscoggan Pulp Mill, which was a real boon to Steep Falls until about 1930. A spur connected the mill with the Maine Central Railroad near the Steep Falls Station, thus adding to the importance of Steep Falls as a rail center.

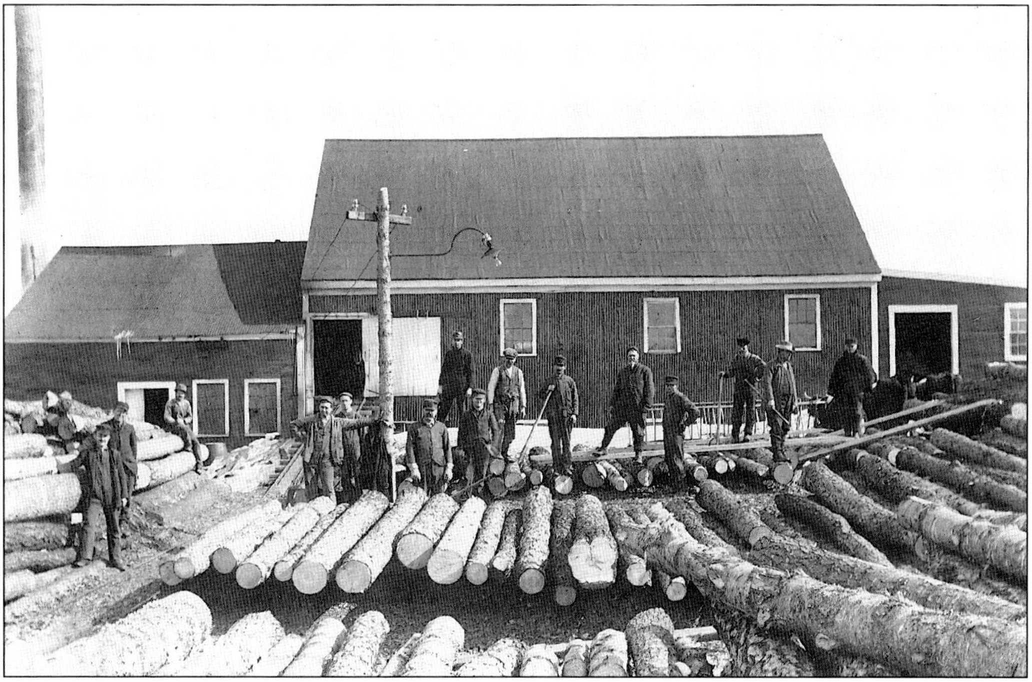

SANBORN'S MILL, *c.* 1935. Sanborn's Mill was built by Marshall Sanborn *c.* 1917 at the end of Mill Street in Steep Falls. Sanborn specialized in making barrel heads, which were shipped out by rail. The mill was purchased by Stuart Gunther and George Jewett *c.* 1950 and, after that, manufactured mostly dowels. In 1978, Beverly Gunther Anderson took it over and made pallets. The mill closed in 1980.

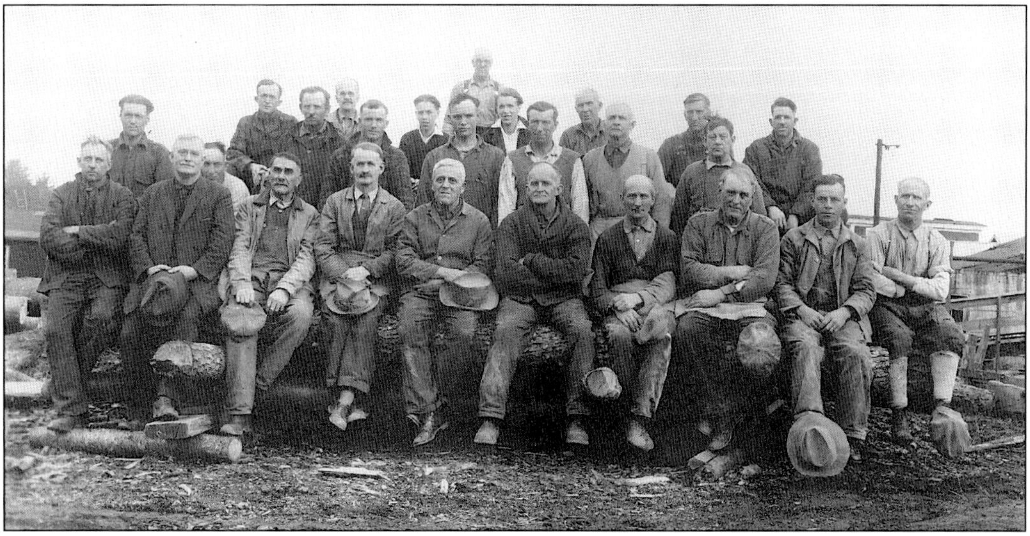

THE WORK FORCE AT SANBORN'S MILL, C.1925. Shown are, from left to right, the following: (front row) I. Bailey, M. Sanborn, W. Ward (behind), E. Richardson, C. Sanborn, C. Nason, S. Christie, D. Graffam, J. Moore, C. Hanscom, and F. Graffam; (back row) A. Perkins, unidentified, G. Sanborn, N. Emery, L. Sanborn, F. Harmon, L. Burnham, T. Graffam, M. Burnham, E. Meserve, C. Moore, R. Ridlon, C. Hunkins, (possibly) A. Perkins, H. Sanborn, and L. Boothby. There are others in the rear, not shown.

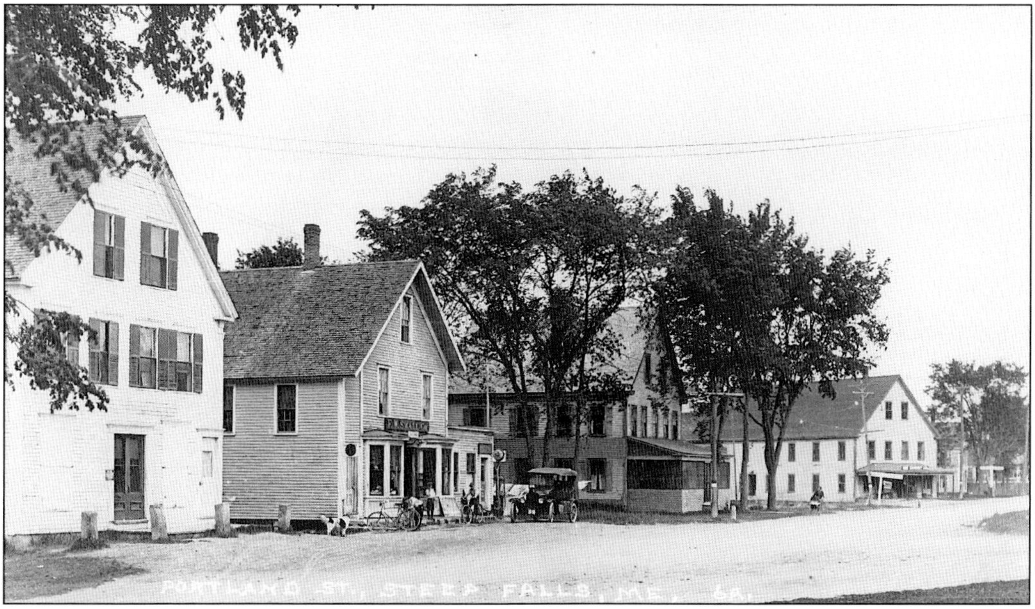

PORTLAND STREET, C. 1910. A row of commercial establishments once greeted those entering Steep Falls from Baldwin and points north on the Pequawket Trail (Route 113). The places shown are, from left to right, the Edwin Wingate Store on the first floor with the Wingate residence on second (originally Cousins and Tucker Store and later a post office and store), the Frank Strout residence, the Mitchell residence, and the Mitchell Grain Mill and Store (now Steep Falls Market).

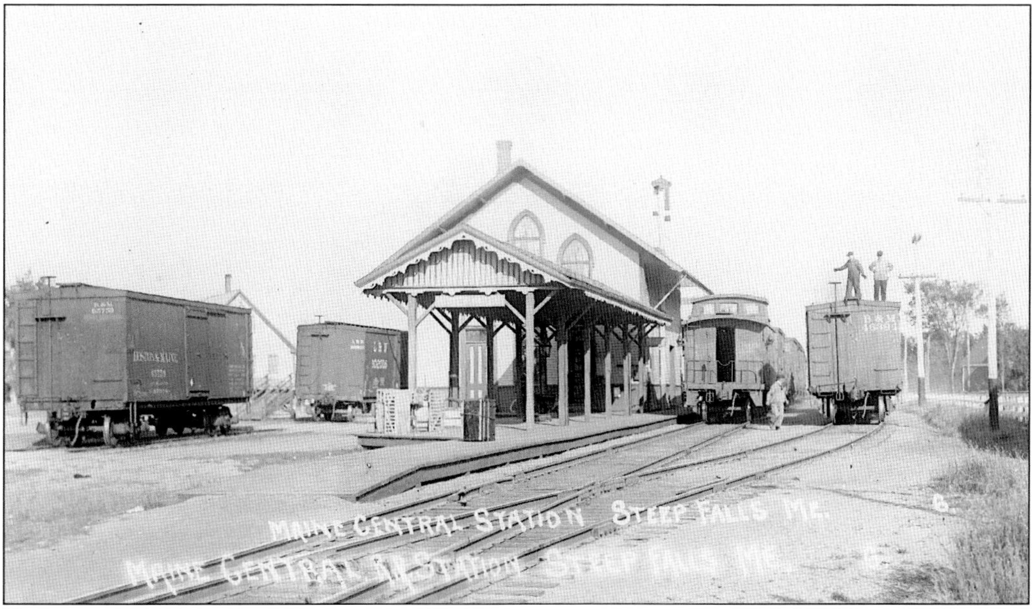

THE STEEP FALLS STATION, C. 1935. The Steep Falls Station was built with $3,000 donated by Tobias Lord, a prominent lumberman in the community, as an enticement for the Portland & Ogdensburg Railroad to run its tracks through Steep Falls. Regular passenger service between Portland and Steep Falls (24.6 miles) began on November 7, 1870. The second floor of the station, demolished in 1961, was originally a dance hall.

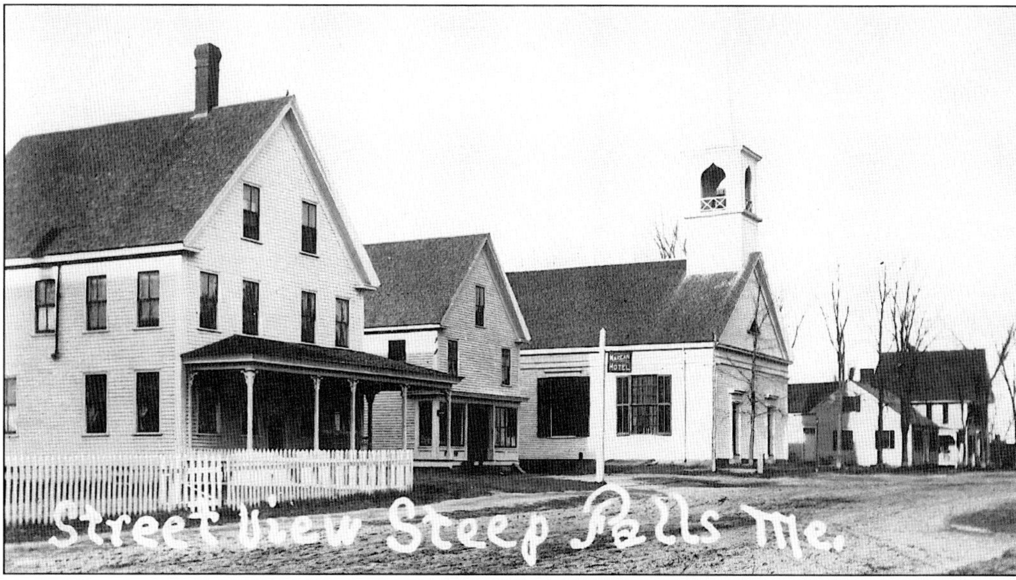

MAIN STREET, STEEP FALLS, C. 1900. The buildings shown here are, from left to right, the Marean Hotel, Marean's Store with a stable in back, the First Baptist Church, the home of Woodbrey Wadleigh, and a duplex containing the homes of Steven Wood on the left and Mabel Ridlon on the right. The Marean complex went up in flames the night that Franklin Delano Roosevelt was elected president. It is claimed that when the fire alarm sounded, local residents failed to respond, thinking it was rung to celebrate the election of the new president.

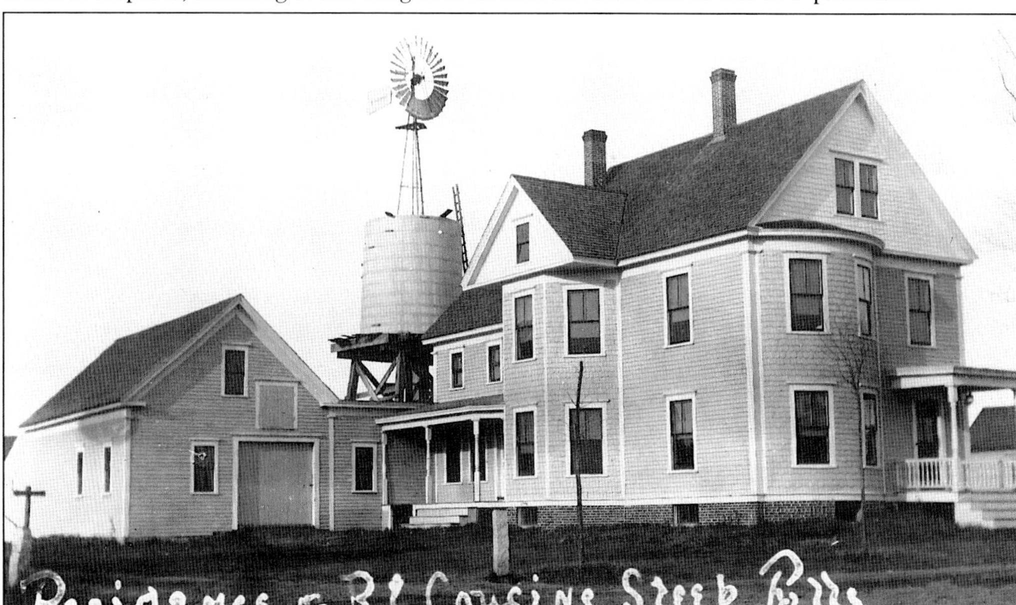

STEEP FALLS WATER CO. C. 1920. Ben Cousins erected this windmill, which towers above his two-and-a-half-story house off Main Street (Route 11) in Steep Falls. For many years he pumped water from Tucker Brook, near his house, into the large storage tank above the ell and provided water for himself and for many of the local residents without wells. It is said that on Mondays (washday), the flow of water into subscribers' houses was reduced to a trickle.

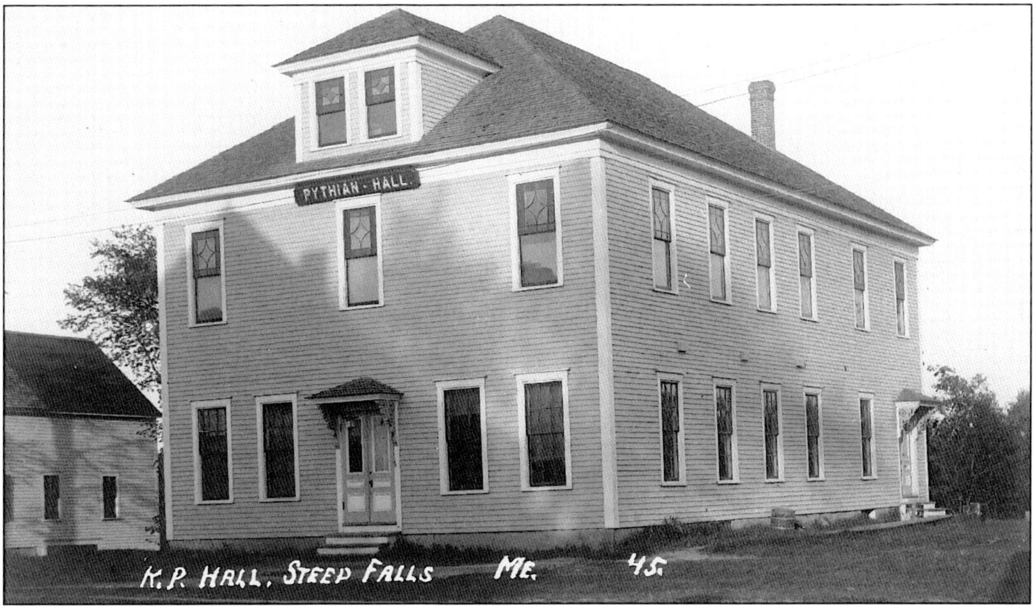

THE KNIGHTS OF PYTHIAS HALL, 1945. The Crescent Lodge No. 20 Knights of Pythias in Steep Falls was chartered on July 11, 1879. This secret organization, named after the legendary Damon and Pythias of 4th-century Syracuse (Sicily), adopted as its motto "Friendship, Charity, and Benevolence." Unable to stem the tide of declining membership, this lodge closed *c.* 1975. The building is now owned by Davis and Hanscome Incorporated.

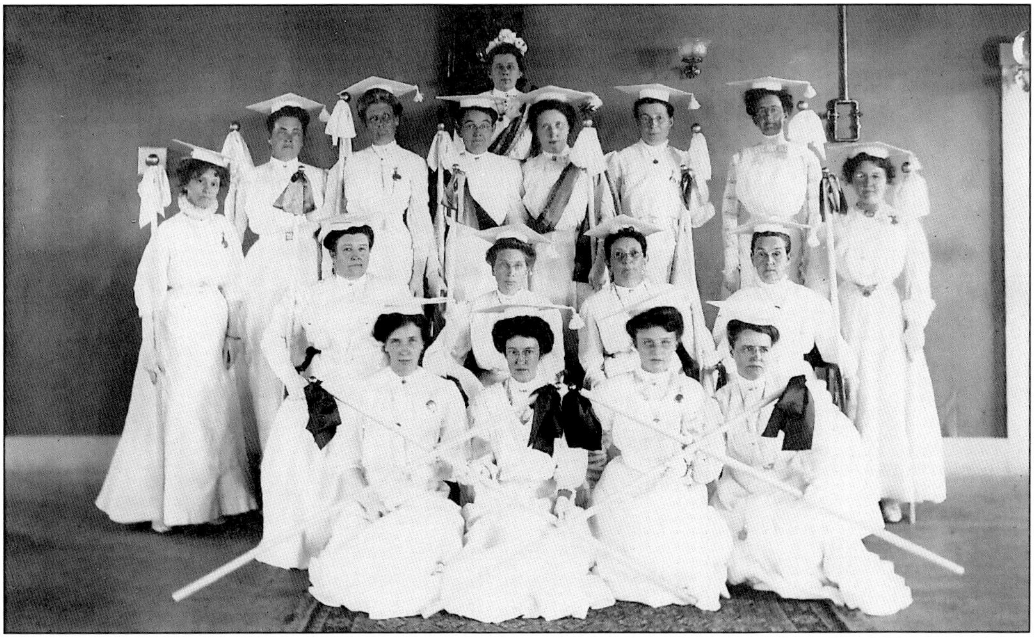

CROWN TEMPLE AT STEEP FALLS, C. 1900. Shown are, from left to right, the following: (first row) Laura Meserve Burnham, Lillian White Norton, Hattie Burnham Meserve, and Annie Marean; (second row) Rose Porter, Sadie Ridlon, Mandy Brackett, and Ida Baker; (third row) Mrs. Chadbourne, Abbie Emery, Carrie Ridlon, Ava Meserve Haley, Ida Berry, Mamie Hartford, and Bessie Chadbourne; (fourth row) Mabel Elwell.

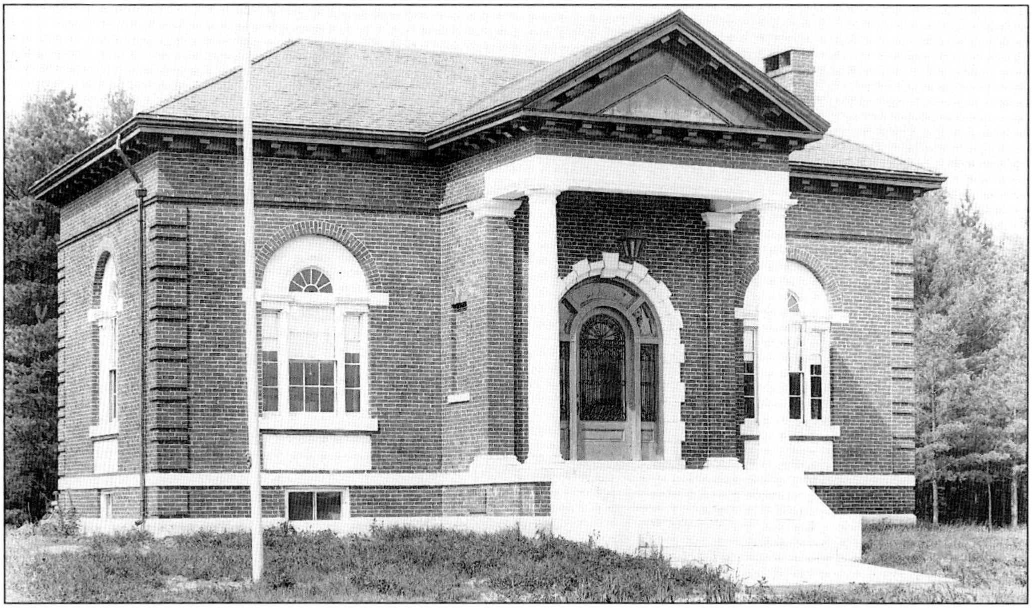

THE STEEP FALLS LIBRARY, C.1920. Steep Falls has always prided itself in having one of the most imposing libraries for a community its size in Maine. This original portion was constructed in 1916 from funds bequeathed by Henry Pierce, native to the community, who made a fortune in sundry enterprises in California during the Gold Rush days.

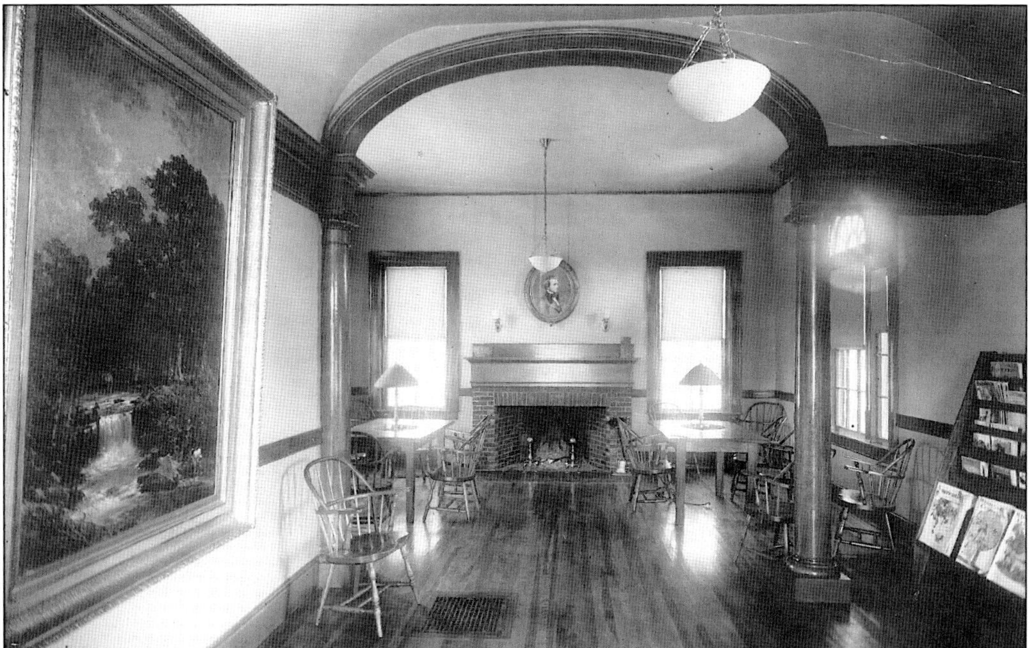

THE LIBRARY INTERIOR. The interior of the Steep Falls Library radiates warmth and grace. The splendid landscape in oil accenting a waterfall refulgent in moonlight is entitled *A Wary Moment*. Painted by Thomas Hill, it was-sold to the California wine merchant Ernest Gallo in 1985 for $50,000. A portrait of George Pierce hangs over the fireplace. Pierce's niece Henrietta Pierce Watkinson provided the funds for the construction of the children's annex in 1925.

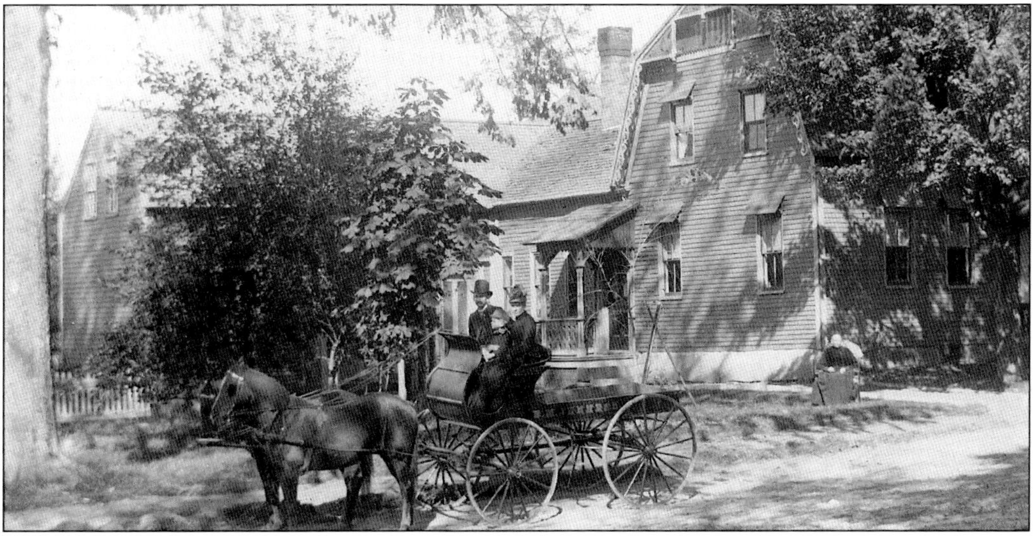

THE PARKER JENNESS PLACE, 1888. Ben Jenness, his wife, and their son appear to be headed for a funeral. Jenness was a funeral director and undertaker for many years in Steep Falls. At the apex of the influenza epidemic during World War I, he was inundated with funerals. This lovely old house with a gamboled roof and filigree overhang on Main Street is currently the home of Dr. Neil Corson and his wife, Anna.

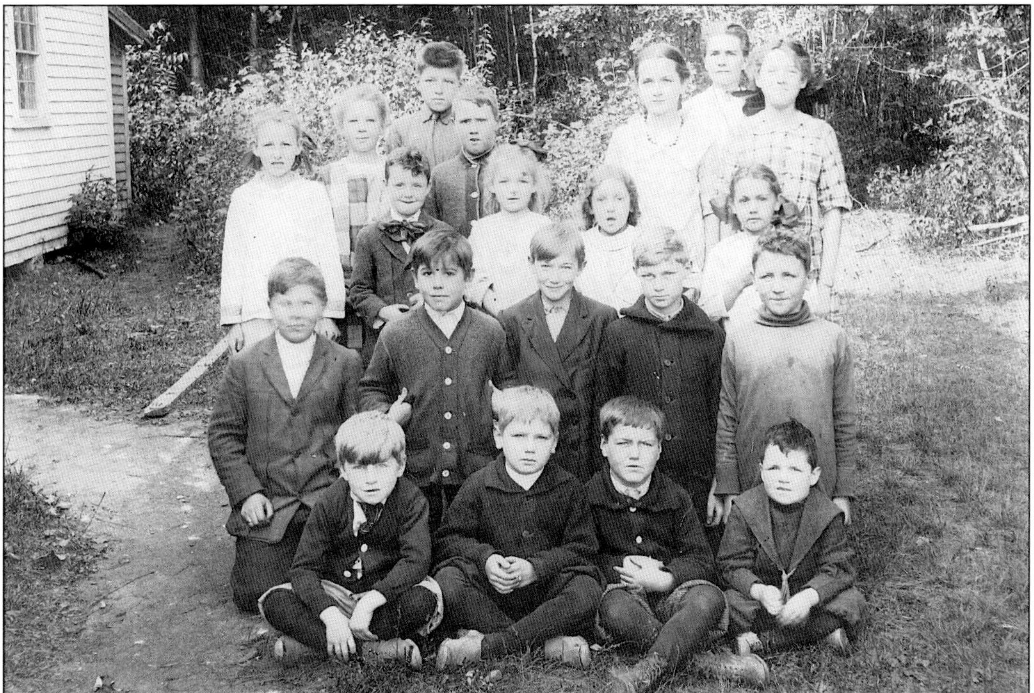

STEEP FALLS SCHOLARS, C. 1910. Pictured are, from left to right, as follows: (first row) Gordon Fraser, Phil Sanborn, Ervin Perkins, and Lawrence Rand; (second row) Ed Coolbroth, Guy Coolbroth, Lester Chute, Lawrence Cousins, and Arthur Gallant; (third row) unidentified, Warren Rand, unidentified, Thelma Gallant, and Eva Gallant; (fourth row) Bertha Sanborn, Raymond Strout, Paul Gallant, unidentified, (possibly) Edith Usher, and Rachel Strout.

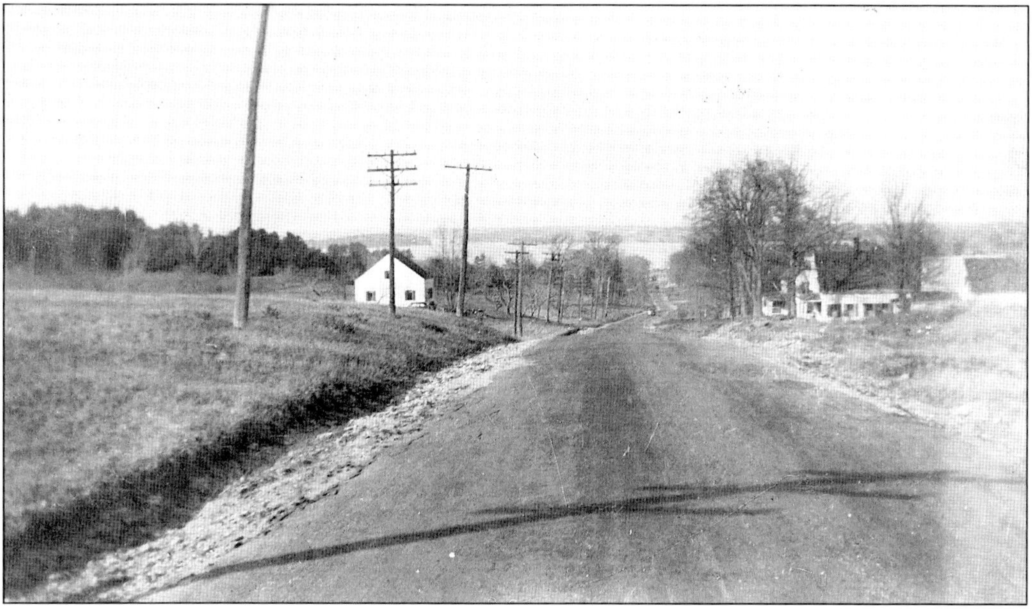

SEBAGO LAKE, C. 1935. A splendid panorama from Hillcrest on Route 35 of the Lower Bay of Sebago Lake, often referred to as the Queen of Inland Waters, unfolds as one begins the descent to Sebago Lake Village. The Simon Moulton house and the apple orchard are on the left. Elmer and Ina Glidden lived in the first house on the right, which is now owned by Richard Walker. Below that is the Herbert Carr farm, which was later purchased by Ben Blake and is now the home of Robert and Mildred Walker.

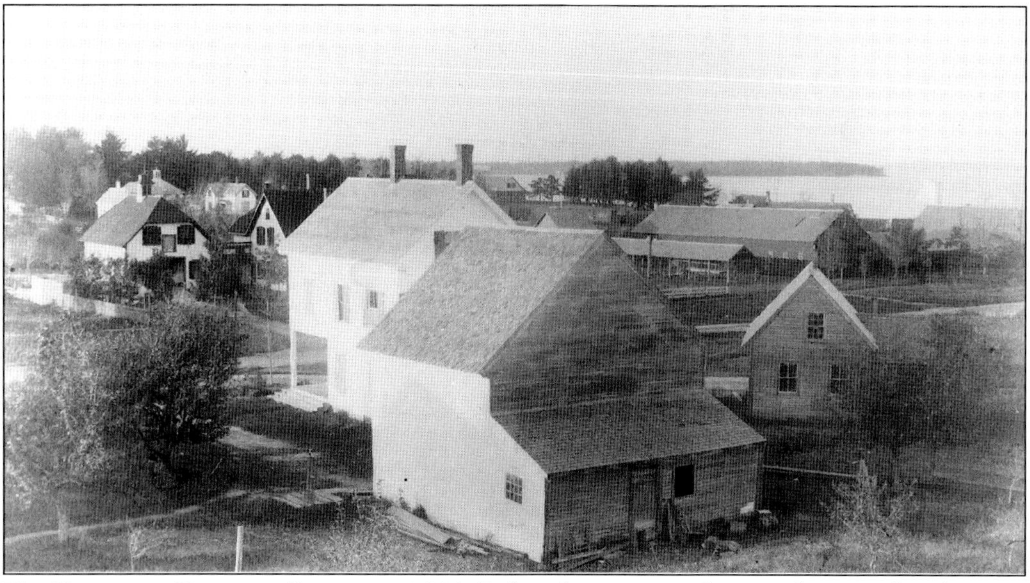

THE PORTLAND PACKING COMPANY, 1883. Before the memory of anyone living today, this corn shop, operated by the Portland Packing Company, provided welcomed seasonal employment and a ready market for corn. The corn was grown locally and was processed and shipped on the Portland & Ogdensburg Railroad to Commercial Street in Portland.

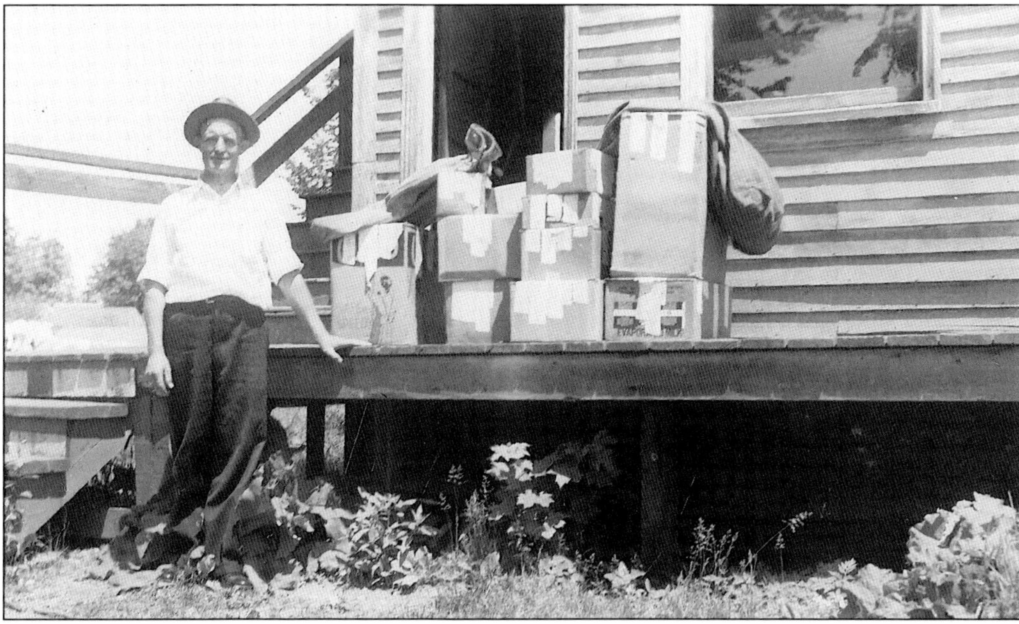

THE MAILMAN, 1943. For many years John R. Edgecomb served as a rural mail carrier, who delivered mail by automobile in all kinds of weather all the way up Route 114 as far as the end of Long Beach in East Sebago. Here, he poses in front of the Sebago Lake Post Office platform, piled high with the last mail and equipment from the North Gorham Post Office. The building, originally owned by Lem Rich, is now TJ's Sandwich Shop.

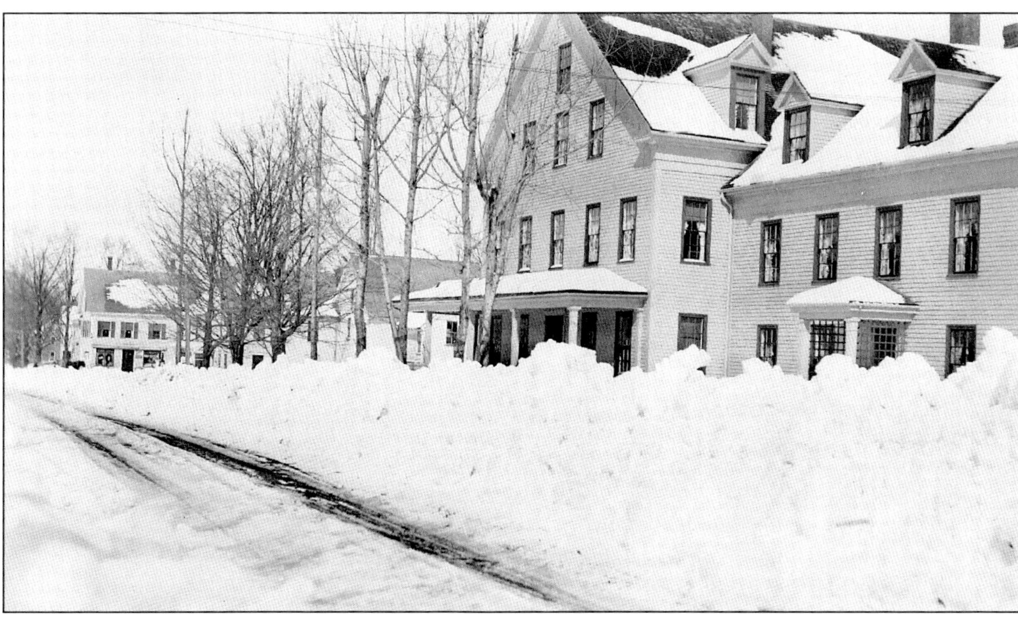

SEBAGO LAKE VILLAGE, C. 1938. The Sebago Lake House, for many years a thriving summer resort, looks lonely and forlorn with the snowbank mounting higher and higher in front of it on Route 114. Next to it, where Routes 114 and 35 converge, is Sam Hill's hardware store. On the opposite side of the intersection is Lem Rich's grocery and hardware store.

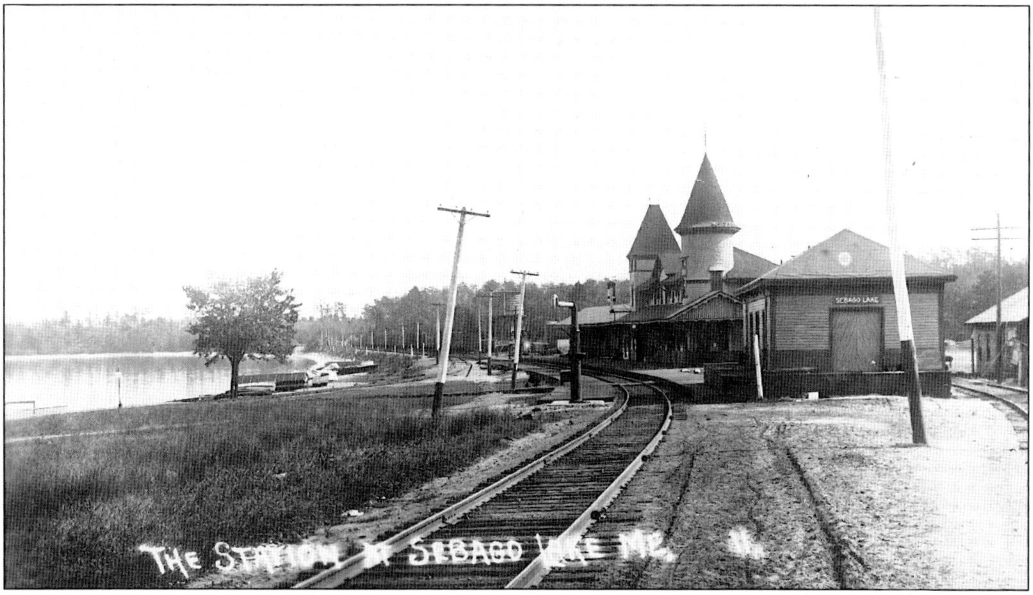

SEBAGO LAKE STATION, C. 1925. Soon after the first regular passenger service commenced from Portland to Sebago Lake on September 12, 1870, on the Portland & Ogdensburg Railroad, Sebago Lake underwent a remarkable transformation. This elaborate and ornate station with a rectangular and a round tower was constructed to handle the huge influx of excursionists who arrived and departed from Sebago Lake, especially during the summer months.

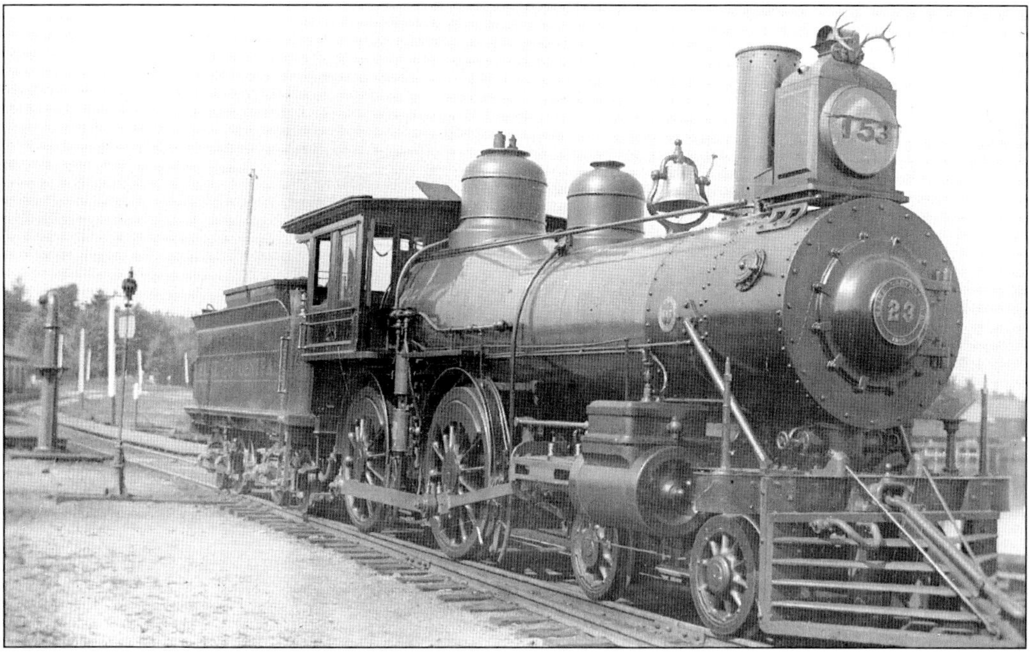

SIDETRACKED AT THE STATION, C. 1900. Locomotive 153, built in 1894 by the Schenectady Locomotive Works, sits idly on a sidetrack at Sebago Lake Station. A large turntable was constructed here at the lake so that special trains to the station could be turned around and headed back to Portland. Beginning on August 31, 1888, the line was known as the Maine Central Mountain Division.

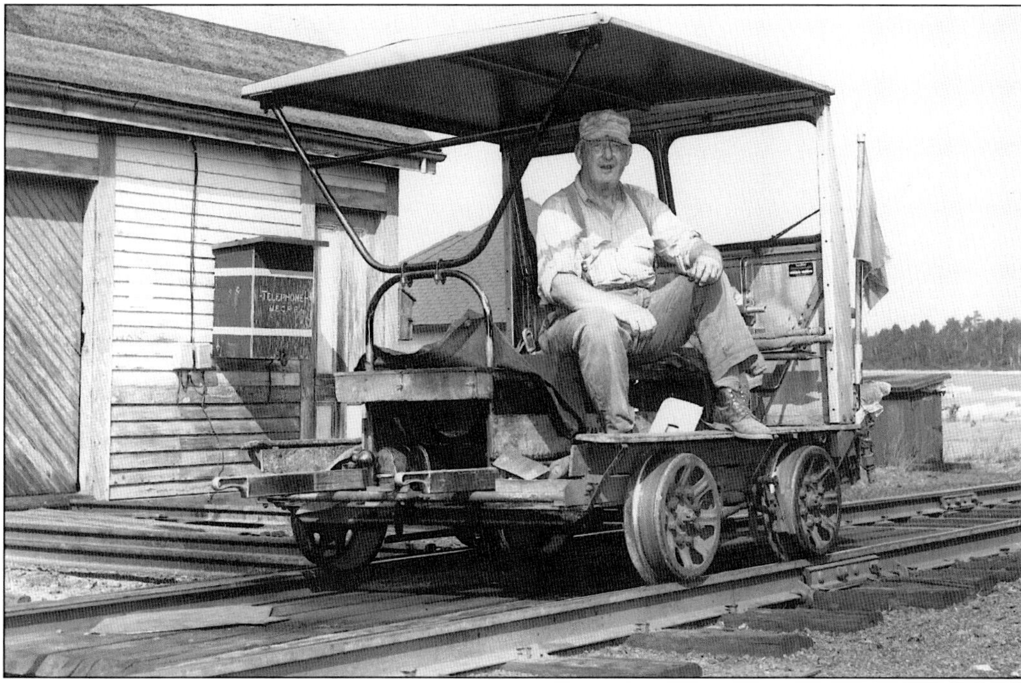

THE SECTION FOREMAN, C. 1950. For many years, Ben Blake, seated on his section car at Sebago Lake Station, was a section foreman for the Maine Central Mountain Division Railroad. It is said that engineers on the line reported to the head office in Portland that they could always tell when they hit Ben Blake's section because it was so smooth.

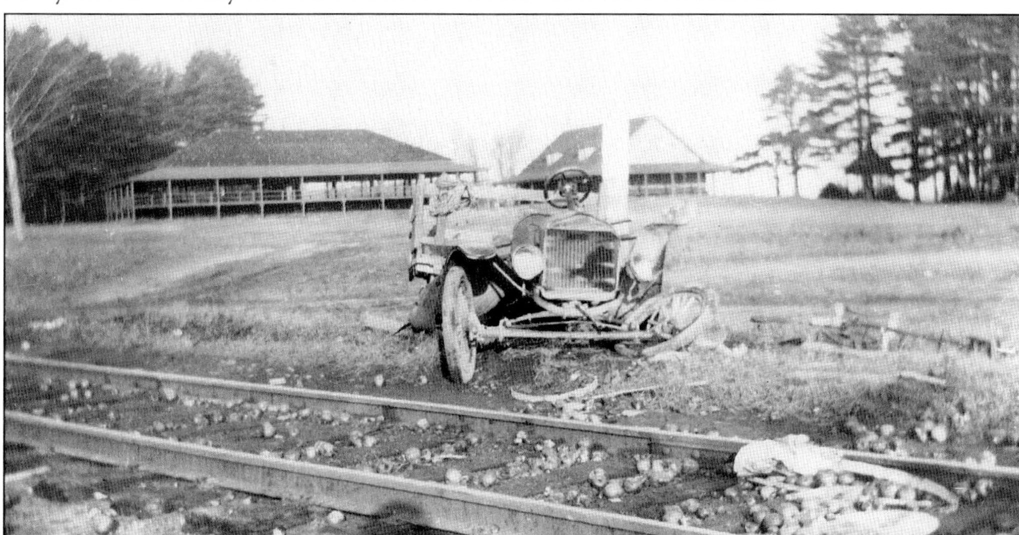

ACCIDENTS DID HAPPEN, FALL, 1922. This accident ("upsetting the applecart"), took place at the Maple Street crossing at Sebago Lake. The first recorded accident occurred on June 28, 1871, near here at Otter Pond when an empty passenger train sent up from Portland to pick up Westbrook students on an outing plowed into a flatcar loaded with rocks. The large building to the rear of the baseball field was the railroad-owned dance pavilion. The smaller structure was the concession building where lunches were served.

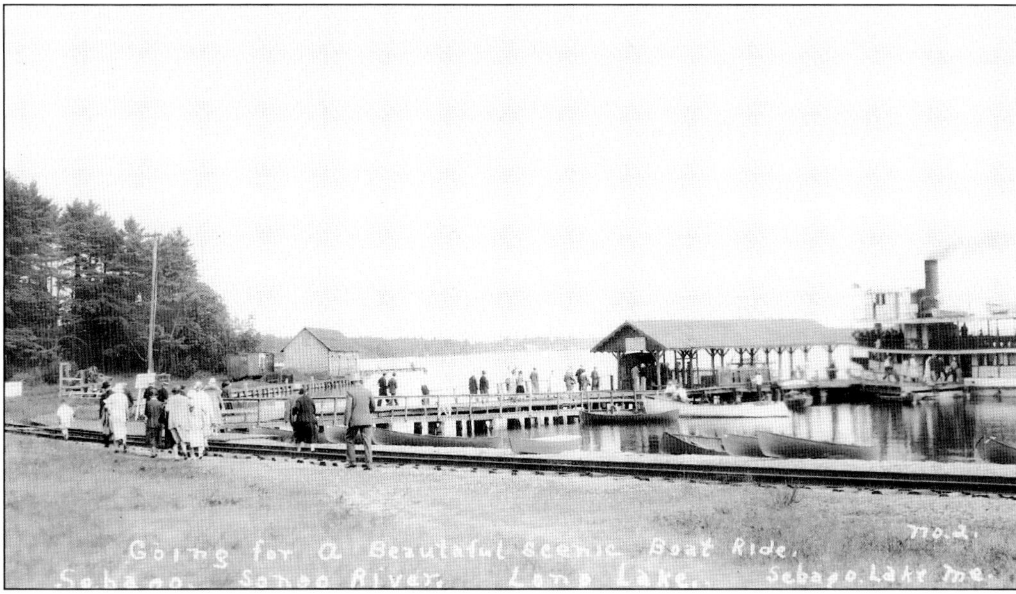

THE SEBAGO LAKE STEAMBOAT WHARF, C. 1920. The Maine Central ran a spur parallel to the station so that both freight and passengers could be easily transferred to the steamers at the 124-foot-long wharf. Passengers could go all the way to Harrison by steamboat, take the lilliputian 2-foot Bridgton & Saco River Railroad to the junction in Hiram, and return to Portland via the Central Maine Mountain Division Railroad.

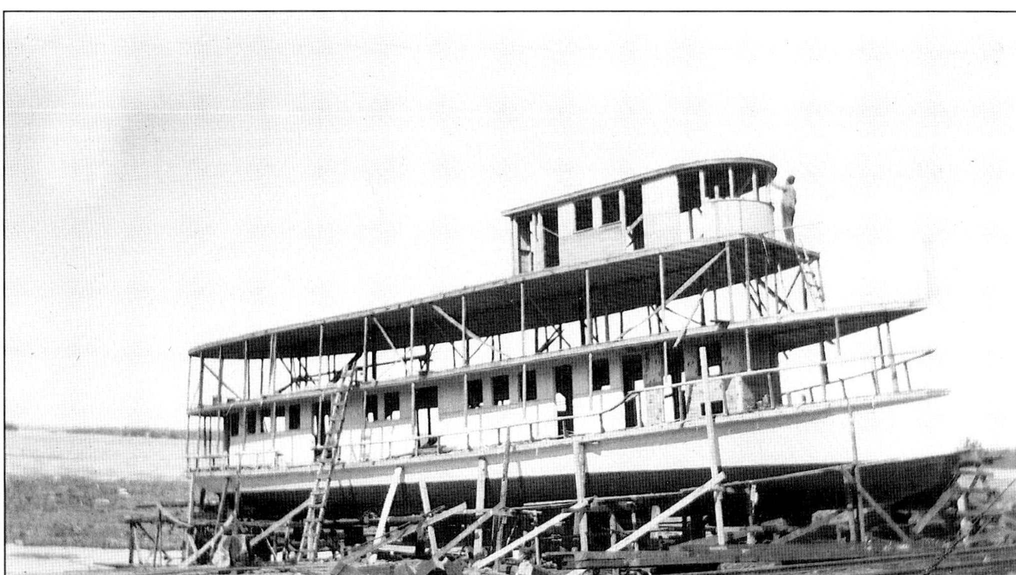

ASSEMBLING THE *GOODRIDGE*, 1912. Soon after S.D. Warren purchased the Sebago Steamship Company from Charles E. Gibbs of Bridgton in 1892, Charles L. Goodridge acquired the line and changed the name to the Sebago Lake, Songo River, and Bay of Naples Steamboat Company. The *Goodridge*, the last and largest to be added to the fleet, was built by the Bath Iron Works and assembled at Sebago Lake.

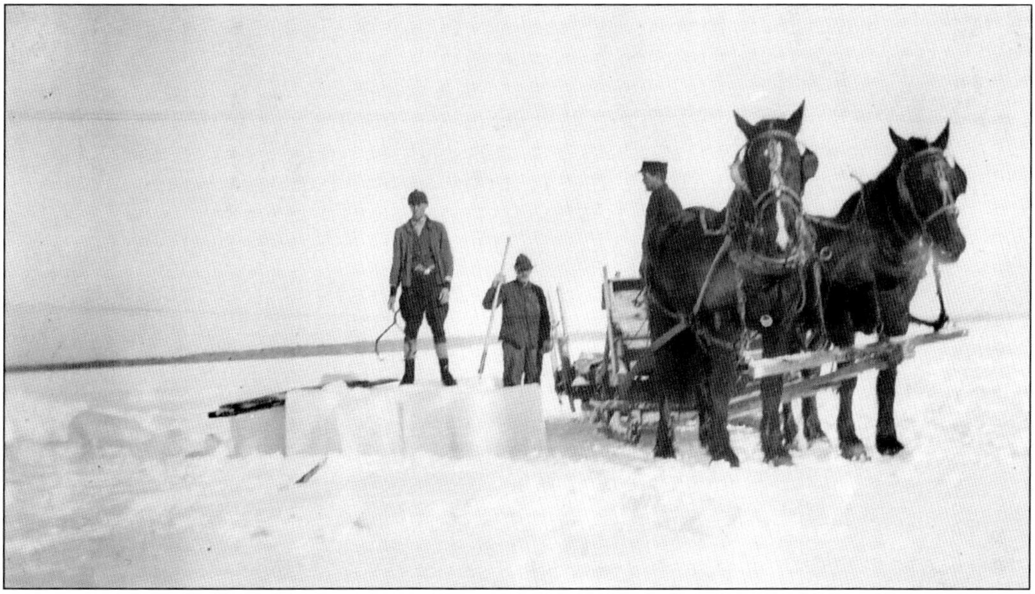

THE ICE HARVEST, FEBRUARY 1923. Beginning in 1880, when the Clark & Chaplin Ice Company erected a mammoth complex of icehouses on the edge of the lake at Sebago Lake Village, harvesting and storing ice became a major commercial enterprise. The same rail spur that ran to the steamboat wharf was extended to the complex, and boxcars were loaded almost daily with the "white gold" and transported to Portland and beyond.

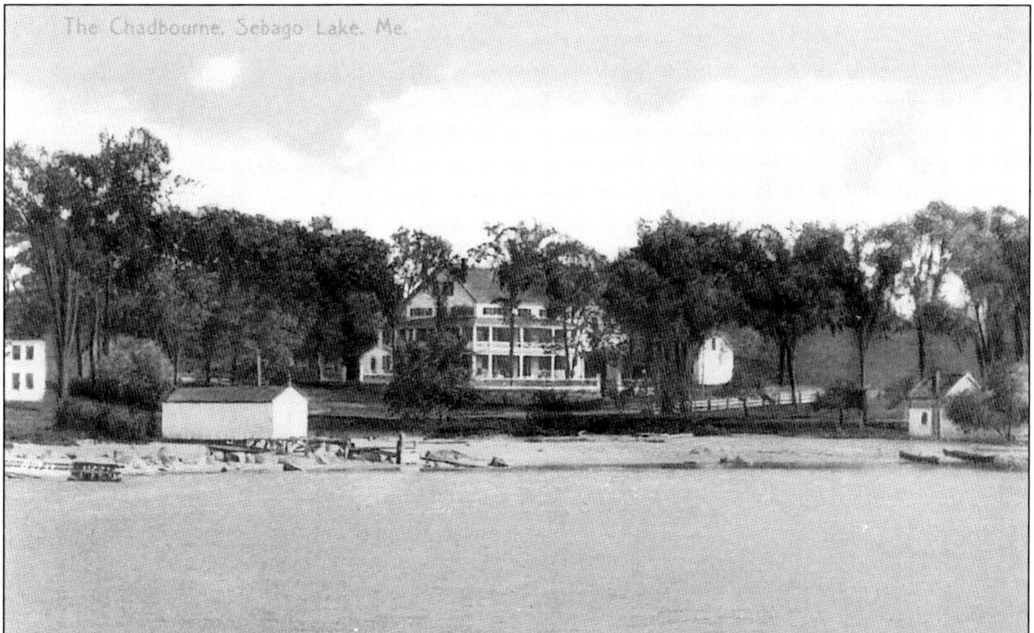

CHADBOURNE LANDING, C. 1910. For nearly three quarters of a century, the gracious Chadbourne House and Landing near Sebago Lake Station (16 miles from Portland) was a popular hostelry for weary travelers who arrived either by stagecoach, the Cumberland & Oxford Canal, or steamboat (dating back to 1847 when the lake's first steamboat, the ill-fated *Faun* docked here with dignitaries).

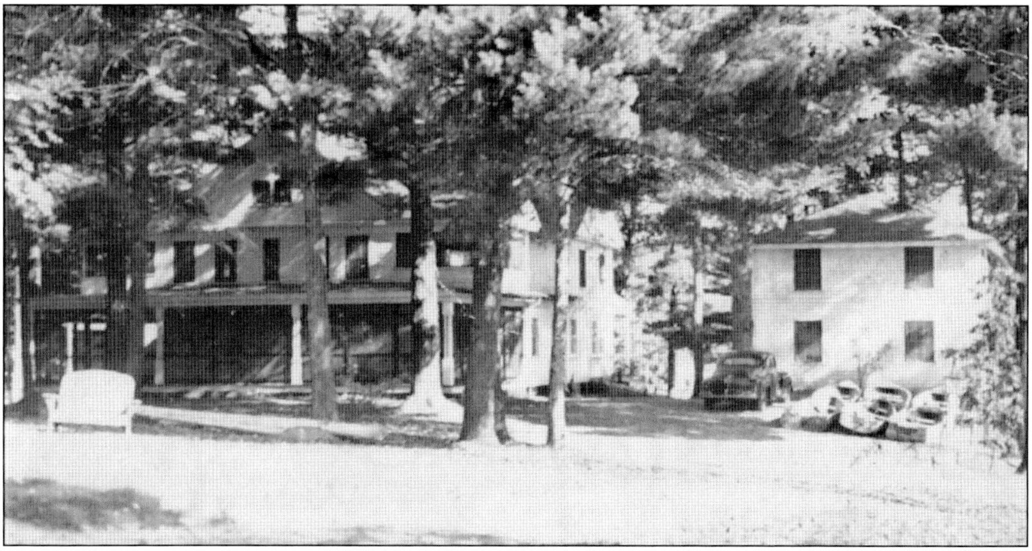

Burton Lodge and Cottages, c. 1942. The cottages at White's Bridge, overlooking the Sebago Lake Basin, were formerly the private residences of T.A. Kenney of New York City. In the 1950s, the property became Martin's Lodge and in 1985, the Sebago Lake Lodge.

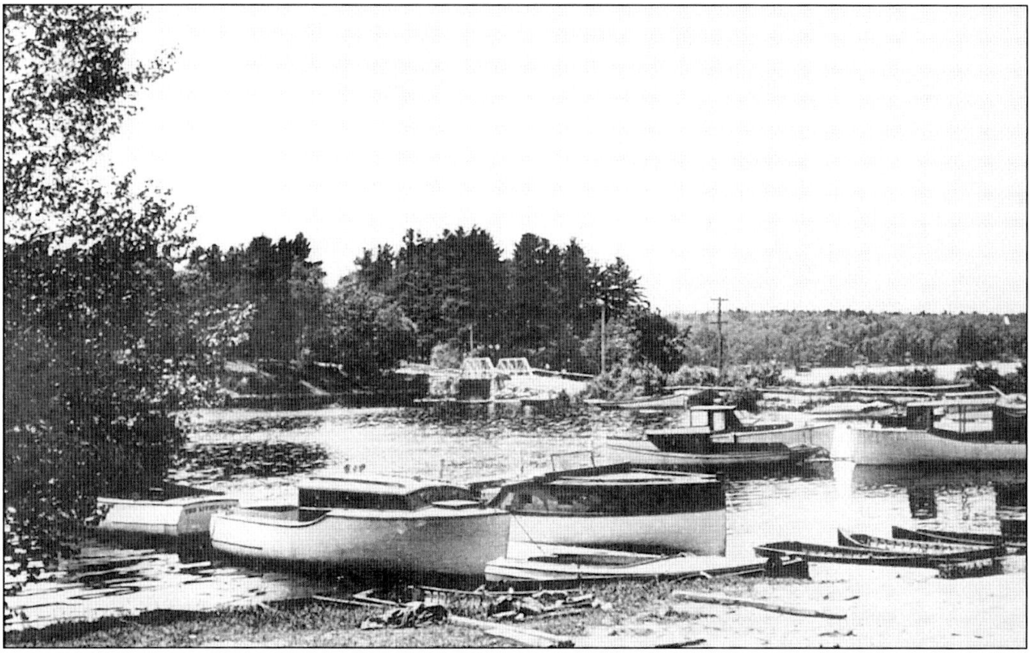

White's Bridge, c. 1935. This is a view of the Standish side of the Sebago Lake Basin at White's Bridge taken from the Windham side, showing the steel bridge that replaced the original wooden bridge in the early 1920s. Because the basin empties into the Presumpscot River—the earliest artery between Sebago Lake and Falmouth (Portland) and from 1830 to 1870, the gateway to the Cumberland & Oxford Canal—it played a vital role in the history and economic development of all the towns in the Lake Region.

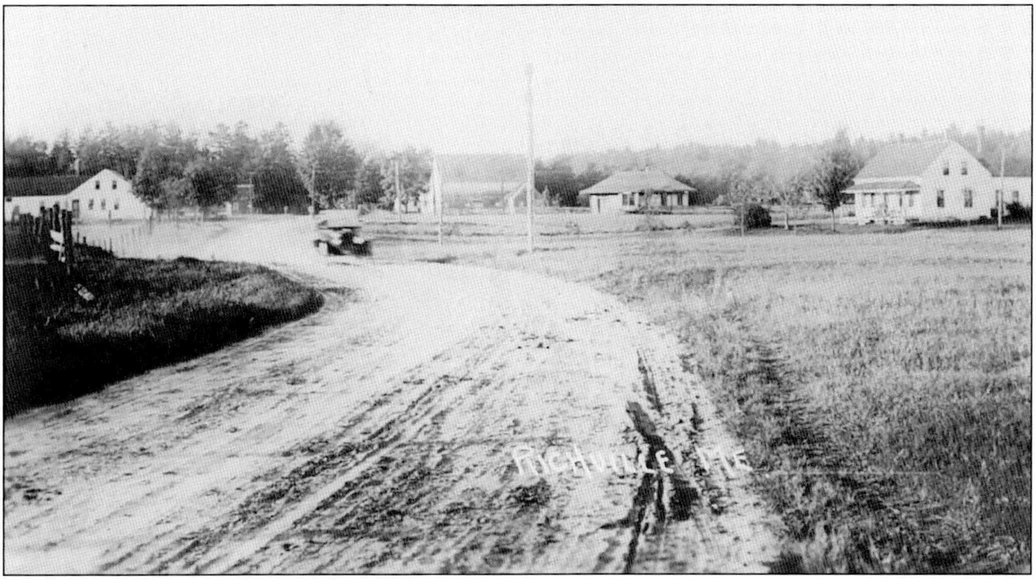

RICHVILLE, C. 1927. Richville is named after Lemuel Rich, who moved with his family on March 12, 1788, into a cabin on property now owned by Allen Hawkes. Soon afterward the Rich family moved up to Rich's (Harmon's) Hill and settled there permanently. This view, taken looking up what is now Route 114 shortly before it was surfaced, shows on the left the farm owned by Ed Pendexter, whose wife, Elsie Pendexter, ran a store here in later years. On the the right are the Everett Lombard house and store, the Richville Railroad Station, and the Clyde Rand farm.

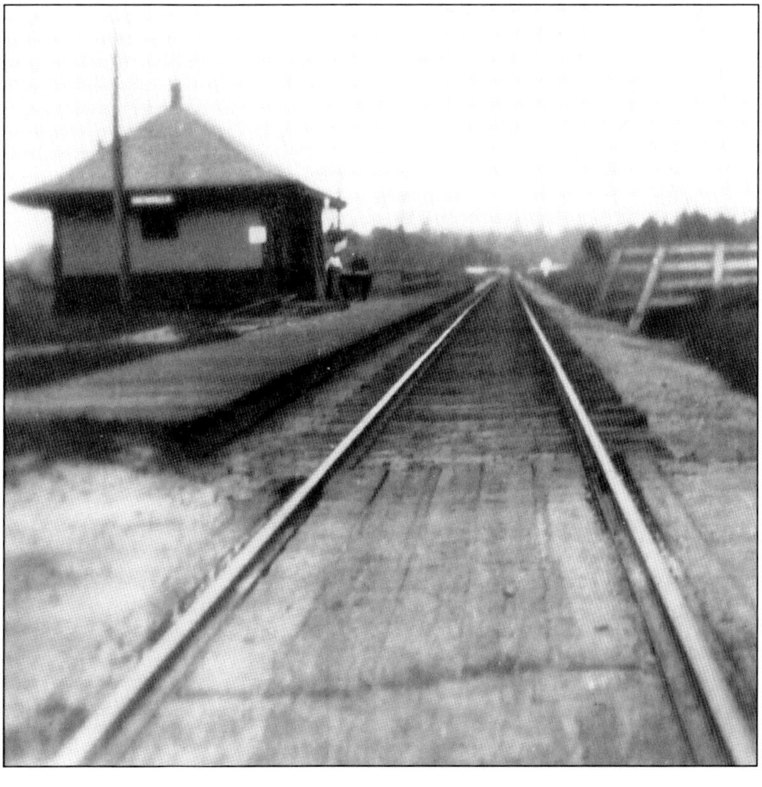

THE RICHVILLE STATION, C. 1930. This view of the Richville Railroad Station was taken looking east toward the Sebago Lake Station, which is a little more than 3 miles down the track. The Richville Station was erected in 1910, primarily to accommodate the growing summer population at the lake. Within a decade, the automobile superseded the railroad and the station was closed on January 21, 1921.

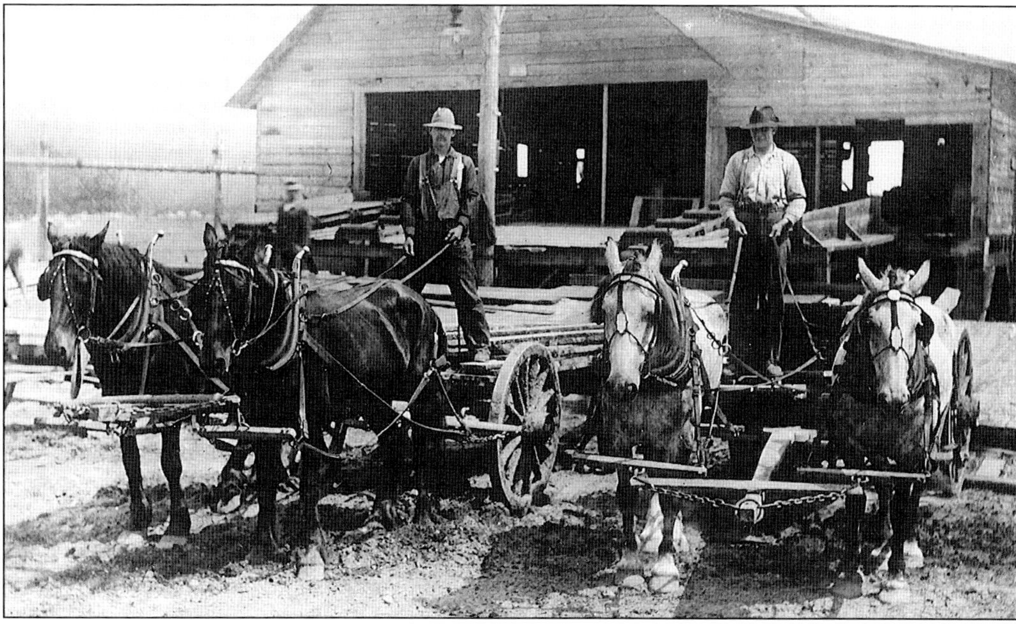

SMITH'S MILLS, 1910. Benjamin F. Smith set up a sawmill in 1888 near the lake in the section of Richville that still bears his name. In 1907, E.I. Dupont purchased the mill and property, greatly expanded the complex, and manufactured packing boxes for munitions that were shipped by rail to the Dupont Powder Mill in Wilmington, Delaware. During World War I, Smith's Mills became a boomtown with a population of some 500 people. The Portland Water Company purchased the mill and the entire community in 1922, and Smith's Mill vanished like vapor.

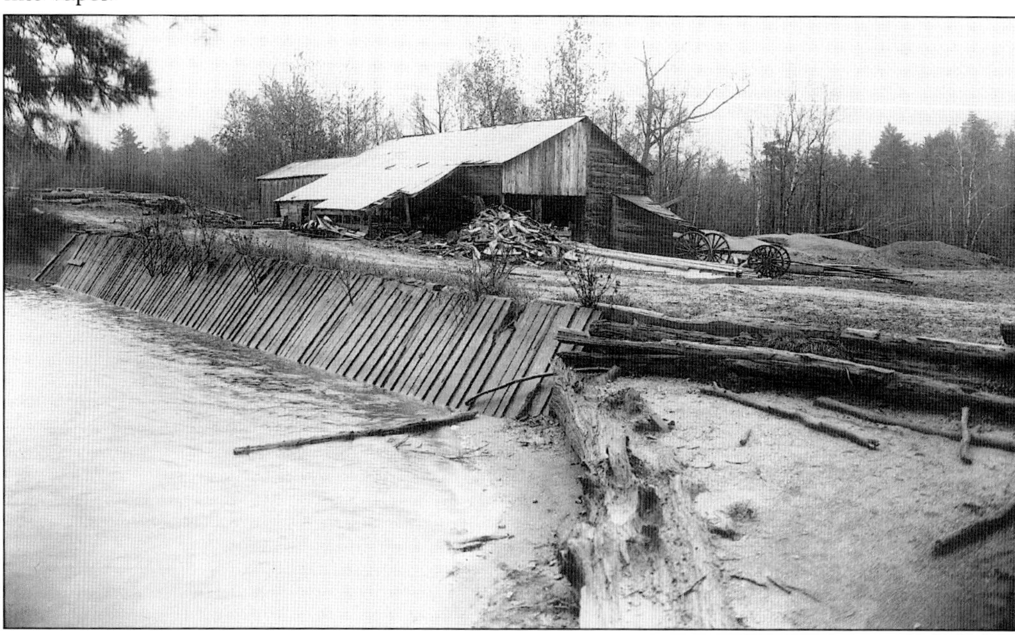

RICH'S MILL, C. 1920. For well over a century, logs were sawed on this site in Richville, starting at a mill owned by William Rich. The water mill was destroyed by fire three times. Delmont Hawkes purchased the mill from Emory Rich and operated it until his death in 1974.

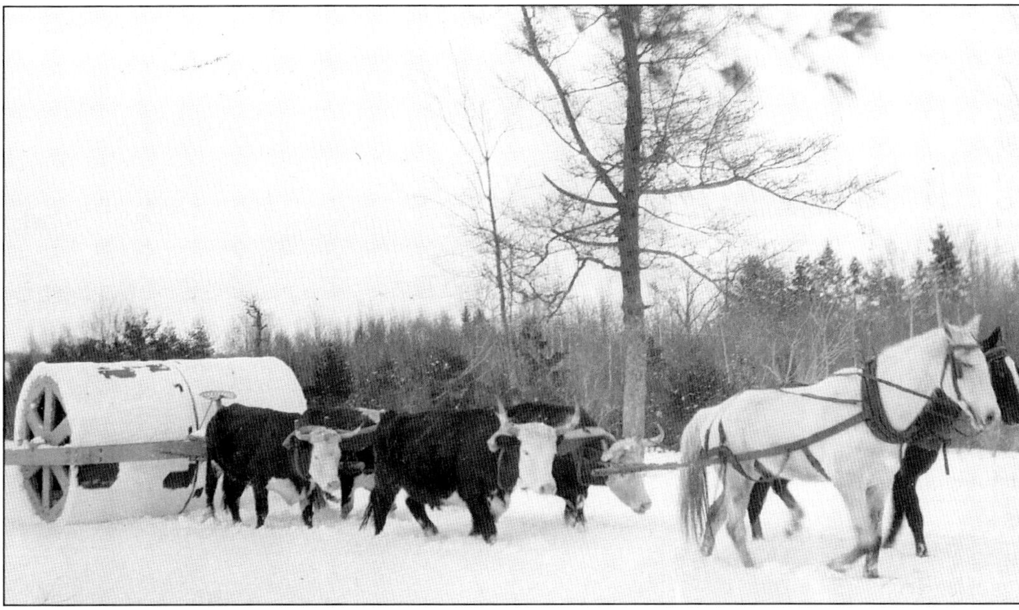

PACKING DOWN THE SNOW, c. 1910. Throughout much of the 19th century and into the late 1920s, roads in rural Maine, such as this one in Richville, were rolled and the snow was packed down by horse- and ox-drawn rollers. Fresh teams of horses and yokes of oxen replaced the weary teams along the way. The mixture of horses and oxen in this picture is a bit unique.

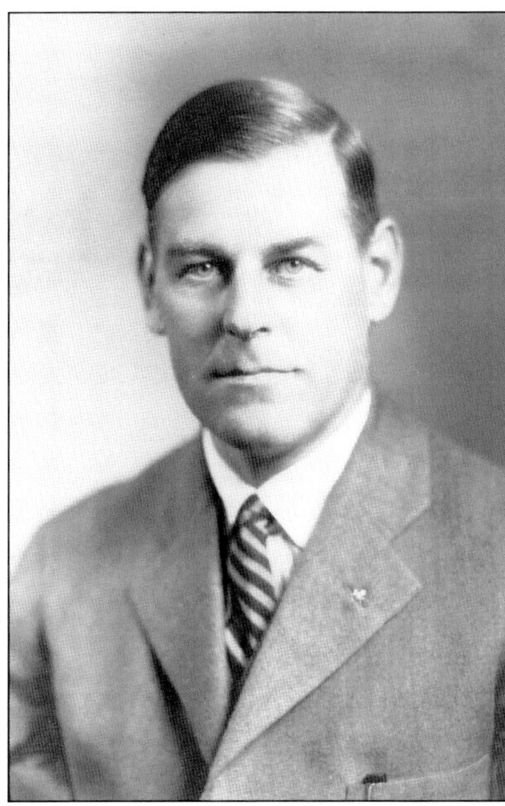

DELMONT HAWKES, 1927. Delmont Hawkes was born in Richville in 1886 and, except for spending some winters in Florida, lived all of his life on the farm in Richville where his grandson Allen Hawkes now resides. He attended Standish High School and graduated from Bridgton Academy. He later briefly attended Westbook Seminary. In 1927, at the age of 39, he was elected to the 83rd Maine Legislature and later served two more terms. He also served on the Standish School Committee and the Standish Board of Selectmen. He was a trustee of the Old Red Church at Standish Corner and a member of the Richville Grange. He spent much of his life in the lumber business and ran Hawke's Lumber Company in Richville. He was married to Pearl Wilson from the town of Sweden. He died in 1974.

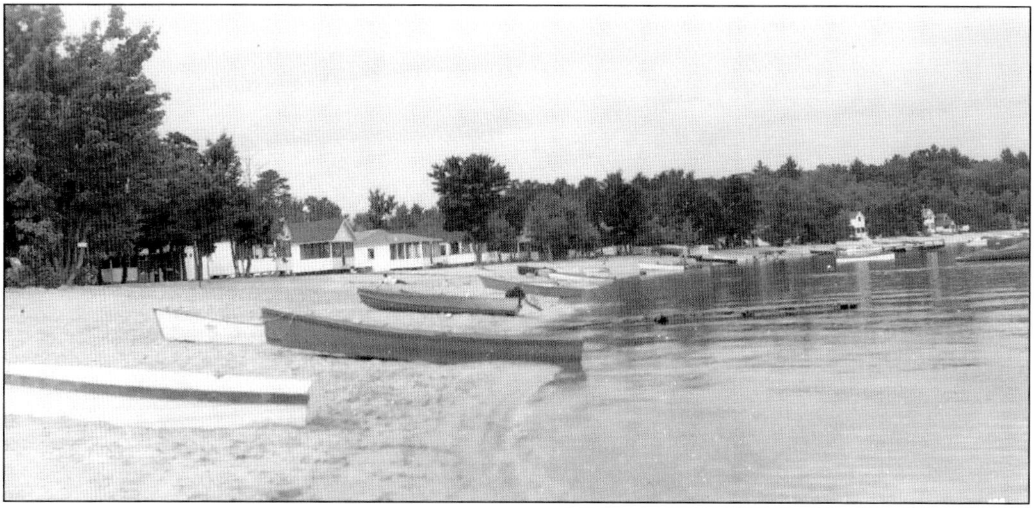

Harmon's Beach, c. 1940. Because of its fine stretch of sandy shoreline on Sebago Lake, Harmon's Beach was dotted with cottages by the early 1920s. The first cottage in the Richville area, however, was built by Dr. Charles A. Dennett in 1899 on Long Point. Besides Harmon's Beach, there is Harmonsville, Harmon Road, and Harmon Hill in Richville. Mulbry Harmon was one of Richville's earliest settlers.

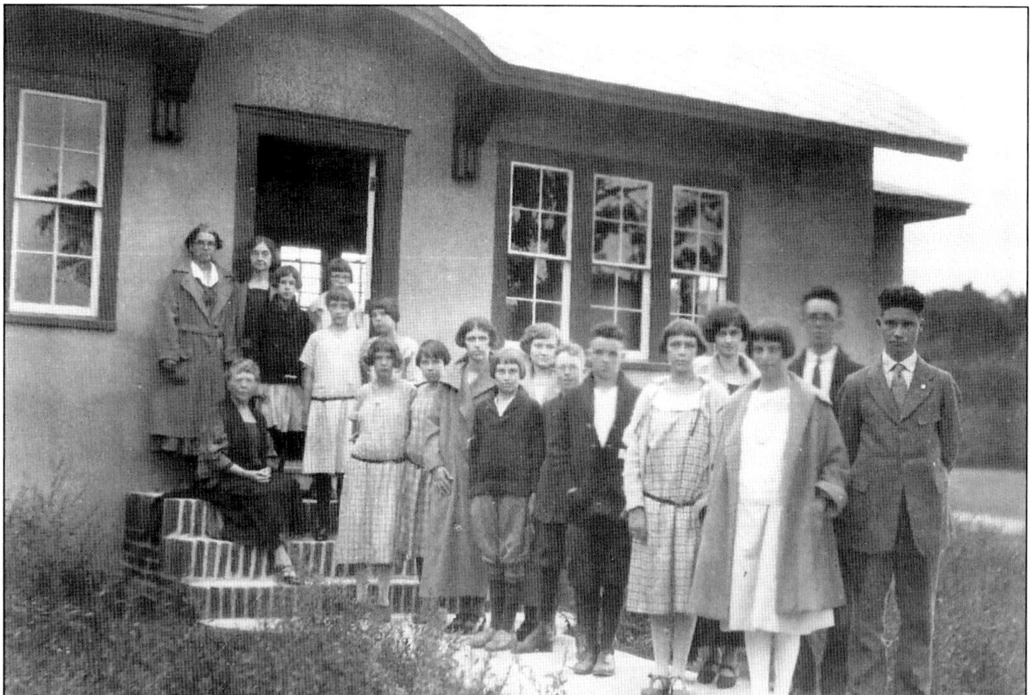

The Osmunda Club, c. 1922. The club's local young members gather with their founder, Edna Wadsworth Moody, seated, and librarian Gertrude Swift, left, in front of the original Richville Library, which was built largely with contributions from summer residents. The organization was based on Christian values stemming largely from the teachings of Dr. Norman Vincent Peale. Edna Moody, a writer, and her husband Herbert R. Moody, a chemistry professor, summered on Long Point.

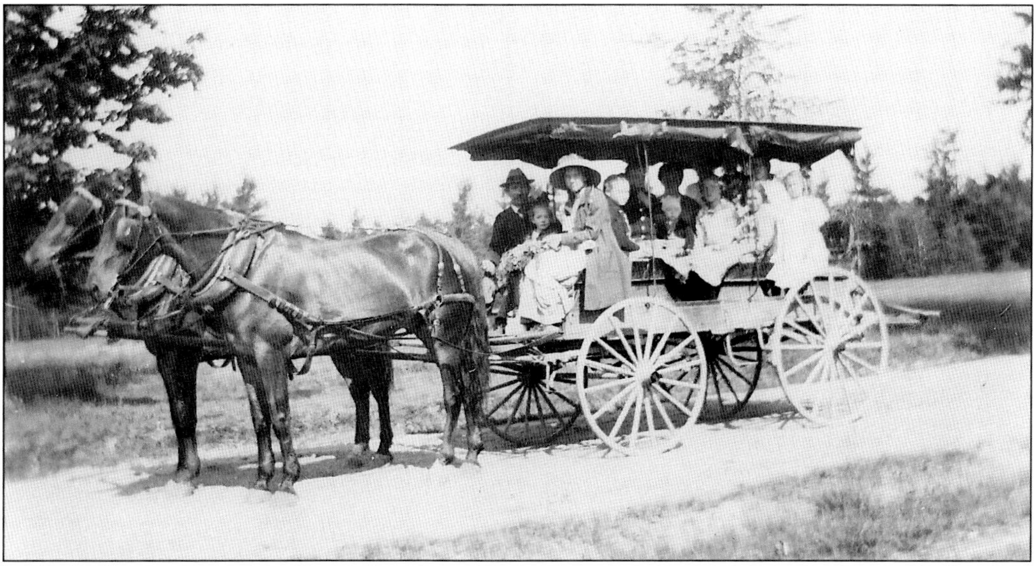

THE LOCAL SCHOOL BUS, C. 1914. Ed Rackliff drives his team Don and Dandy with a surrey full of students and their teacher Gertrude Swift, the local librarian, seated in front next to Rackliff's daughter Edna, down the dusty road to the District 5 Richville school.

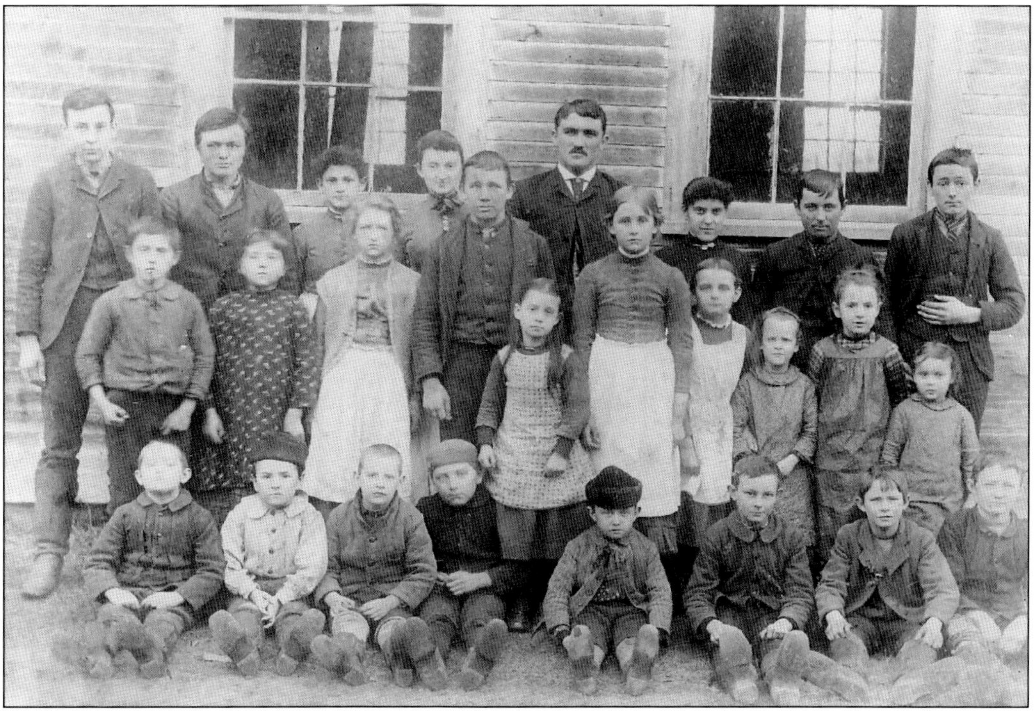

THE RICHVILLE GRAMMAR SCHOOL, C. 1880. The earliest reference to a school in Richville was recorded in a book in 1816 by John Rich II, who may have been Richville's first teacher. He agreed to teach for two months for $14. A school was built in 1825 and rebuilt on the same site three different times as the enrollment increased. This school was eventually moved to Delmont Hawke's farm, where it can still be seen. The last school closed in 1951 when the George E. Jack Consolidated School was opened near Standish Corner.

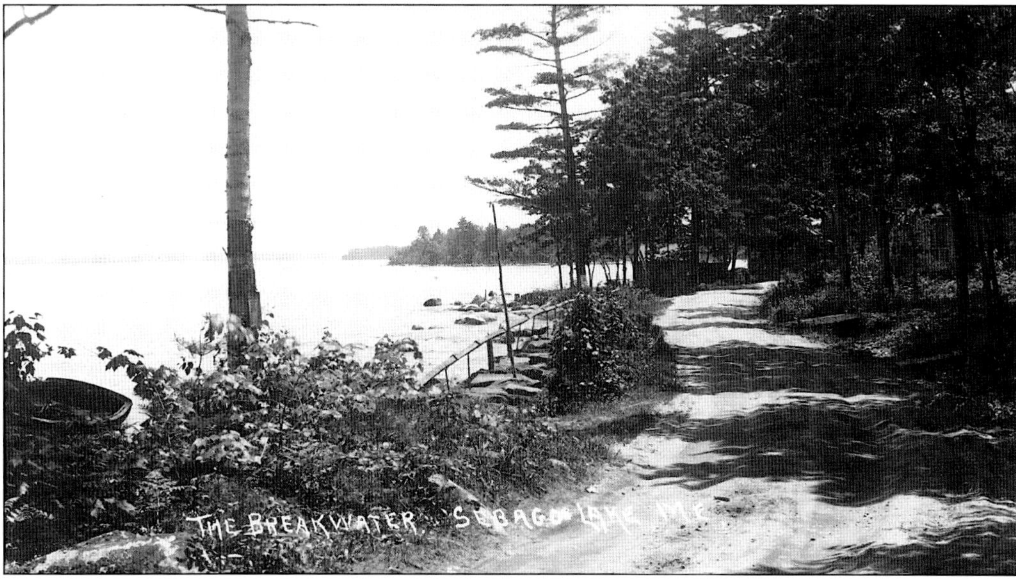

WARD'S COVE, C. 1935. Until 1931, shortly before this photograph was taken (probably near the Norton cottage named the Breakwater), this narrow, winding road was the main route to Portland. Today, it is the Wards Cove Road off Route 114 in Standish. The building at the bend in the road was once a store. Beyond the first point is Snug Harbor. Long Point is visible in the distance.

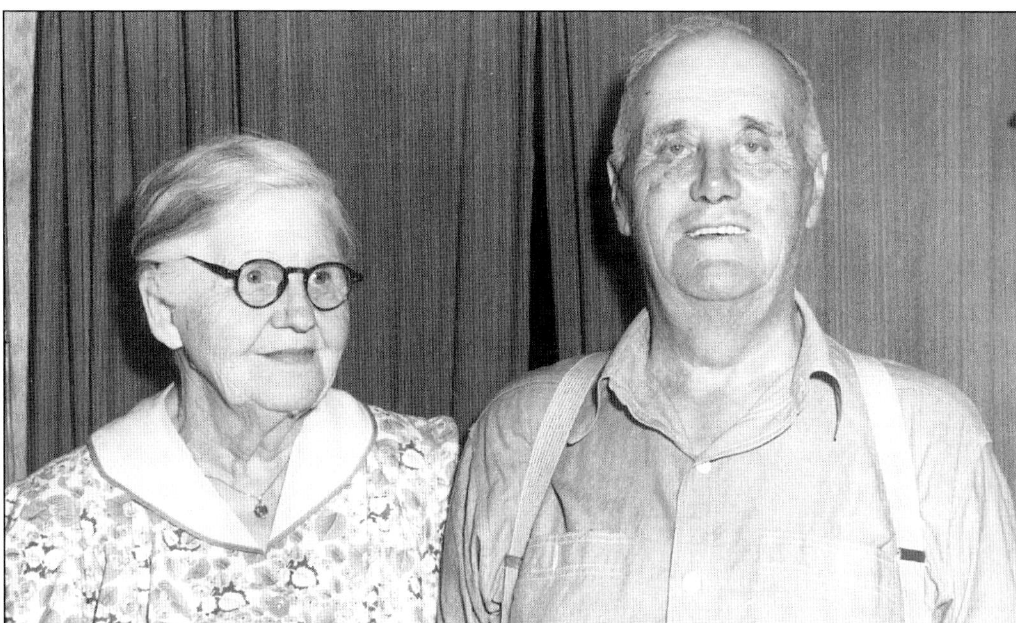

CHARLOTTE AND GEORGE NORTON, C. 1938. The Nortons lived on St. John Street in Portland and spent their summers at the Breakwater, which they built at Ward's Cove c. 1935. George was a conductor on the Maine Central Mountain Division Railroad and an avid fisherman. Their granddaughter Joan Stanford and her husband spend their summers at the Breakwater, and their grandson Bennett and his wife own a year-round home across the road from the Breakwater.

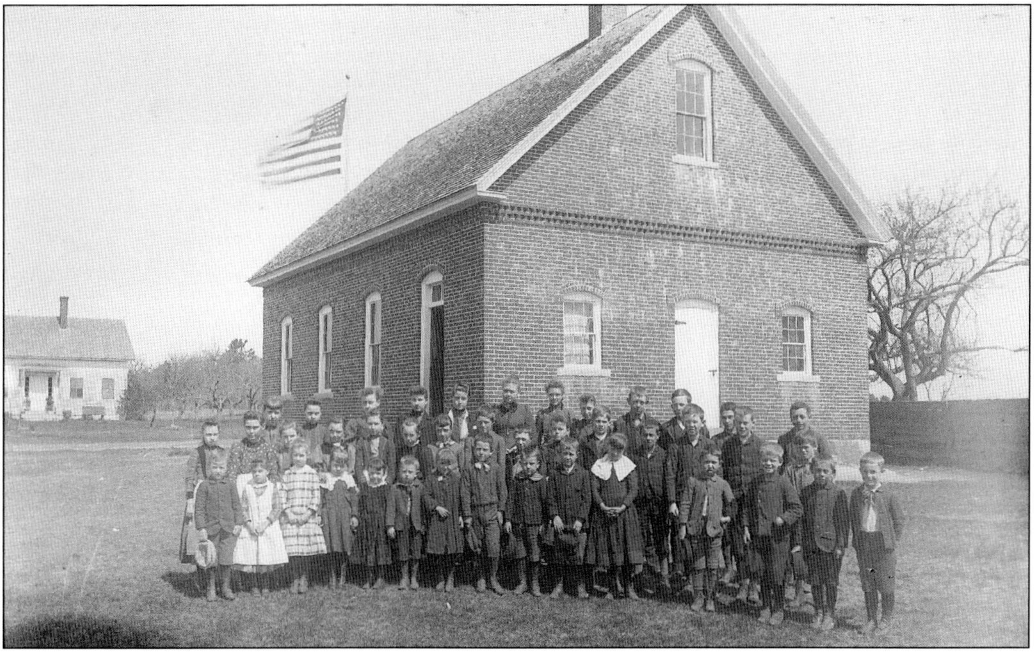

THE BRICK SCHOOL, C. 1910. Before the first school was constructed two years after Standish was incorporated as a town and the district school system was established, children received some sort of instruction either at home from their parents or an itinerant teacher or in the nearby home of a teacher. This sturdy brick school, now part of a private home, was located on Hillcrest, overlooking Sebago Lake. It was closed in 1923.

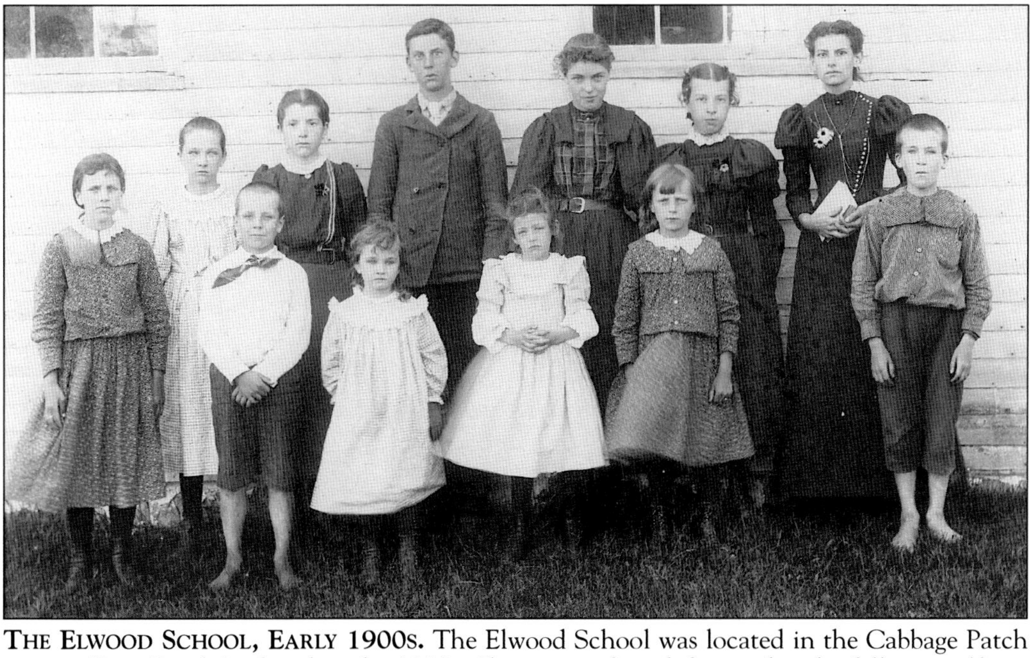

THE ELWOOD SCHOOL, EARLY 1900S. The Elwood School was located in the Cabbage Patch area on Dow Road. It closed in the 1930s. Shown are, from left to right, the following: (front row) Luena Chaer, Selden Chaer, Alice Berry, Lora Chaer, and Fred Robbins; (back row) Inez Berry, Pearle Dow, Perley Fogg, Maude Hadley, Vena Dow, and teacher Ida Cole.

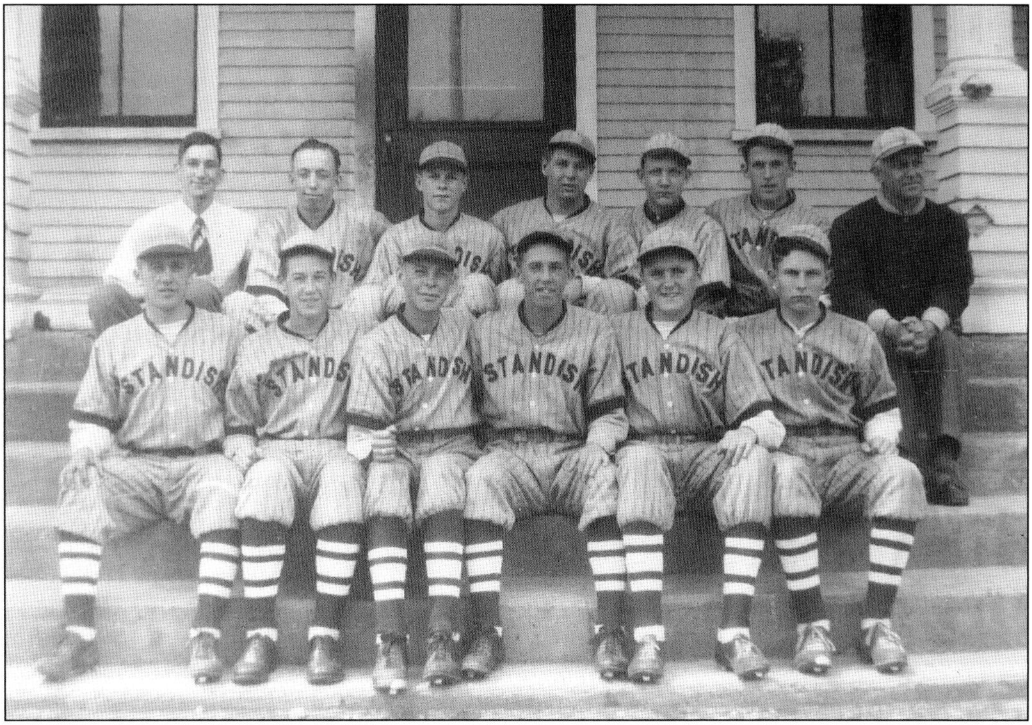

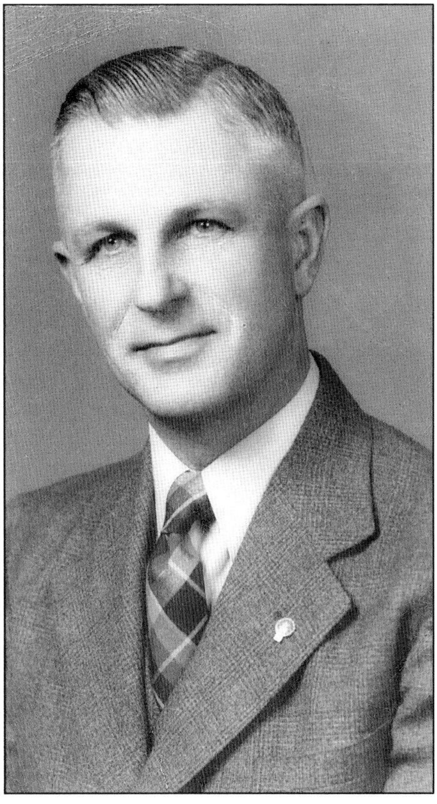

TRIPLE C CHAMPS, 1945. Seated on the steps of Standish High School, which was constructed at Sebago Lake in 1914, are, from left to right, as follows: (front row) Neil Shaw, Ernest Rines, Victor Woodbrey, Arthur Rines, Roger Mead, and Paul Burnell; (back row) Leopold Irish, manager; Jack Barnes, captain; Herbert Woodbrey; Phil Coolbroth; Richard Gaisford; Rodney Warren; and Rupert Johnson, coach. Missing is Gordon Warren.

RUPERT J. JOHNSON, (1902 -1974). Rupert Johnson, widely known in his later years as the "Grand Old Man" of sports in Maine, was principal, teacher, and coach at Standish High School. He served in that post from 1925 until Standish joined with Buxton, Hollis, and Limington, and Standish High School became Johnson Junior High School. He continued to serve as teacher and athletic director at the new district Bonny Eagle High School until his retirement in 1965. A native of Brownfield, Johnson attended Fryeburg Academy and Bowdoin College, where he excelled academically as well as in baseball and basketball. He organized the Triple C League in 1926 and was a leading member of the Maine State Principals Association for 36 years. In 1978, he was voted into the Maine Sports Hall of Fame.

Two

Baldwin

First Settled: *c.* 1773
Incorporated: 1802
Population: 1,300
Area: 36.40 Square miles
Principal Settlements: East Baldwin, West Baldwin, North Baldwin, Old Baldwin

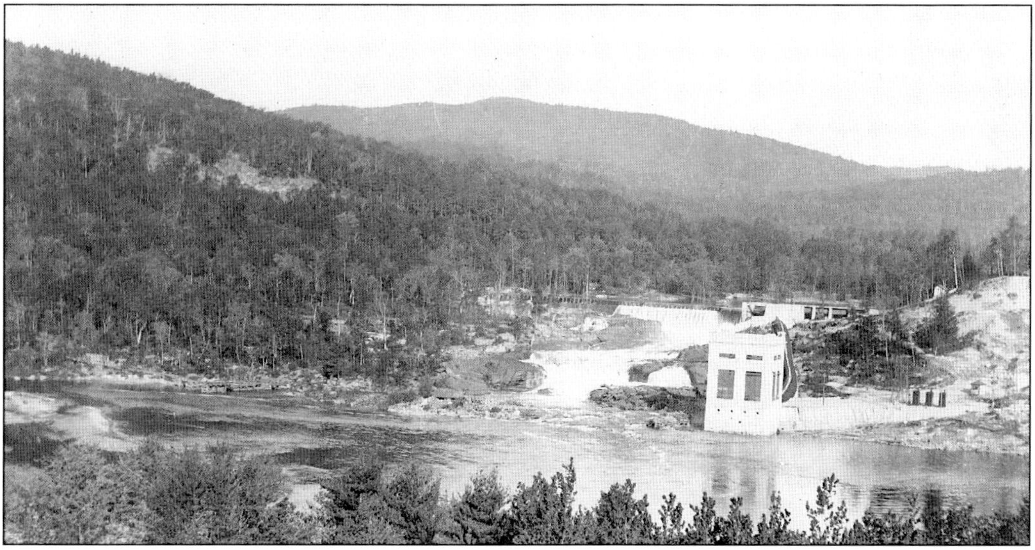

THE GREAT FALLS, C. 1920. The Great Falls on the Saco River, commonly referred to today as the Hiram Falls—even though the lower half with the power station is in the town of Baldwin––provided power to turn waterwheels and later turbines soon after the first settlers arrived in the area. The river, despite intermittent rapids and falls, was a major artery linking the hinterland to the coast before roads were built. It enabled lumberman to harvest the valuable white pine trees, brand them, and float them down the river to the mills that sprouted up along its banks and then to the coast to be loaded onto schooners. At one time, ferryboats ran from Ingalls Pond, just above the falls, to Fryeburg. The power station and dam were built by the Cumberland Power and Light Company *c.* 1918.

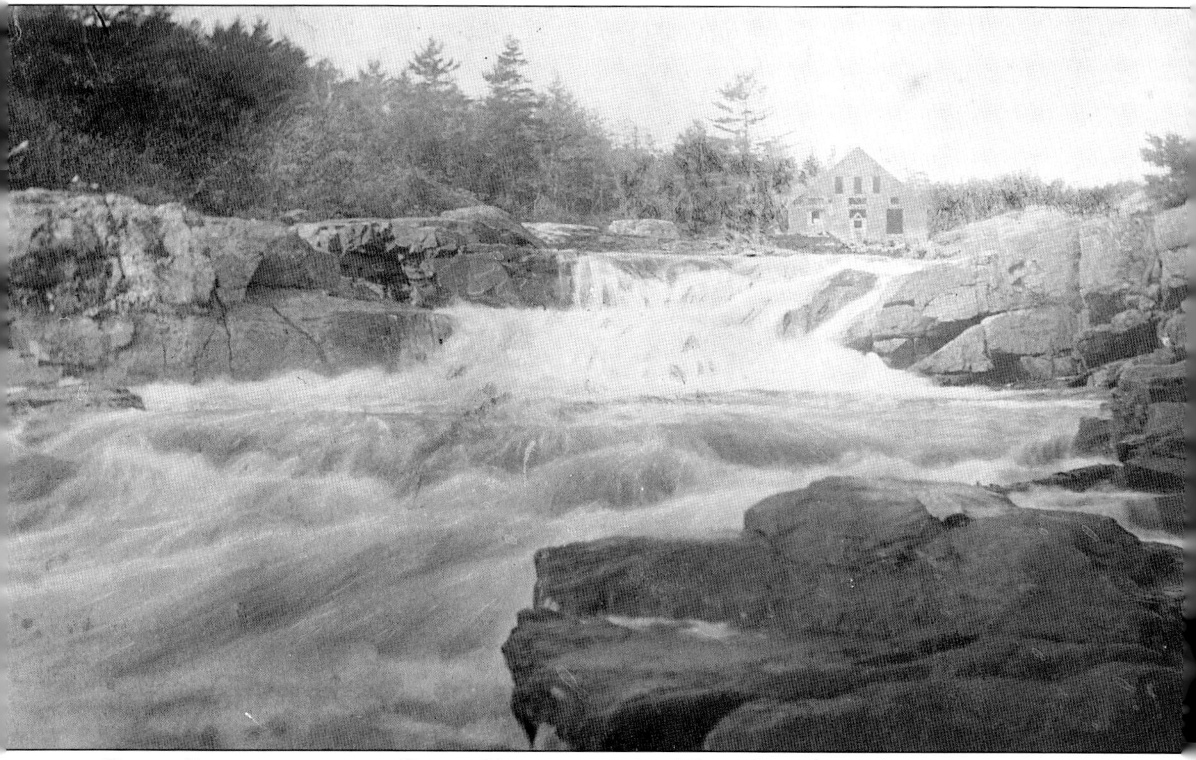

EARLY INDUSTRY AT THE GREAT FALLS, C. 1887. There has always been a paucity of good farming land in much of Baldwin because of the predominance of rugged glacial outcroppings and the sandy lacustrine plains, particularly in parts of Old Baldwin and East Baldwin. Baldwin, however, has always been blessed with superfluous waterpower. Laommi Baldwin and Josiah Pierce built the first dam and sawmill at the Great Falls, said to have been the first in Baldwin, before the town was incorporated. King Philip's War (1675–1676) not only marked the beginning of a long series of conflicts between the British colonials and the Native Americans who soon thereafter were supported and encouraged by the French but also set the wheels in motion that eventually led to the formation of the Flintstown Plantation, renamed Baldwin upon its incorporation in 1802. It was common practice for the Massachusetts Bay Colony to compensate its veterans (or their descendants) for rendering military services with land, since it was beggared of money but possessed vast tracts of unsurveyed wilderness. One of these eligible veterans was John Flint (Flynt) of Concord. But since he died in 1687, it remained for his son and namesake (and others) to petition the Massachusetts Bay General Court for a township, which they were granted in 1735. However, in the ensuing dispute between Massachusetts and New Hampshire, 28 townships—including the one involving John Flint—were awarded to the latter in 1738 by King George II, acting as arbiter. Consequently, Flint & Company and countless other veterans ended up empty-handed. It remained for Samuel Whittemore and Amos Lawless to petition the Massachusetts General Court in 1774 on behalf of Flint and the others for compensation. The township of Flintstown was officially granted them on June 16, 1780, including not only what is today Baldwin but also the part that became Sebago in 1826 and the 800-acre Prescott Grant that was transferred to Hiram in 1790. Among those who played an important role in the early development of Baldwin were Samuel Whittmore, Amos Lawless, Laommi Baldwin, Josiah Pierce, David Brown, Peter Harwood, Zachariah Fitch, John C. Flint, Eleazer Flint, and Benjamin Ingalls, Baldwin's first settler. Then, too, there was the legendary Lazarus Rowe, veteran of the French and Indian Wars and the Revolutionary War, who lived to be 104.

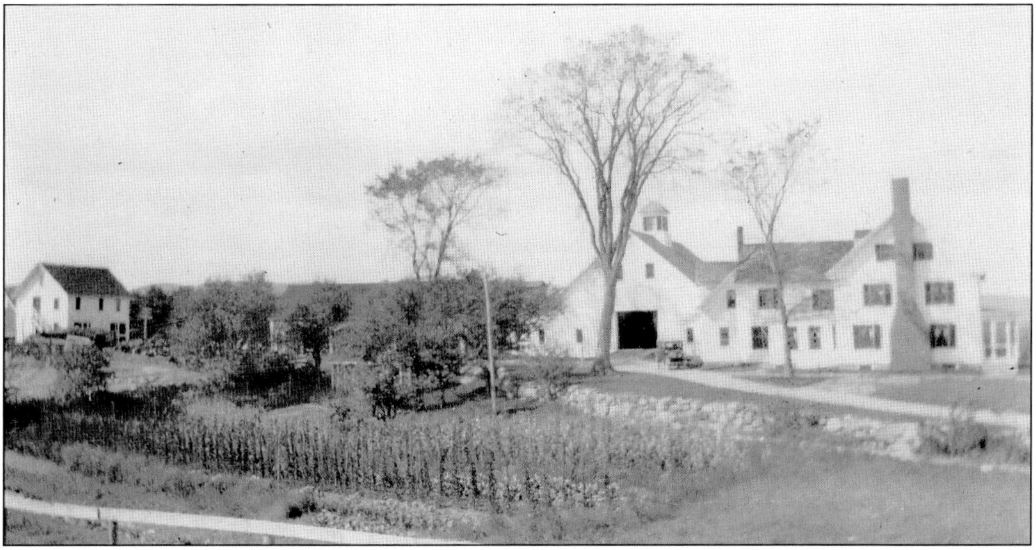

THE PEQUAWKET, c. 1925. The Pequawket, located on the Chase Road in West Baldwin, was built in 1785 by Capt. John Flint shortly after the Flint homestead—just off Route 5 where Deacon Ephraim Flint erected the granite horse trough—was constructed. Except for a period of time when it was operated as an inn, the Pequawket has remained in the hands of the Flint's descendants. It is currently owned by Donald Flint.

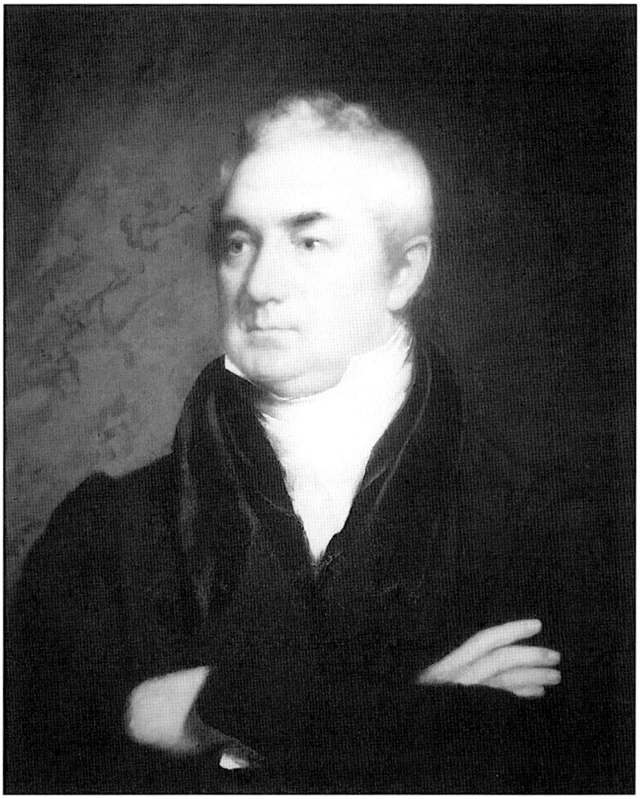

LOAMMI BALDWIN. Loammi Baldwin (1789–1838), [oil on canvas, by Chester Harding, 1827], was the son of Col. Loammi Baldwin of Woburn, Massachusetts, for whom the town of Baldwin was renamed in 1802 and for whom the Baldwin apple is named. The colonel, along with his partner and fellow proprietor Josiah Pierce, at one time owned much of what today is Baldwin and traded lumber and potash for commodities, such as woolens, tobacco, and tea. When Colonel Baldwin was a young man, he worked as a cabinetmaker. Later, he became a self-taught engineer and was the chief engineer, as well as one of the proprietors, of the Middlesex Canal, which did for western Massachusetts and southern New Hampshire what the Cumberland and Oxford Canal did for the Sebago Lake area.

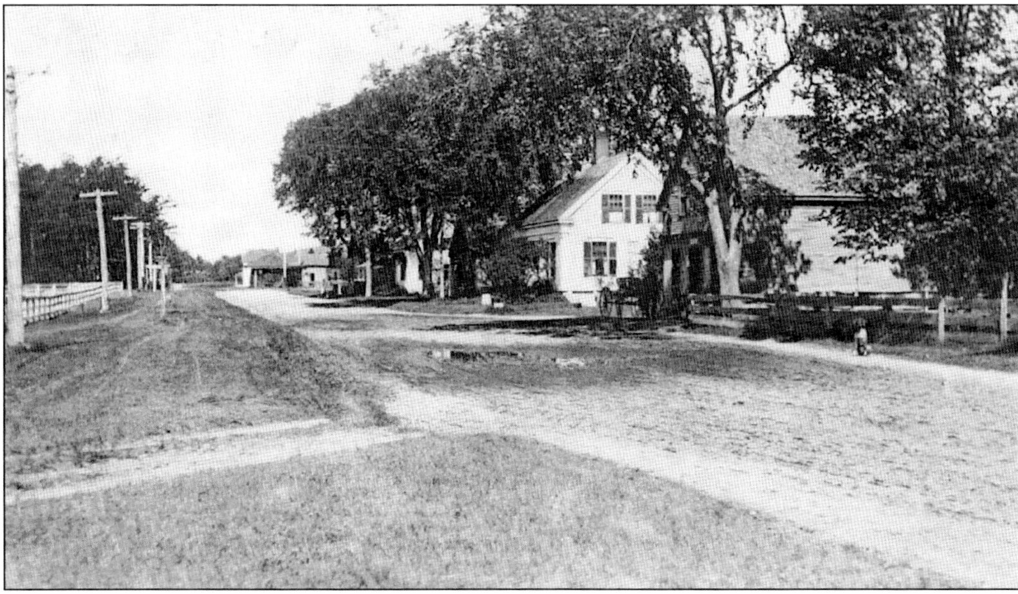

EAST BALDWIN, C. 1905. East Baldwin is still referred to by many locals as Mattocks, named in honor of Civil War hero Brig. Gen. Charles P. Mattocks, who at the time of this photograph owned a large estate (part of which is now Ed Labbe's Auto Repair) in the village and specialized in breeding thoroughbred swine and sheep.

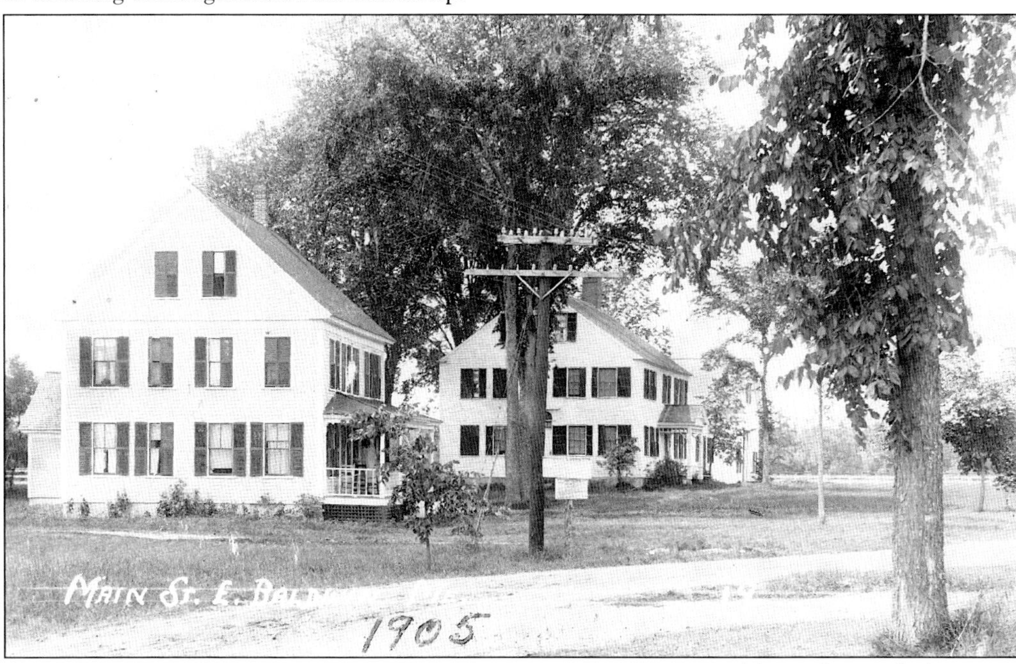

MAIN STREET, EAST BALDWIN, 1905. Main Street in East Baldwin featured these two magnificent Federalist homes, visible today from Route 114. The house and barn on the right were constructed *c.* 1831 by Joshua Chadbourne, tinker and postmaster. The house on the left was built by Chadbourne's oldest son, Josiah (named after Josiah Pierce and the only one of five brothers not to leave for California during the Gold Rush) for his son Joseph as a wedding present when he married Emma Douglas in 1883.

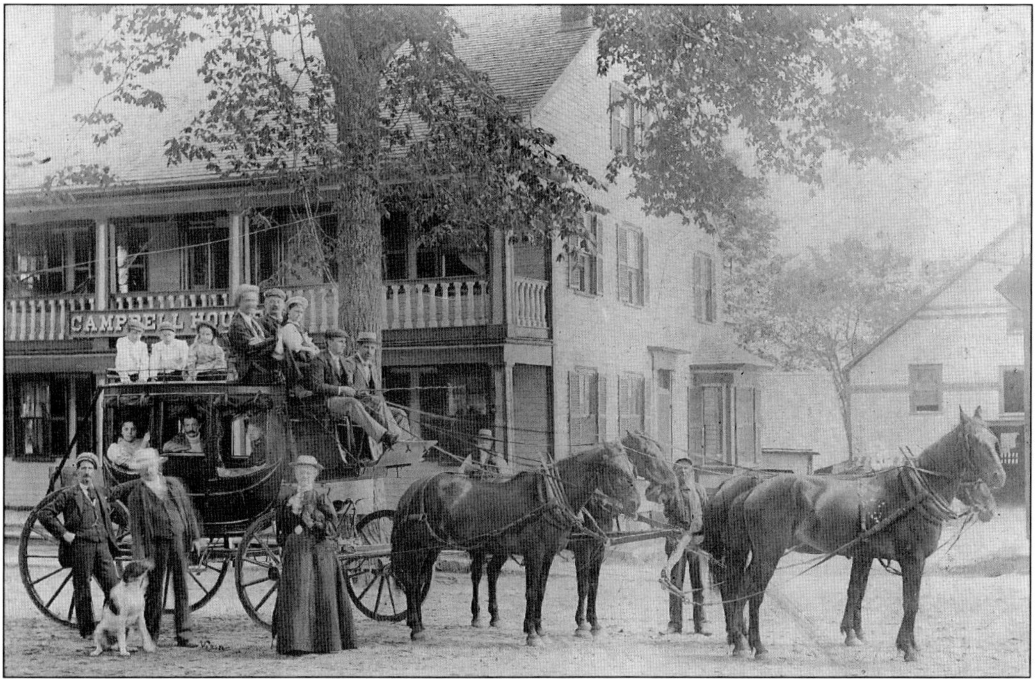

THE CAMPBELL HOUSE, C. 1870. The Campbell House, a popular stagecoach and teamster stop located in the area of the Brown Memorial Library in East Baldwin, burned in 1875. After a good night's rest and generous repast, these passengers seem ready to continue the bone-jarring journey either to Portland or up to Fryeburg and perhaps the White Mountains.

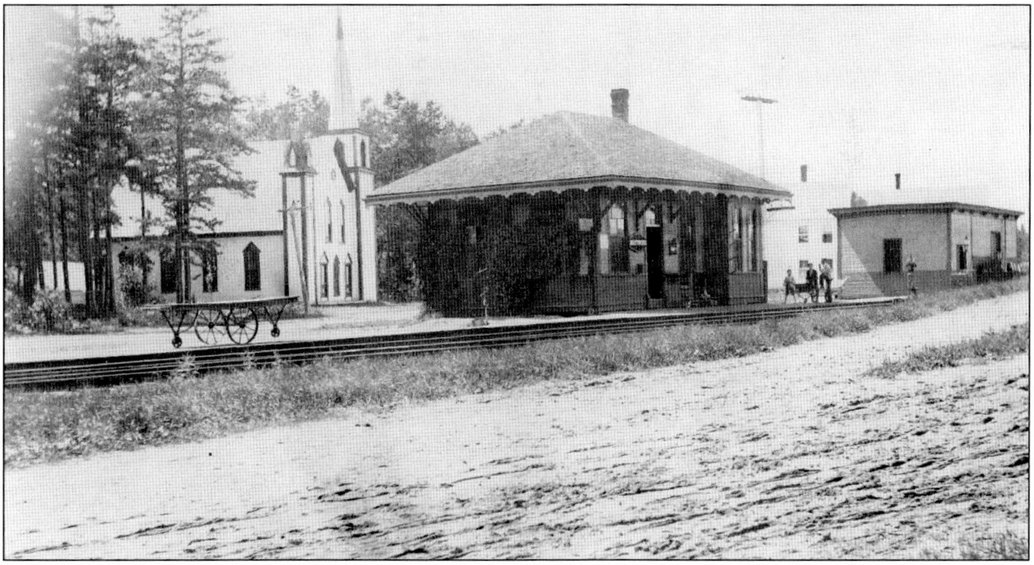

MATTOCKS STATION, C. 1908. This railroad station, originally called the East Baldwin Station, was renamed Mattocks Station on December 30, 1888. Until it closed on March 8, 1933, mailbags for Sebago and Naples, as well as East Baldwin, were dropped off here. Next to the station is the freight shed. On the opposite side of Main Street is the Congregational church built in 1877 as a replacement for the old Emerson meetinghouse, erected near Meadow Brook in 1833.

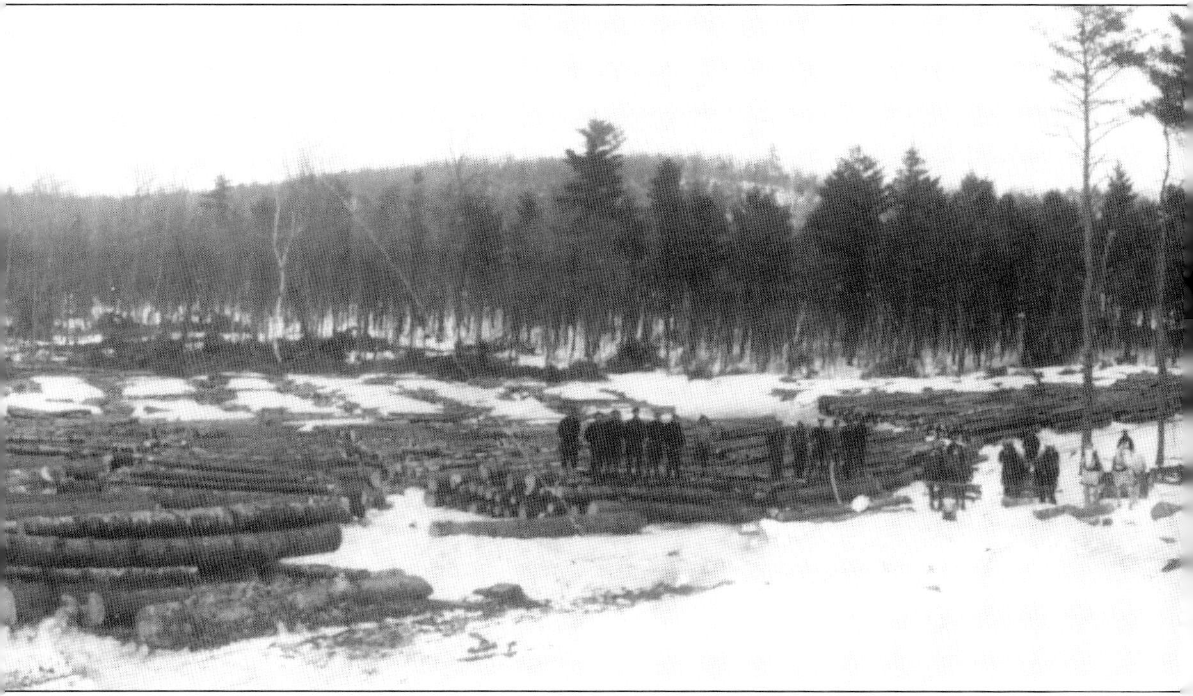

YARDING LOGS, C. 1923. Thousands of feet of white pine are being yarded out by teams of horses to be sawed into rough timber at the Fox Brothers et. al. Electric Mill Operation in East Baldwin, thereby greatly reducing the weight before hauling the boards out by horses and oxen to the nearest railroad or finishing mill. Portable mills remained popular in areas too remote

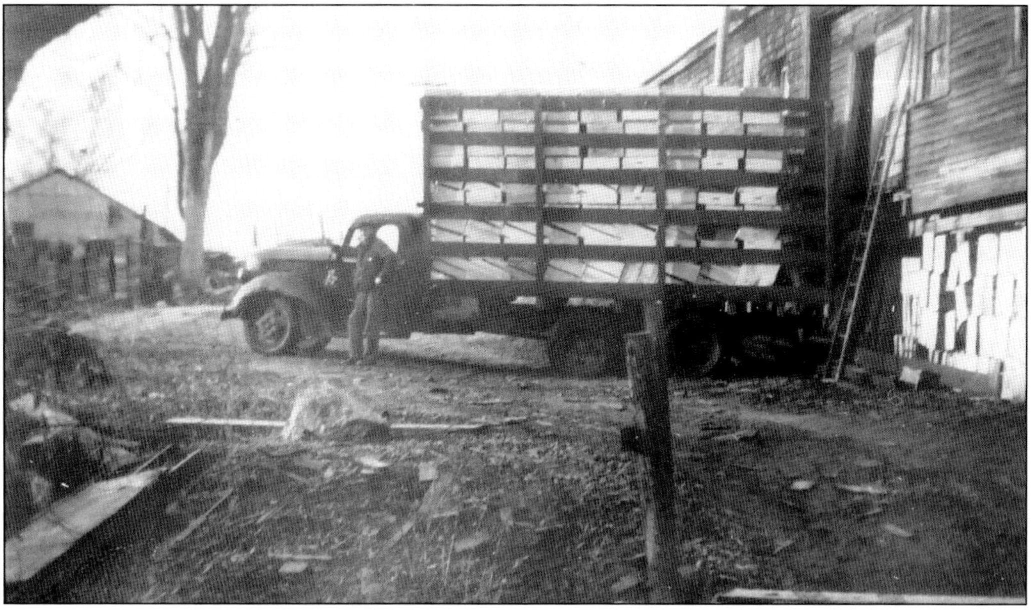

F.E. WOOD AND SONS, C. 1950. For over 40 years, F.E. Wood and Sons of East Baldwin has specialized in processing deciduous logs into pallets. Frank E. Wood, whose father, Frank W. Wood, purchased the mill in 1900, is getting ready to drive this truck loaded with pallets to the Quincy Market in Boston.

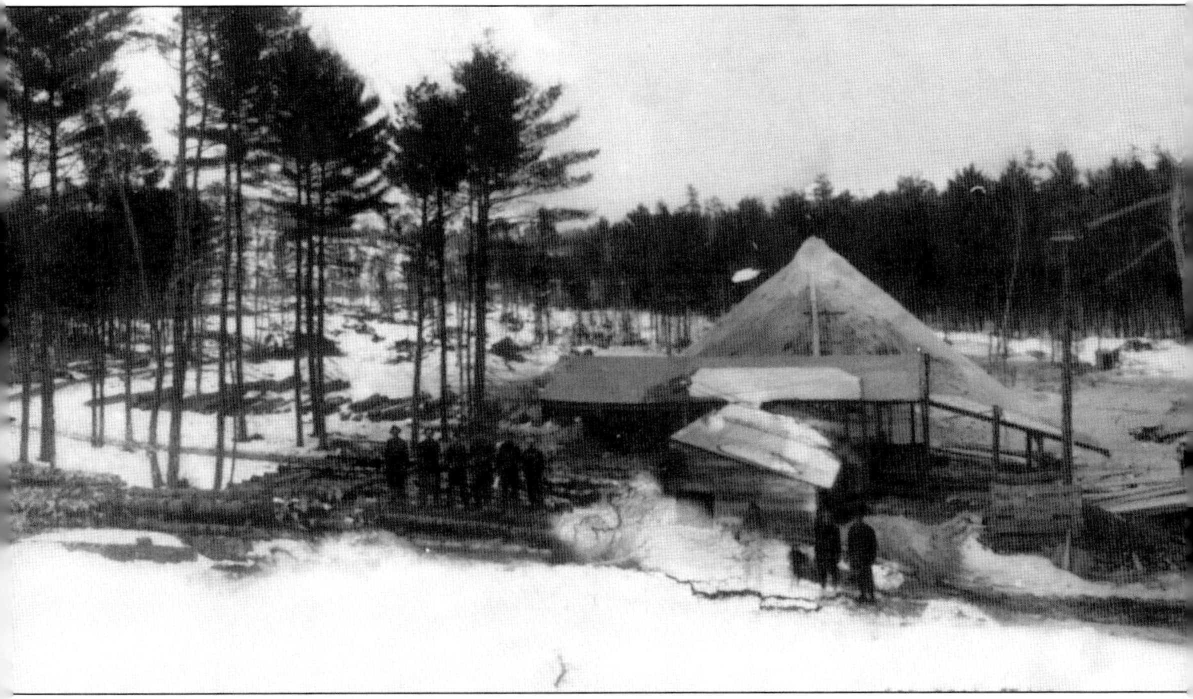

from waterways until modern logging technology following World War II made it easier and more feasible to transport logs directly to the mill to be completely processed from a primary resource to a secondary resource ready for the carpenter. Logging and wood products were and continue to be of primary importance to Baldwin's economy.

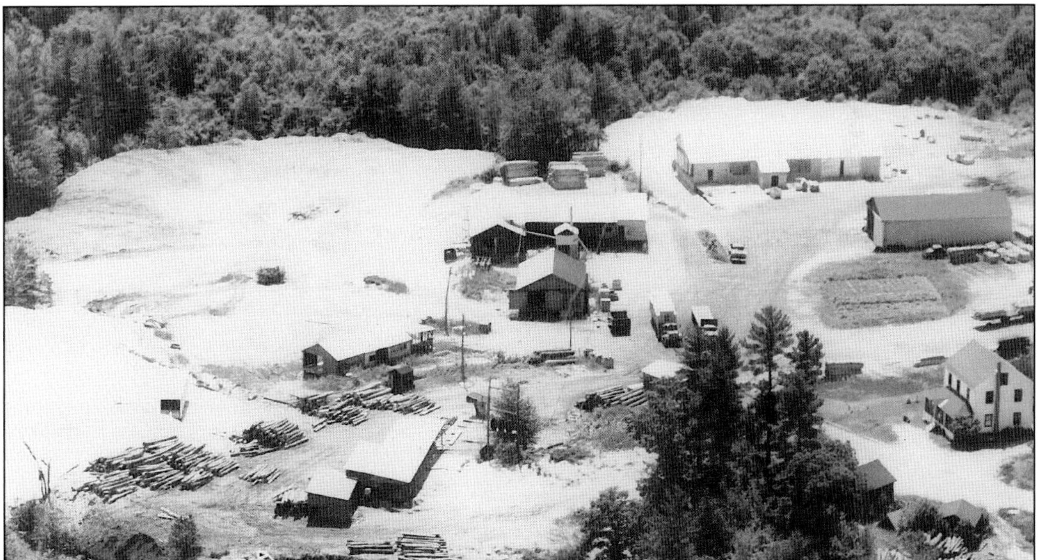

F.E. WOOD AND SONS, C. 1970. Ever since 1789 when Laommi Baldwin and Josiah Pierce erected a water-powered mill here on Quaker Brook in what was then Flintstown, softwood and hardwood logs have been converted into various forms of wood products from rough lumber to pallets. Wood's Mill, as it is known locally, is now a fully automatic sawmill currently operated by the fourth generation of the Wood family.

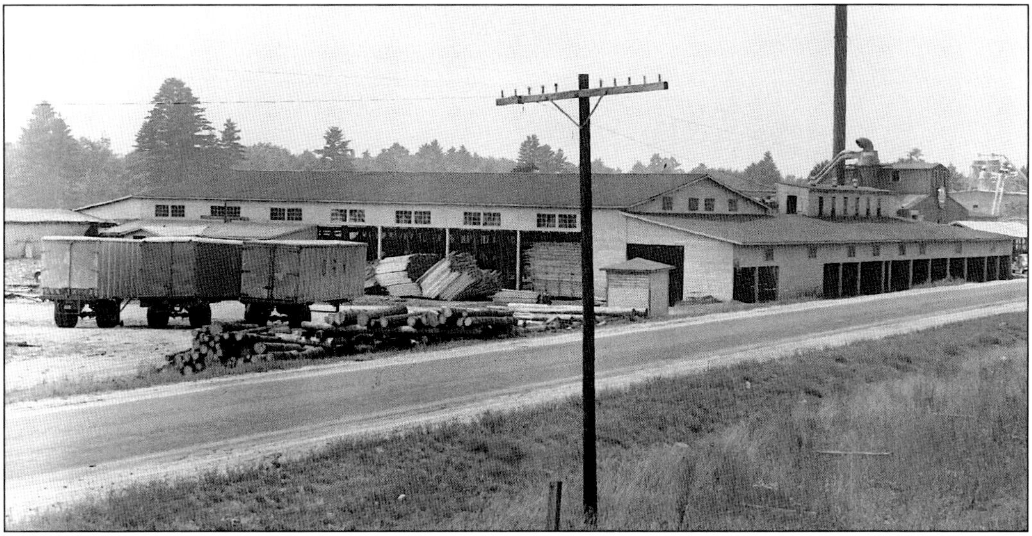

SEBAGO FORESTRY, C. 1960. This sprawling mill complex in East Baldwin was owned and operated by the three Gunther brothers, Ted, Jack, and Stewart, from the early 1940s until 1978. Processing white pine logs into paneling and molding was the mill's specialty. Molding was shipped by rail to famed Levittown, Long Island. The sawdust was sold to the Congoleum Company next door to the mill on Route 113, which dried, bagged, and shipped it to the company's linoleum plant in New Jersey.

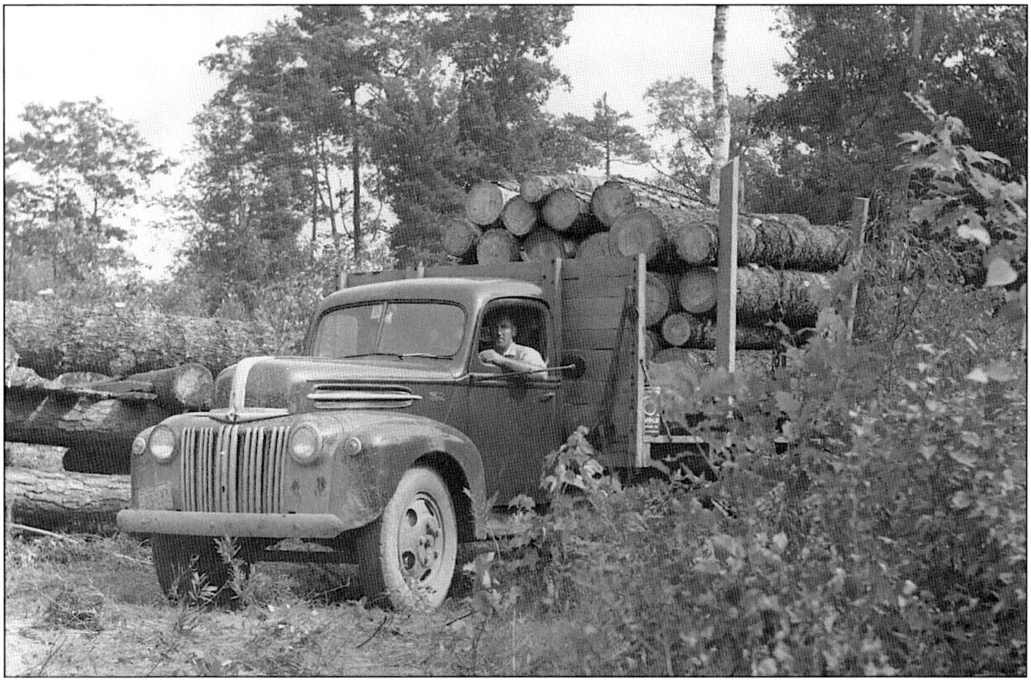

HEADED FOR THE MILL, 1948. Harold Jordan, now retired and living comfortably with his wife, the former Laurette Riley of Old Baldwin, on the shores of Pequawket Lake in Limington, heads out from Don Chadbourne's woodlot on the Old Baldwin Road in a 1944 Ford truck with a load of white pine logs for Sebago Forestry. For 24 years Jordan managed the mill in Steep Falls owned by Stewart Gunther and George Jewett.

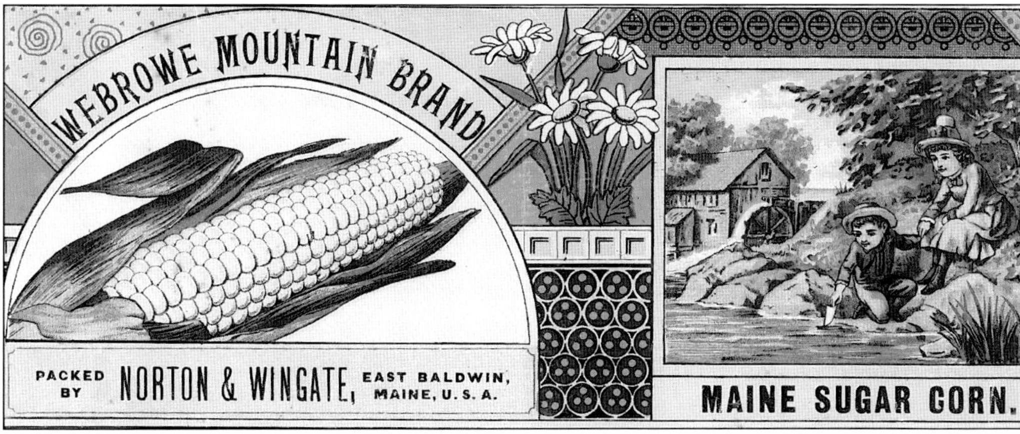

THE CANNING INDUSTRY, C. 1890. In 1871, shortly after the Portland & Ogdensburg Railroad was constructed, Burhnam and Morrill of Portland opened a canning factory in East Baldwin and for a number of years canned corn, presumably raised by local farmers on the rich alluvial soil along the Saco River Valley and possibly North Baldwin. Charles P. Mattocks owned the factory for a time, before it was taken over by Lorenzo Norton and Mr. Wingate and named for Webrowe Mountain in North Baldwin.

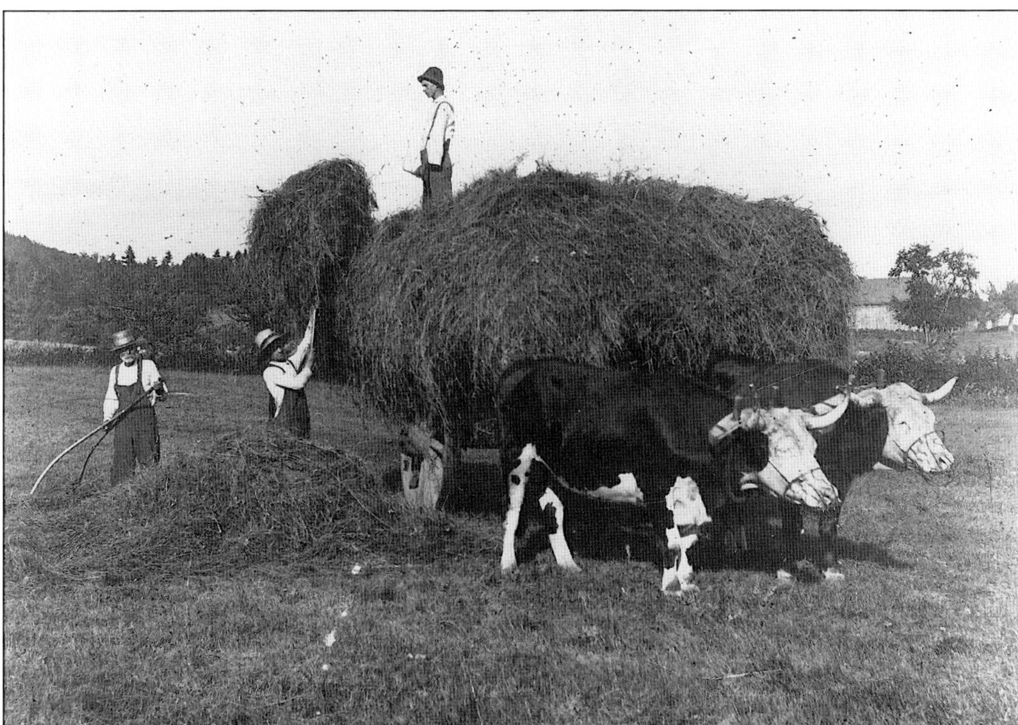

HAYING TIME, C. 1890. Haying was a slow, labor-intensive procedure here in Maine before mechanization about a half century ago. A loafer rake is being used to rake up the scatterings while the final few pitchforks of hay are being tossed up to the young man waiting with his fork to pack it down, before this evenly matched pair of horned Herefords trundles it up the hill to the barn.

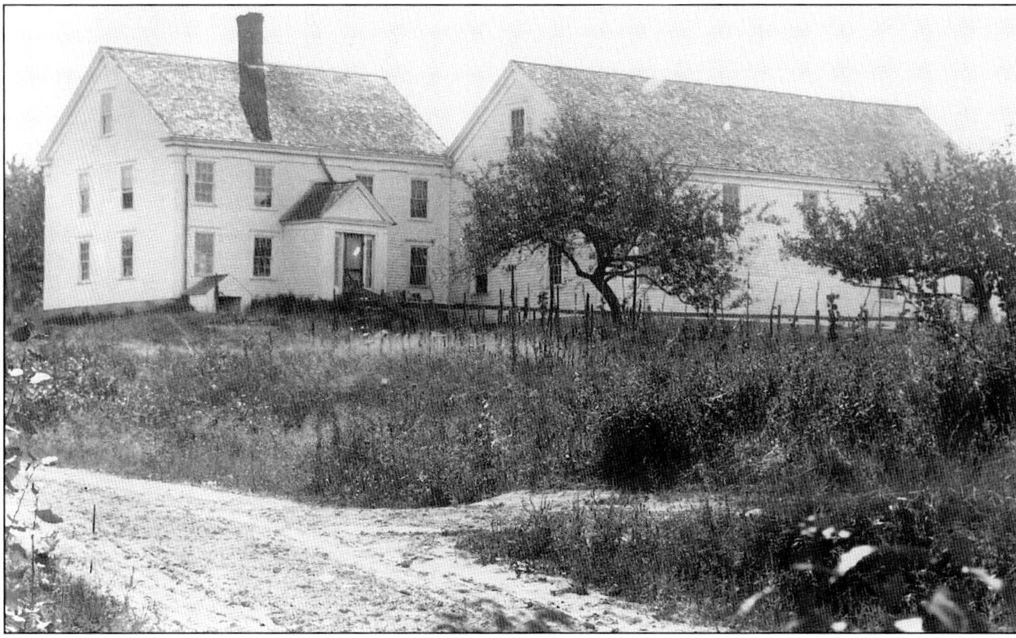

The Old Milliken Place, 1930. The Old Milliken Place, located on Rocky Dunn Hill in West Baldwin, was built by Charles Henry Harding in the 1780s and sold to James Milliken in 1813. It was once a tavern and a favorite stop for passengers on the White Mountain stagecoach. In the early part of the 20th century, Frank Milliken made wooden barrel hoops here. One of Baldwin's oldest houses, it begs to be restored.

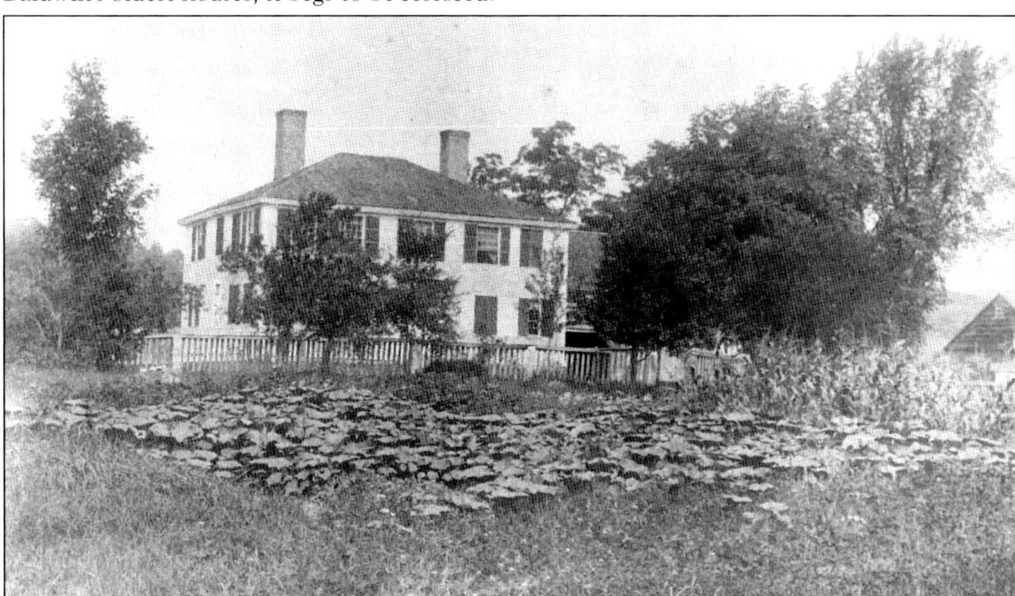

The Pierce Place, c.1913. This magnificent Federalist dwelling, one of the oldest extant houses in Baldwin, was constructed in 1785 by the firm of Baldwin and Pierce of Woburn, Massachusetts, and lived in by Josiah Pierce, who brought his wife, Phoebe Thompson, up on horseback from Woburn in 1787. In 1922, a sizable extension was added. Six generations of Pierces have lived in West Baldwin.

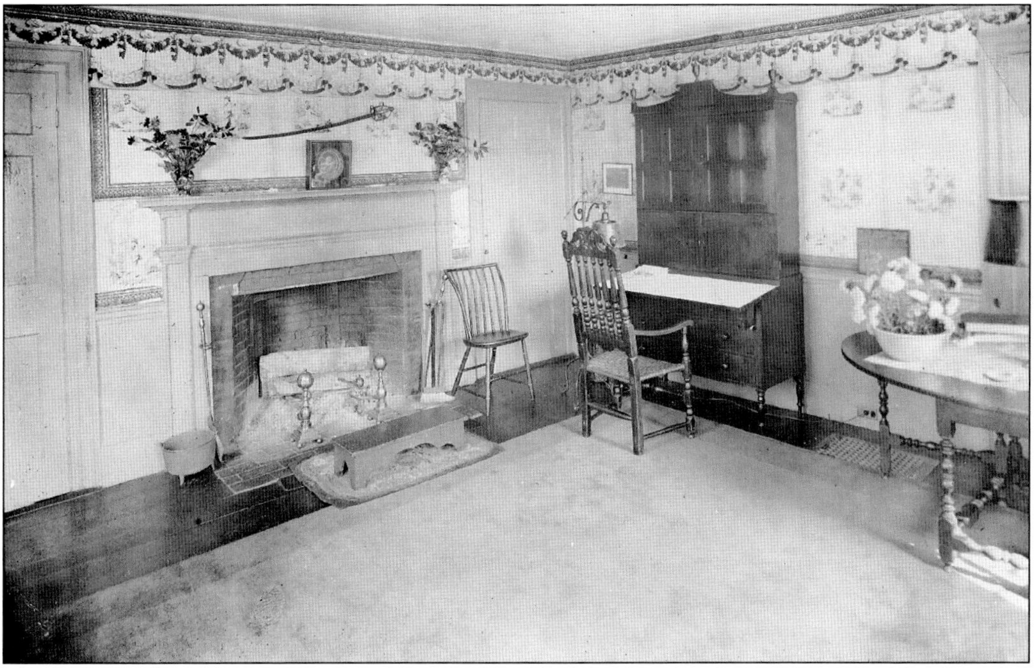

THE PIERCE PLACE, C. 1913. This room, which served as a store in the early years that the squire resided here, and the other original seven rooms have been painstakingly maintained to the present. The squire's sword, worn during the Revolutionary War and Shay's Rebellion, hangs over the fireplace, one of eight in the house built according to the formula prescribed by Benjamin Thompson (Count Rumford). The table accompanied the squire's parents, Josiah and Ruth Simon Pierce (the count's mother) when they moved up from Woburn shortly before the father's death in 1799. The secretary is thought to have been made in Baldwin.

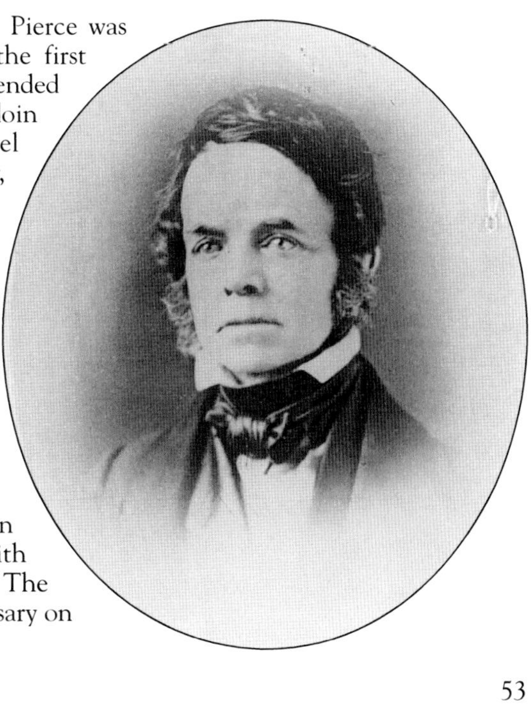

THE HONORABLE JOSIAH PIERCE, C. 1820. Pierce was the son of Josiah and Phoebe Pierce and the first male Pierce to be born in Baldwin. He attended Bridgton Academy, and graduated from Bowdoin College in 1818—a few years before Nathaniel Hawthorne, Henry and Stephen Longfellow, and Franklin Pierce, who was a relative of Judge Pierce. Josiah was judge of probate for Cumberland County, a member of the Maine Legislature, and president of the Maine Senate. The judge's eldest son, Josiah, was appointed by Franklin Pierce to the legation staff in St. Petersburg, Russia. His younger son, George W., married Anne Longfellow, and their great-grandson William Curtis Pierce (the fourth generation of Bowdoin graduates, the fourth generation of lawyers, and the former chairman of the Bowdoin College Board of Trustees) currently resides with his wife, Elizabeth Gay, at the Pierce Place. The couple celebrated their 70th wedding anniversary on July 29, 1999.

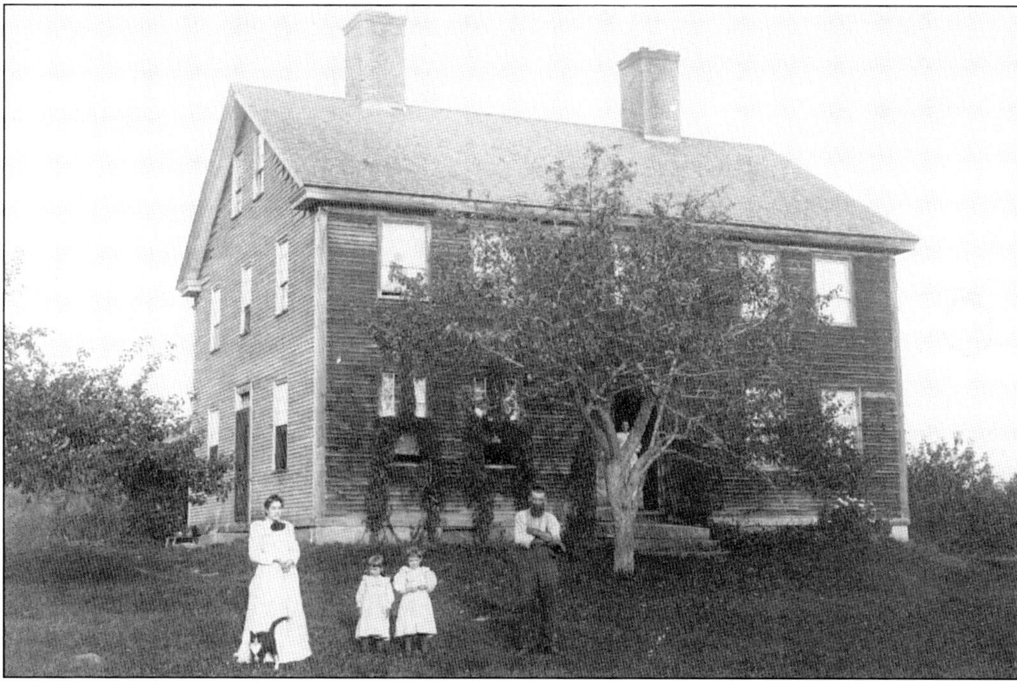

THE OLDEST HOUSE IN TOWN, C. 1890S. Slightly older than the Pierce Place, a few hundred feet away, is this two-and-a-half-story Federalist house that was built in 1784 by Ephraim Batcheldor, who later sold it to a cousin, David Boothby. Boothby's granddaughter Lillian, pictured here with her daughters Thelma and Nellie and her parents, Joseph and Lydia Ann, married Elmer Black, who took over the farm in 1898 and lived to be 92. Black's great-granddaughter Maggie Black is the present owner of the house.

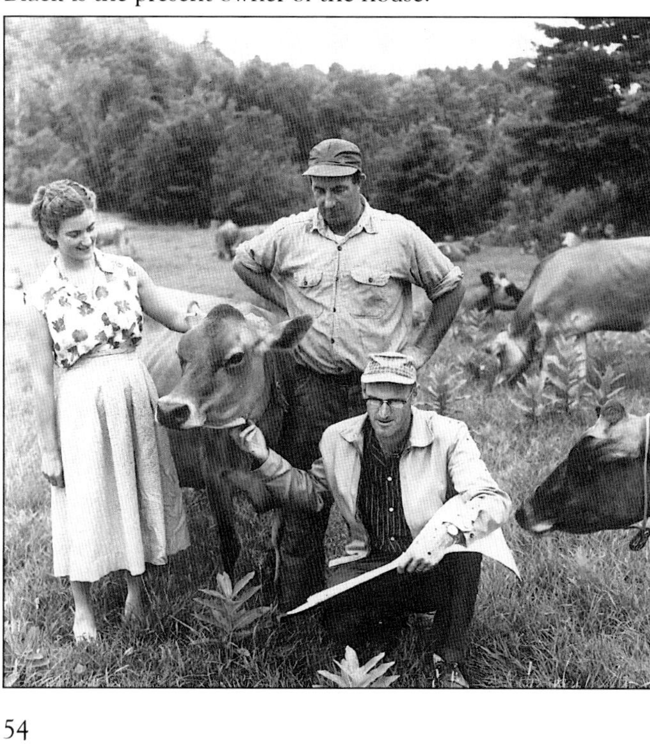

BRIARCLIFF FARM, C. 1950. Helen and Henry Black and Harry Bell, the Cumberland County agent, inspect one of Briarcliff Farm's registered Jersey cows. Black took over the family farm *c.* 1943 and made many innovative changes over the years, such as replacing conventional stanchions with "loose housing," enabling the herd to move about freely and eat hay at will. At one time, the 400-acre farm supported 260 head of registered Jerseys and a sizable flock of Dorset sheep. In 1957, Black was one of 59 Jerseymen in the nation to be awarded the highly prestigious Constructive Breeder Award given out by the American Jersey Cattle Club.

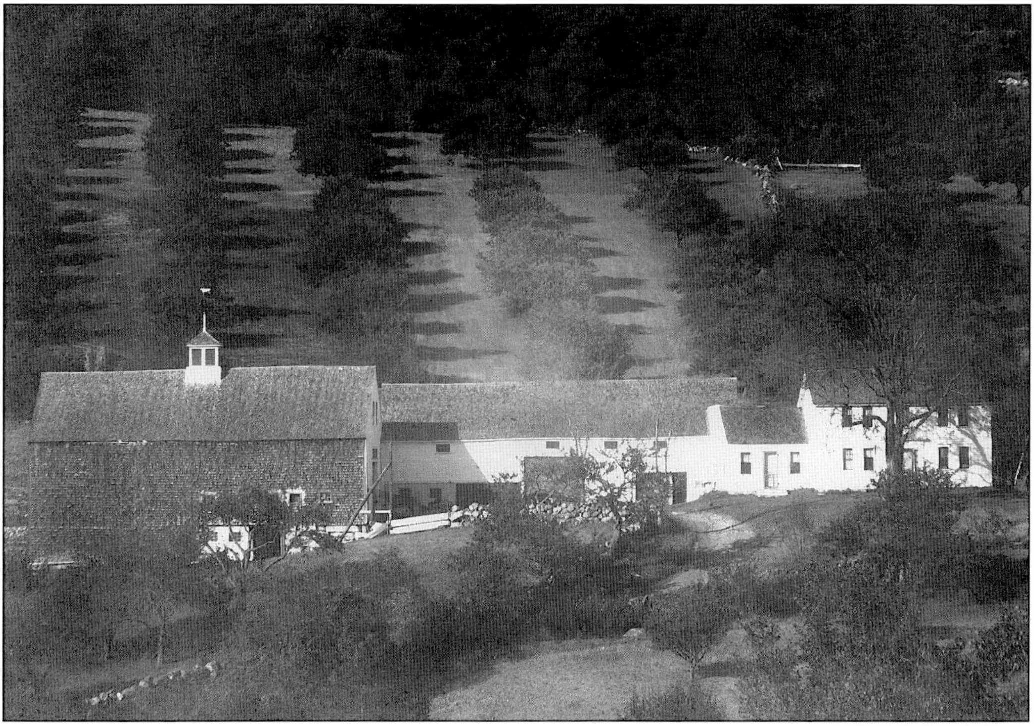

DIRIGO FARM, c. 1925. The undulated landscape, particularly in West and North Baldwin, was ideally suited to growing apples and grazing livestock. Dirigo Farm, owned by Elmer E. Usher and located on the Douglas Hill Road in West Baldwin, like Briarcliff and numerous other farms that once operated in Baldwin, did both. Dirigo Farm had one of the finest Holstein-Friesian herds in the country and advertised breeding stock nationally. Dirigo Farm also had a fine apple orchard until the winter of "the big freeze" in 1933–34 devastated it and other orchards in Baldwin and much of Maine. The famous Baldwin apple was particularly hard hit. Until then, almost every farm in the area raised some apples, and this kept the local coopers busy making barrels and hoops. Cider mills were also common. Locally grown apples primarily were transported by rail and sold to Hannaford Brothers in Portland, to be shipped to London and Liverpool.

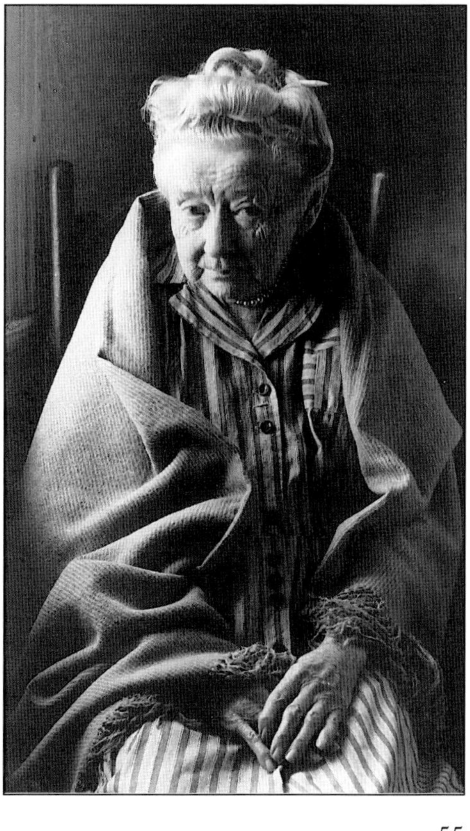

ALMA USHER, c. 1950 Alma Usher was the wife of Elmer E. Usher and lived at Dirigo Farm in West Baldwin. She was about 90 years old when Roger W. Flint took this photograph. In 1952, she and Elmer Black were the two oldest citizens of Baldwin.

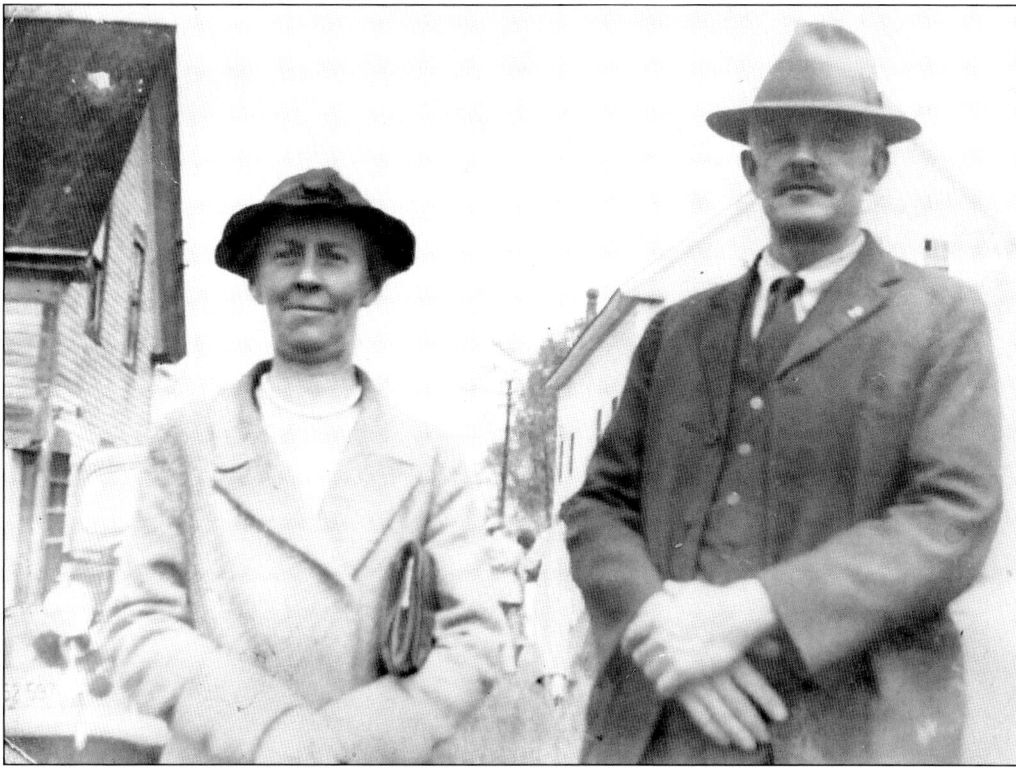

EVA AND ROSCOE SPENCER, C. 1940. The Spencers lived on the Douglas Hill Road in West Baldwin on the farm now owned by Fred and Earlene Doughty. Married for nearly 49 years, Eva (1890–1965) and Roscoe (1894–1978) were both extremely active in town affairs and were familiar faces at most local social functions. He was a colorful auctioneer and a selectman for many years. "The town couldn't run without Roscoe," commented one West Baldwin senior citizen.

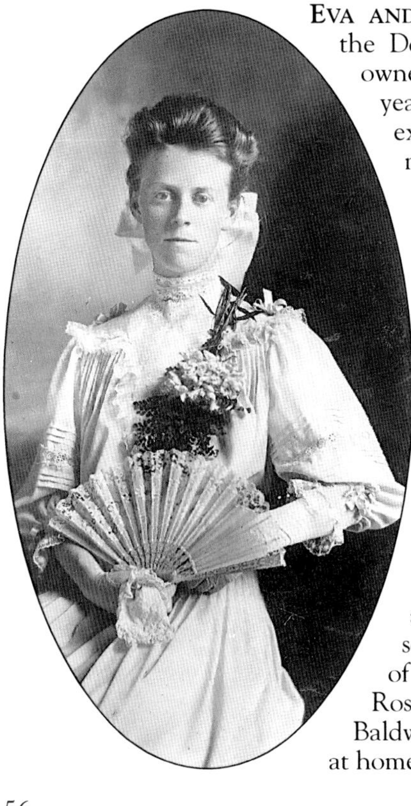

EVA PUGSLEY SPENCER, C. 1907. Eva Pugsley Spencer was born in 1890 on the family farm on High Road in Cornish, and this Victorian portrait was probably taken at her graduation from Cornish High School. She taught school in Baldwin for a number of years and was the wife of one of Baldwin's leading and most colorful citizens, Roscoe Spencer. She was a devoted member of the West Baldwin Methodist Church and the local grange. It is said that at home, "she ruled the roost."

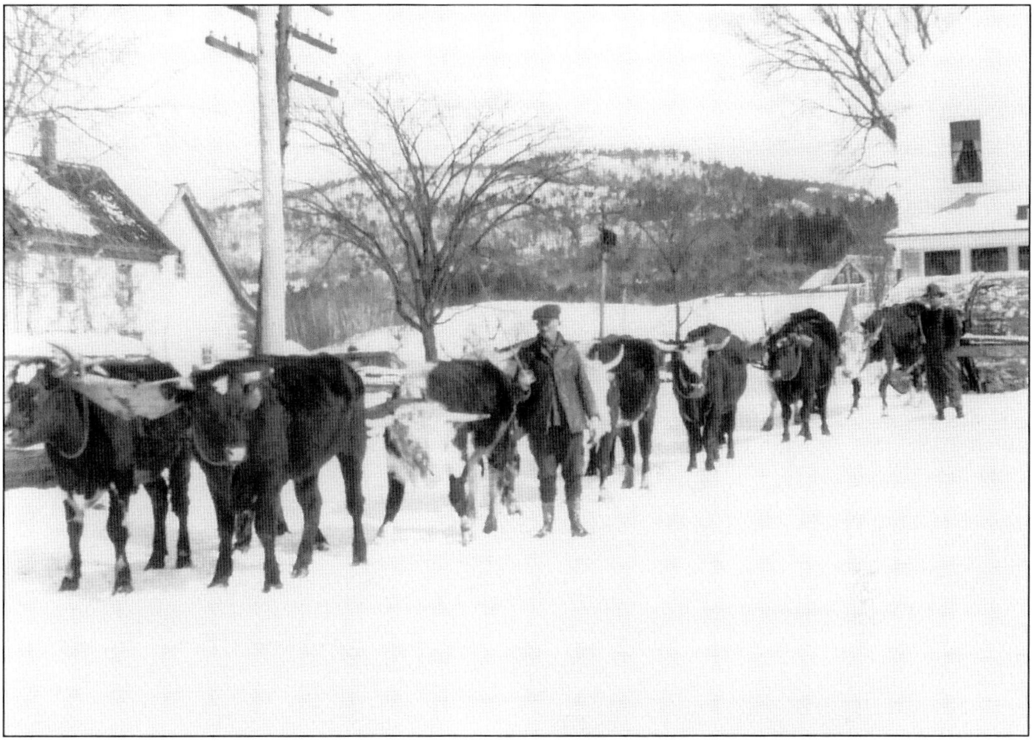

TEAM WORK, C. 1920. Verne Sargent, center, who worked for the Blacks at Briarcliff Farm, and Ellie Locke, right, use goad sticks to guide four yokes of oxen as they pull in unison a huge snow roller along the road through West Baldwin village. Locke is remembered as having built a large wooden V-shaped plow to which he yoked eight pair of oxen and cleared the road down to the Cornish Station. During the winter it was relatively easy to move about on the well-packed roads by horse and sleigh (automobiles were put up for the winter). However, from the time that the ice and snow began to thaw in earnest until the mud dried up, it was nearly impossible for folks to venture beyond their village homes and isolated farms scattered over the hills and along the narrow gauge valleys.

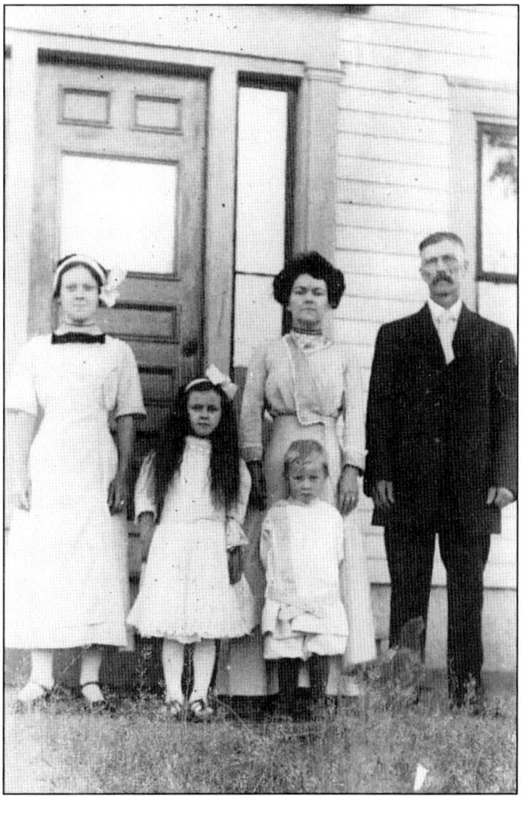

THE ROWE FAMILY, C. 1902. Arthur Rowe Sr., who lived to be 101, and his wife, Addie, who died at 91, stand in front of their home (now owned by the Stackhouses) in West Baldwin with their three children, Mildred, Kathy, and Arthur Jr.

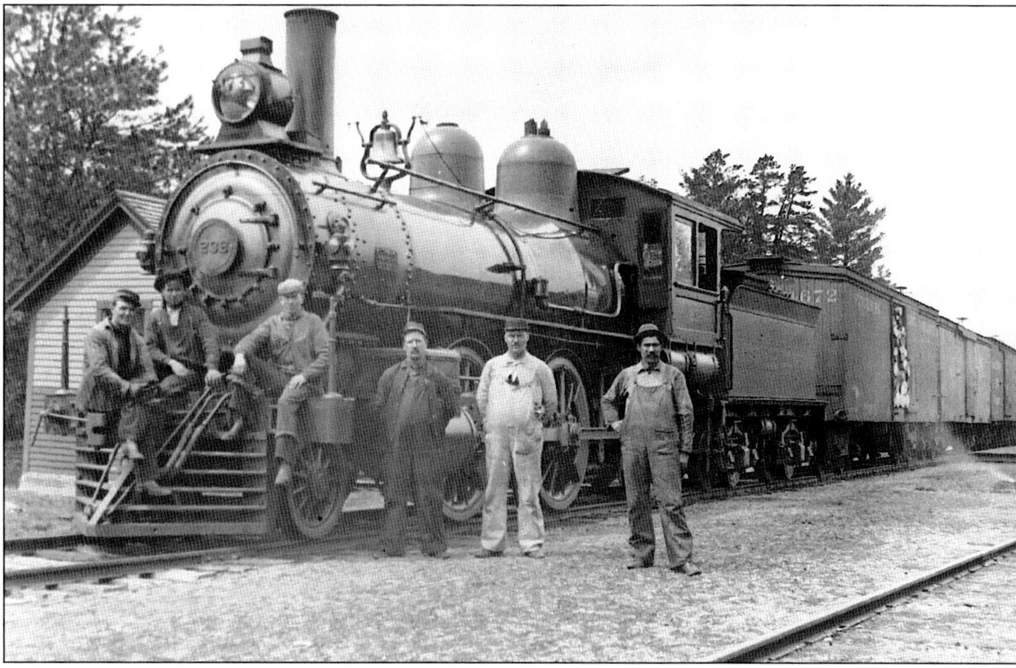

AT THE WEST BALDWIN STATION, C. 1915. This well-polished Schenectady-built Mogul 233 and a long line of freight cars pause for a few minutes at the West Baldwin Station while the crew poses for an unknown photographer before continuing down the line 33.42 miles to Portland. Built in 1894 for the Maine Central Railroad, this handsome locomotive features an ornate kerosene lamp and a single set of pilot wheels.

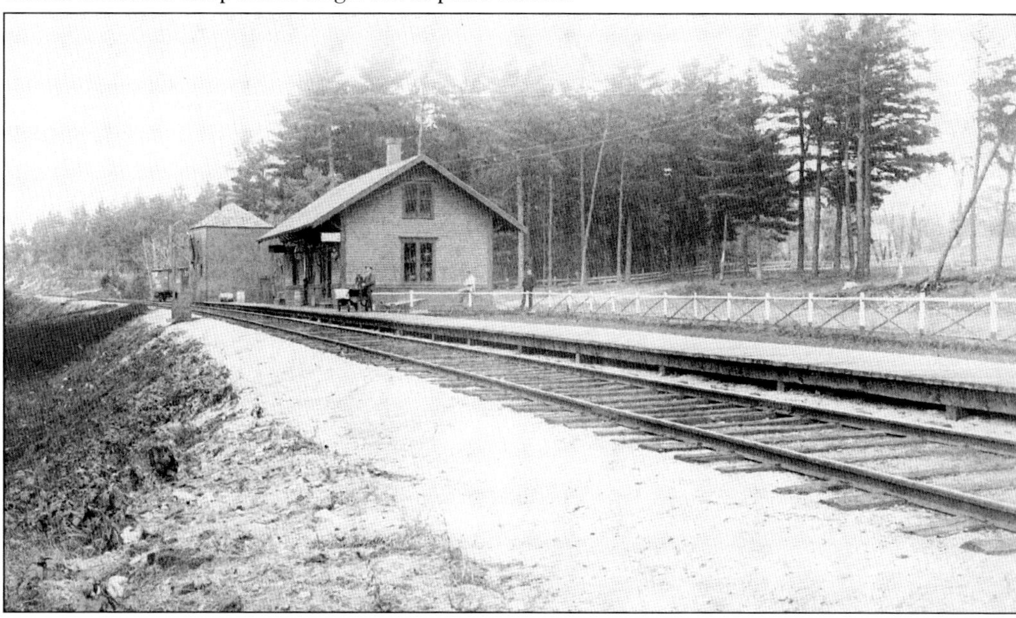

THE WEST BALDWIN STATION, C. 1925. The West Baldwin Station was located about a mile north of the Cornish Station, which prior to December 11, 1888, had been called the Baldwin Station. The West Baldwin Station was closed on September 9, 1930, but the Cornish Station continued to operate until February 14, 1962.

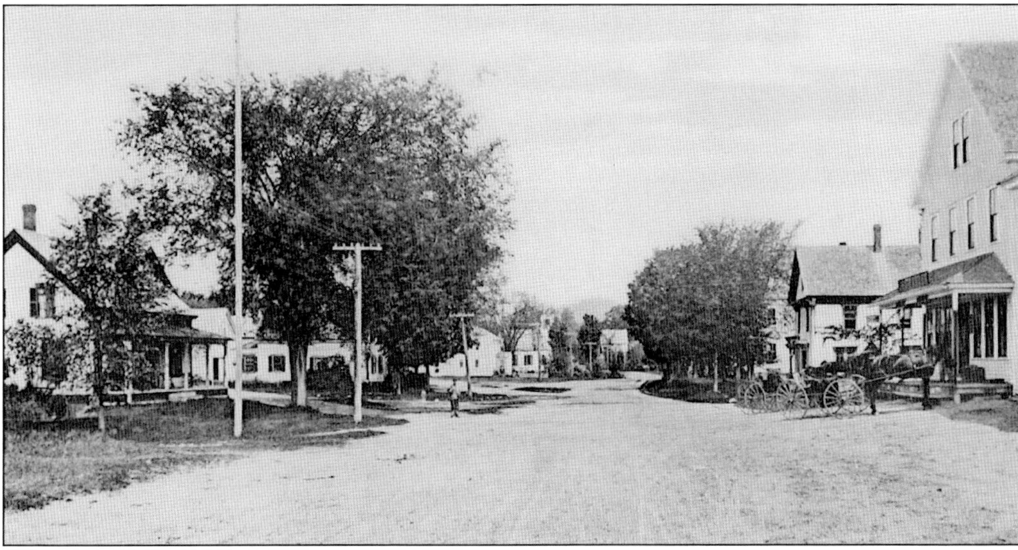

MAIN STREET C. 1900. West Baldwin, straddling the Pequawket Trail (Route 113)—a major artery between Portland and Fryeburg—was once a bustling little community. Visible to the right is Albert Miles's store, Jim Dow's residence, and the grange. Directly across from the store is the Albert Miles's house and farm (originally built by James Lowell and now known as the Locke place), the George Dow residence, Burnell Tavern, and the Methodist church. All these buildings survived the fire of 1928.

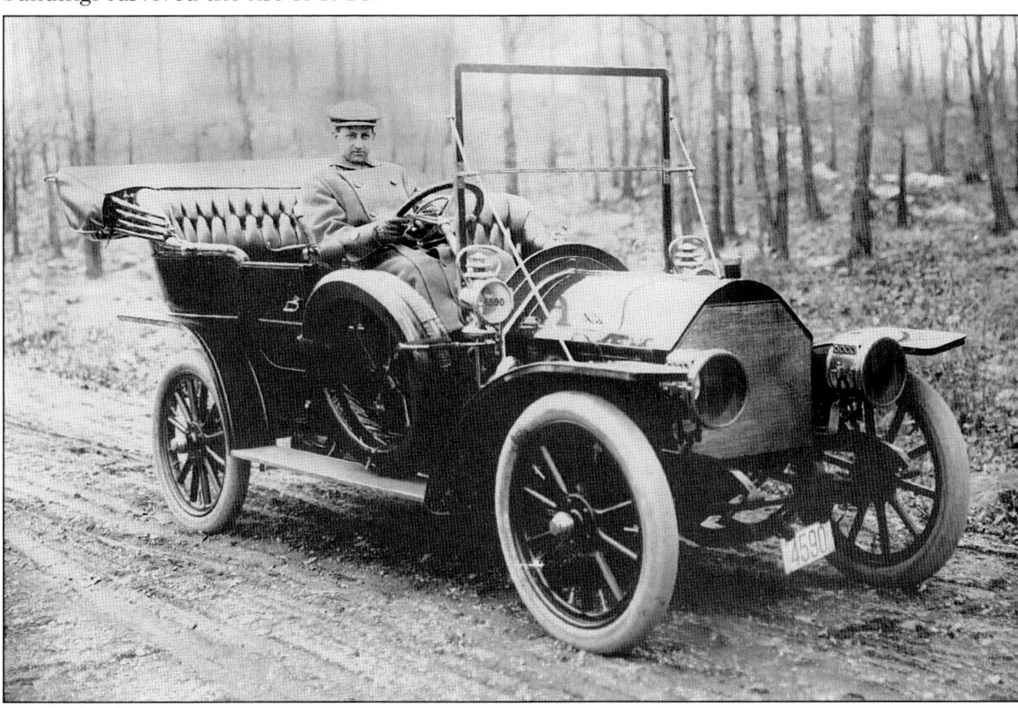

THE THOMAS 40, 1908. This eloquent 1907 Thomas 40 with a Massachusetts license plate, driven by the Sanborn's impeccably dressed chauffeur Roscoe Hillaker, must have attracted considerable attention in West Baldwin. The Sanborns were related to the Burnells of Burnell Tavern.

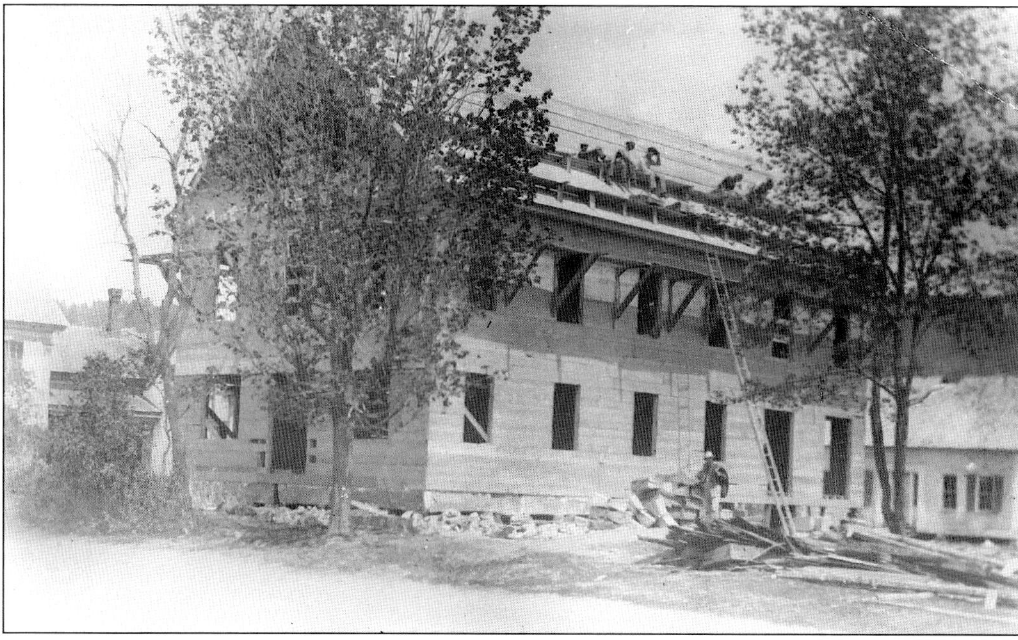

THE WEST BALDWIN GRANGE NO. 374, 1902. The Baldwin Grange was completed just in time for the local ladies to serve a bountiful noon dinner to the invited guests who attended Baldwin's centennial celebration on June 23, 1902. Over the years the large hall became a focal point of social activities and unlike many granges in Maine, it still remains active.

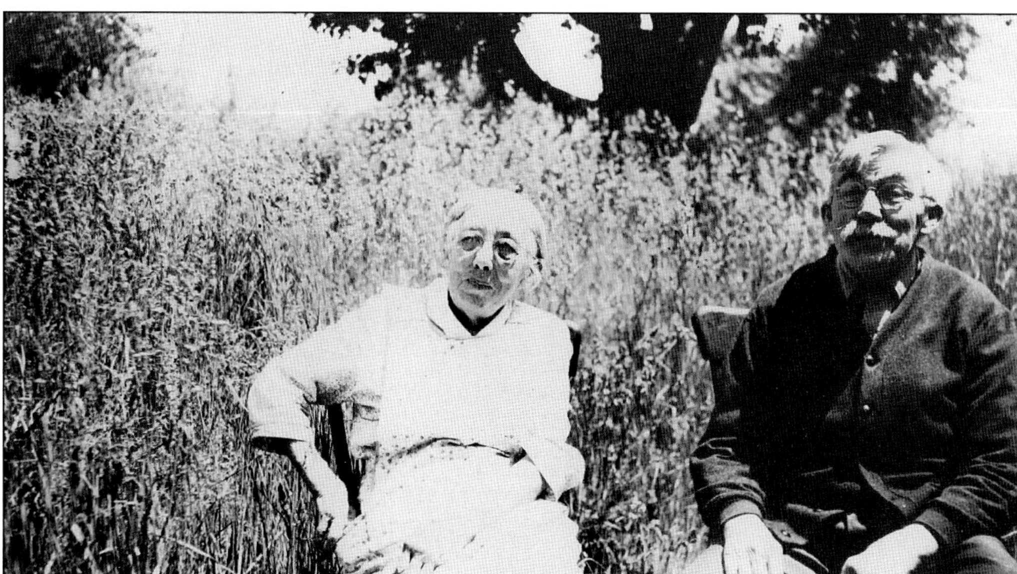

MARY AND WILSON BURNELL, 1947. The Burnells relax in their golden years in front of their farmhouse built by their ancestor and early Baldwin resident Ephraim Bacheldor. Mary (1872– 1957) and Wilson (1875–1953) were brother and sister. Neither ever married, and both continued to live and work the family farm, opposite Henry Black's home, after their parents' death. Both were among the first elected officers of the West Baldwin Grange.

Town of Baldwin

Soldiers Welcome Home Festival

Given by the Town, the Baldwin branches of the American Red Cross and popular subscription

Thusday, Oct. 9, 1919

Program

4-30 P. M. Camp Meeting Grove

BAND CONCERT

PRAYER, REV. M. GERRY PLUMMER

ADDRESS OF WELCOME, HON. C. L. BEEDY

MUSIC, BAND

PRESENTATION OF SOUVENIRS, LORENZO NORTON, M. D.

MUSIC, BAND

6 P. M. Camp Meeting Grove

SUPPER TO ALL RESIDENTS OF TOWN

8 P. M. Pine Grove Cottage

EXHIBITION OF MOVING PICTURES

SONGS, Miss Mansfield accompanied by Miss McPherson

RECITATIONS, Miss Burbank

8 to 12 P. M. West Baldwin GangeHall

SOLDIERS WELCOME, OCTOBER 9, 1919. Nearly a year after the Armistice was signed on November 11, 1918, ending World War I, Baldwin organized a festival to honor its veterans. Most of the activities were held either at the Camp Meeting Grove, located between the Saco River and the West Baldwin Railroad Station, or at the West Baldwin Grange Hall.

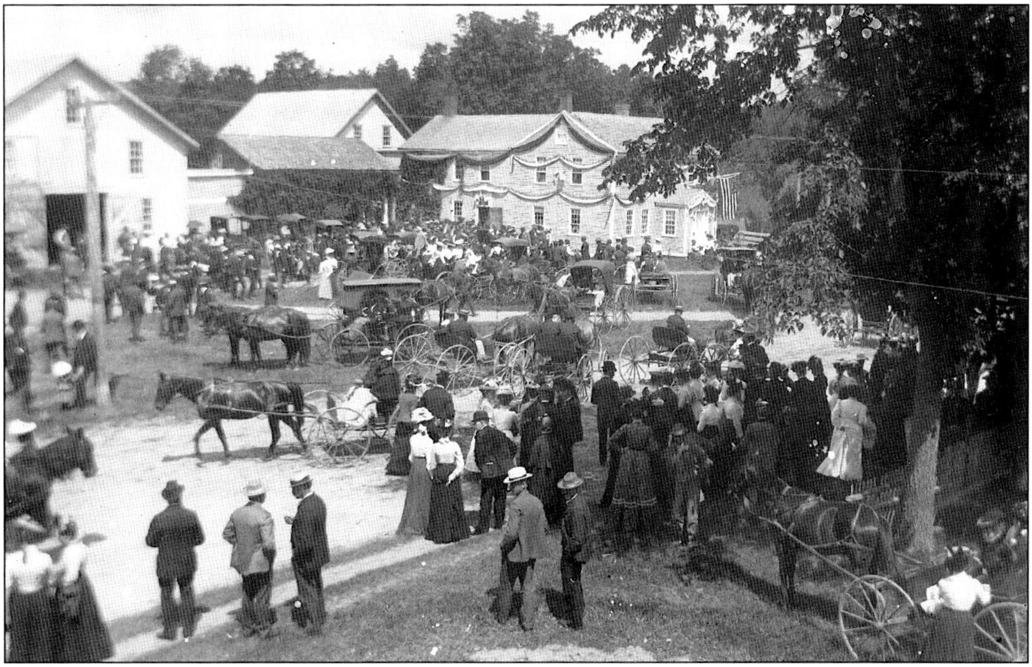

BALDWIN CENTENNIAL, JUNE 24, 1902. The area in front of Burnell's Tavern, decorated with bunting, and the West Baldwin Grange is swarming with people and horse-drawn carriages on this festive day 100 years after Baldwin was incorporated. The celebration was launched upon the arrival of the morning train down at the station with a military parade led by Gen. Charles P. Mattocks.

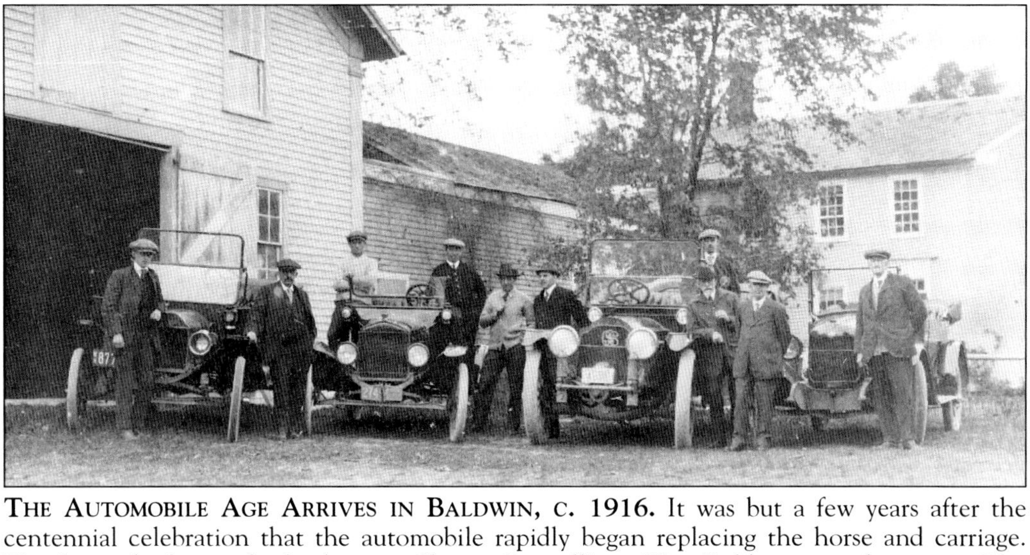

THE AUTOMOBILE AGE ARRIVES IN BALDWIN, C. 1916. It was but a few years after the centennial celebration that the automobile rapidly began replacing the horse and carriage. The four vehicles on display here at Chester Burnell's in West Baldwin varied in price. The automobiles shown are, from left to right, a 1913 Model T, a 1916 Model T (about $590), a 1912 or 1913 Packard ($3,200 to $4,600), and a 1916 Grant Touring Car ($795). The automobile enthusiasts are, from left to right, as follows Earl Burnell, Frank Burnell, Charles Chase, Chester Burnell, Roscoe Hilliker, Mort Cushman, Chas Sanborn, Walter Burnell, and Frank Hilliker.

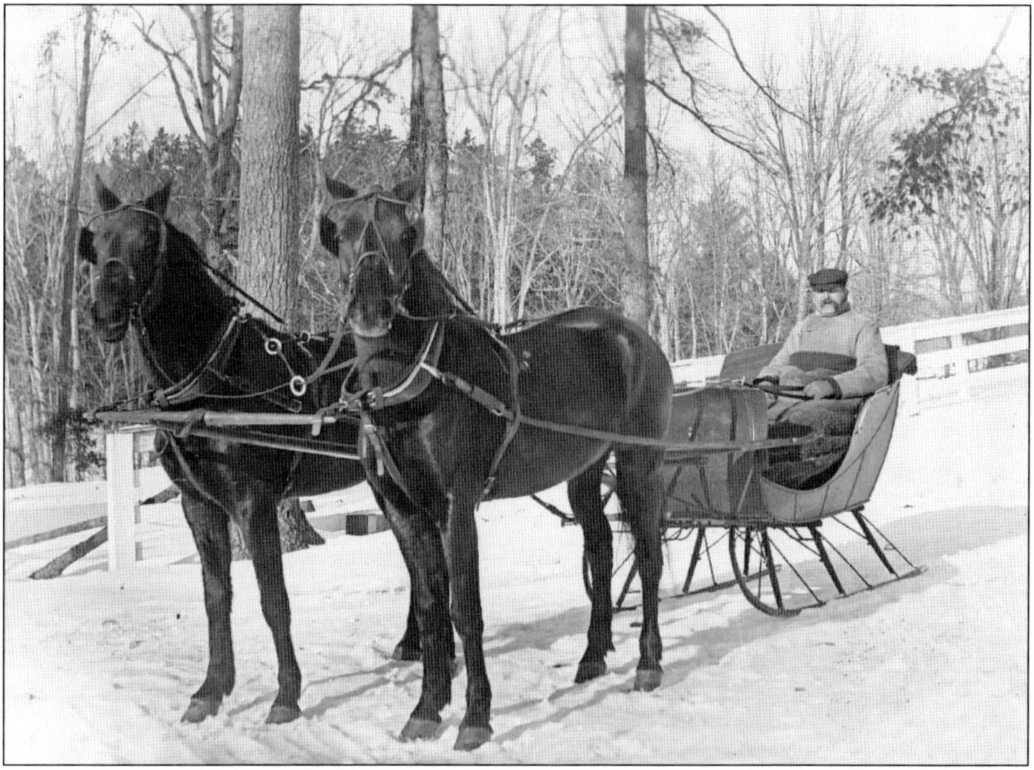

THE INDISPENSABLE HORSE AND SLEIGH, C. 1915. Despite their growing popularity, automobiles were put up on blocks in barns and sheds after the first significant snowfall and remained there until the end of mud season. Here, Chester Burnell has replaced his automobile with a more reliable pair of horses from his stable at Burnell Tavern and is heading out, perhaps down to the Baldwin Station where he reportedly worked as stationmaster.

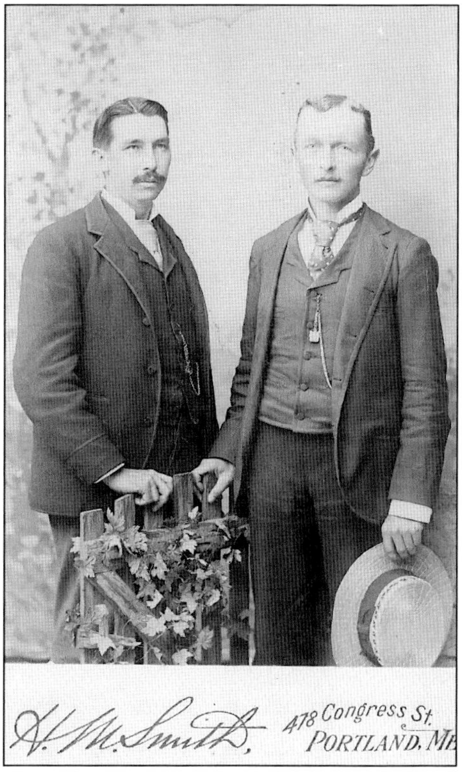

CHESTER BURNELL AND FRIEND, C. 1915. Chester Burnell, left, poses with Johnny Flint at the studio of H.M. Smith in Portland. Burnell (1861–1941) inherited Burnell Tavern, built by his grandfather Enoch Sanborn in the early 19th century. It is said that Burnell's father, Cyrus Freeman Burnell (born in 1819 and married to Elizabeth Sanborn), amassed considerable wealth selling land to the Portland & Ogdensburg Railroad. John Kelly, the owner of a mill in East Hiram, purchased the property after Burnell's death but later sold it to Percy Burnell, a descendent who was married to Olive Stanton and operated the power station at Hiram Falls.

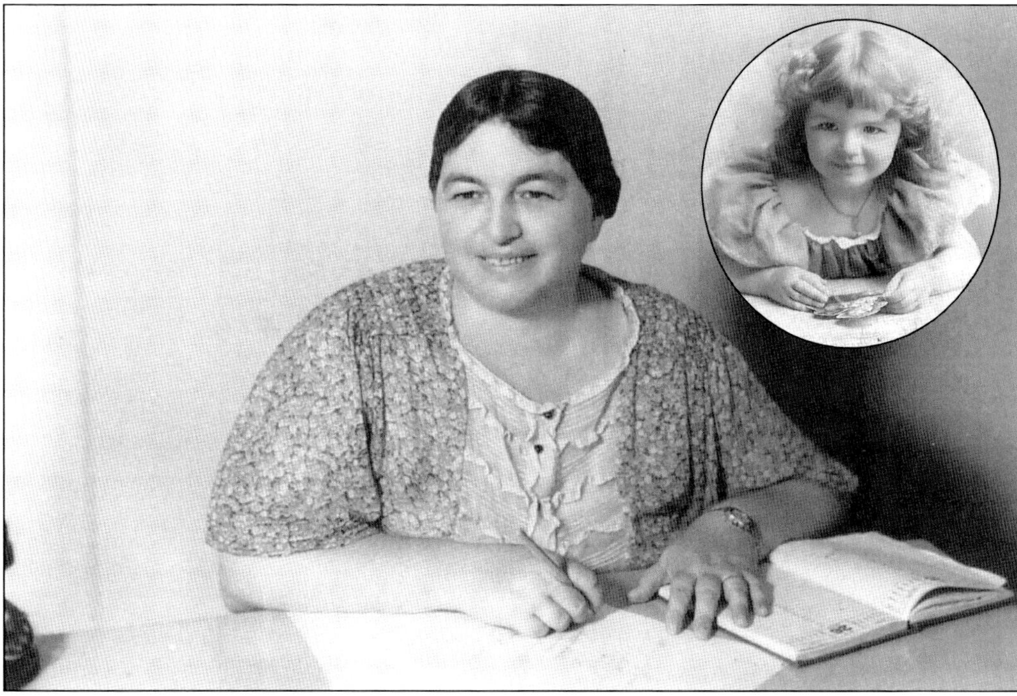

MARGARET FLINT (1893–1960), C. 1935, AND (INSET) AT AGE 2, 1894. Margaret Flint wrote eight novels, all but one of which is set in the Baldwin area. She was born and reared in Orono near the University of Maine campus where her father, Walter Flint, taught civil engineering for 20 years. She was 10 when the family moved to Port Deposit, Maryland, where her father taught at the Jacob Tome School. Soon after she and her brother Ralph graduated from high school in 1908, the Flints moved back to the family farm in West Baldwin and she enrolled at the University of Maine. It was there that she met and fell in love with Lester Jacobs, who was majoring in civil engineering. They were married in 1912 following his graduation. For 30 years Margaret Flint wrote short stories, none of which were ever published. But soon after her husband accepted a position as manager of the Lake Pontchartrain Bridge in Louisiana in 1929, she began working on her first novel, set in West Baldwin, titled *The Old Ashburn Place*. With six children to care for, she took four years to complete it—just in time to be entered in the *Pictorial Review* Dodd, Mead First Novel Contest. In December 1935, she was stunned to hear Walter Winchell announce to the nation that she had won the $10,000 award for her novel. Two years later, her husband died and she and the children moved back to West Baldwin to the farm where Donald Flint now lives. That same year, Dodd, Mead published her *Valley of Decision*, set in Mississippi. Never again, however, did she venture beyond her beloved microcosm, the Baldwin-Sebago area, for grist for her novels. In 1938, *Deacon's Road* was published. In it she portrays the vanished milieu—except for the granite fountain (the Deacon's Fountain) and two granite megaliths at each end of the abandoned Deacon's Road in West Baldwin—of her great-grandfather, Deacon Ephraim Flint. She went on to write *Breakneck Brook* (1939), *Back o' the Mountain* (1940), *Down the Road Apiece* (1941), *October Fire* (1941), and *Enduring Riches* (1943). In 1943, Dodd, Mead also published her *Dress Right, Dress: The Story of the Wacs*. Her collected works are at the Brown Memorial Library in East Baldwin and the Spaulding Memorial Library in East Sebago.

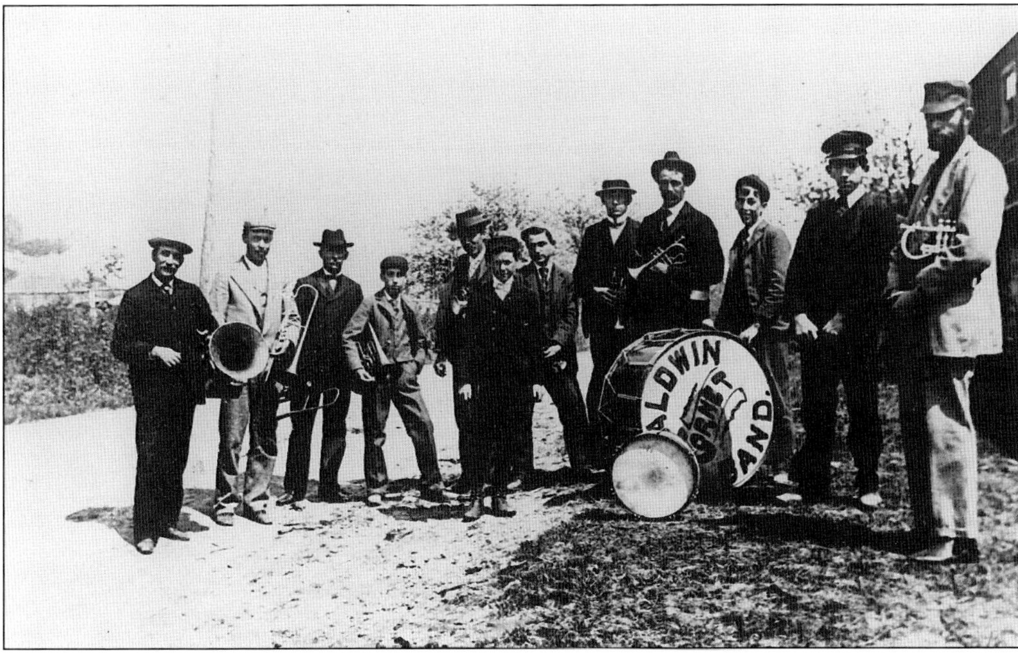

THE BALDWIN CORNET BAND, C. 1900. The Baldwin Cornet Band performed on special occasions in Baldwin and adjacent towns. The disparity in the ages of the members of the band is a reminder that there was a greater interaction between age groups, especially in rural areas, until several decades into the 20th century. Shown here are, from left to right, Irving Chase, Allison Wentworth, Ether Flint, Wilson Burnell, George Jewell, George Murch, Harry Burnell, Leland Boothby, Carroll Chase, Ernest Warren, and Walter Stanton, the leader.

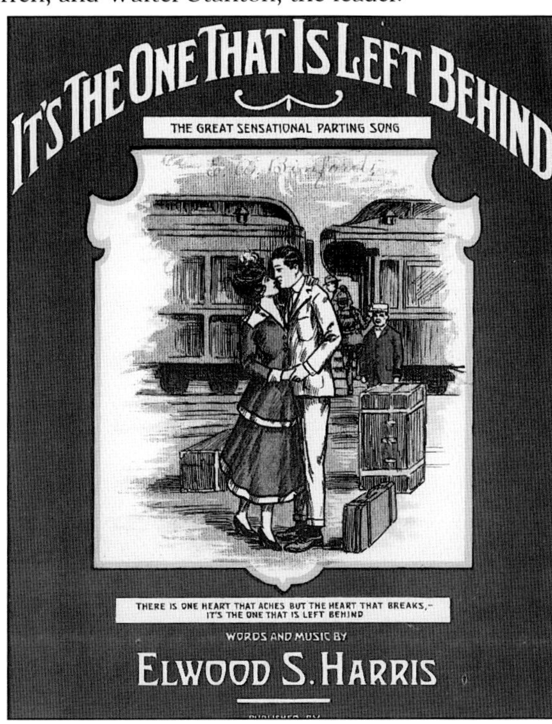

THE MUSIC OF ELLY HARRIS, C. 1918. There are still many residents of Baldwin and neighboring towns who fondly recall the Saturday night dances at West Baldwin's famous Dancemore, constructed in 1928 largely of material from the abandoned mill at Pigeon Brook, and the music of Elwood Harris (1878–1960) and his orchestra, playing from a platform above the dance floor. "Elly" Harris wrote and published music and played the piano at the Dancemore for over 60 years. The Dancemore is still standing. However, the Eatmore lunch stand next door, which was run by Harris's wife, Iva, and the Harris residence are both gone.

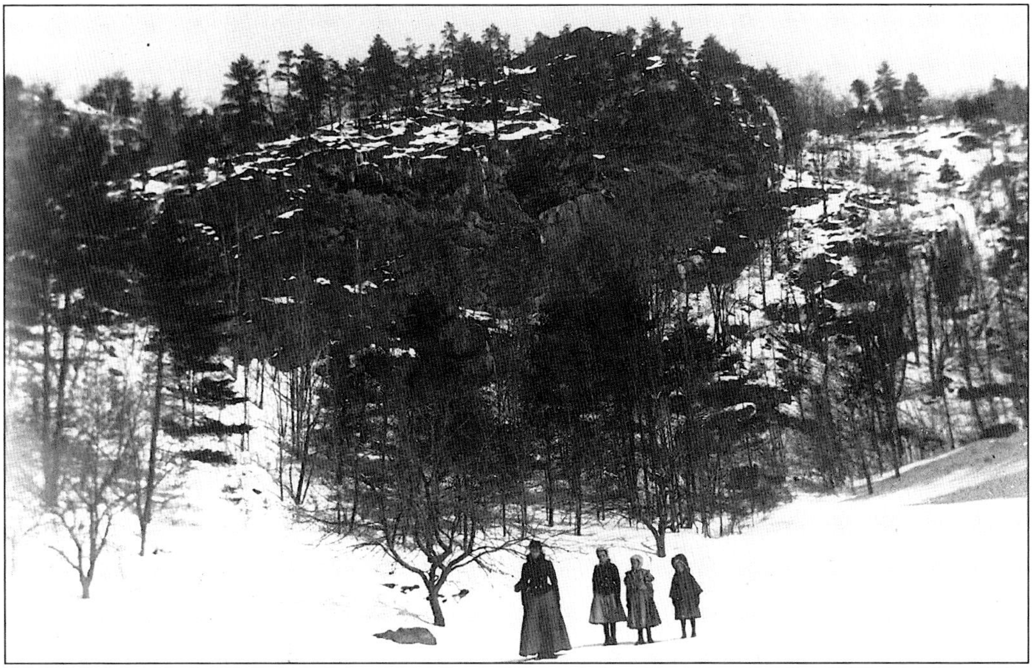

A Winter Outing, c. 1900. An unidentified woman and presumably her three daughters are enjoying a winter walk through an apple orchard in the shadows of these colossal granite outcroppings somewhere in Baldwin.

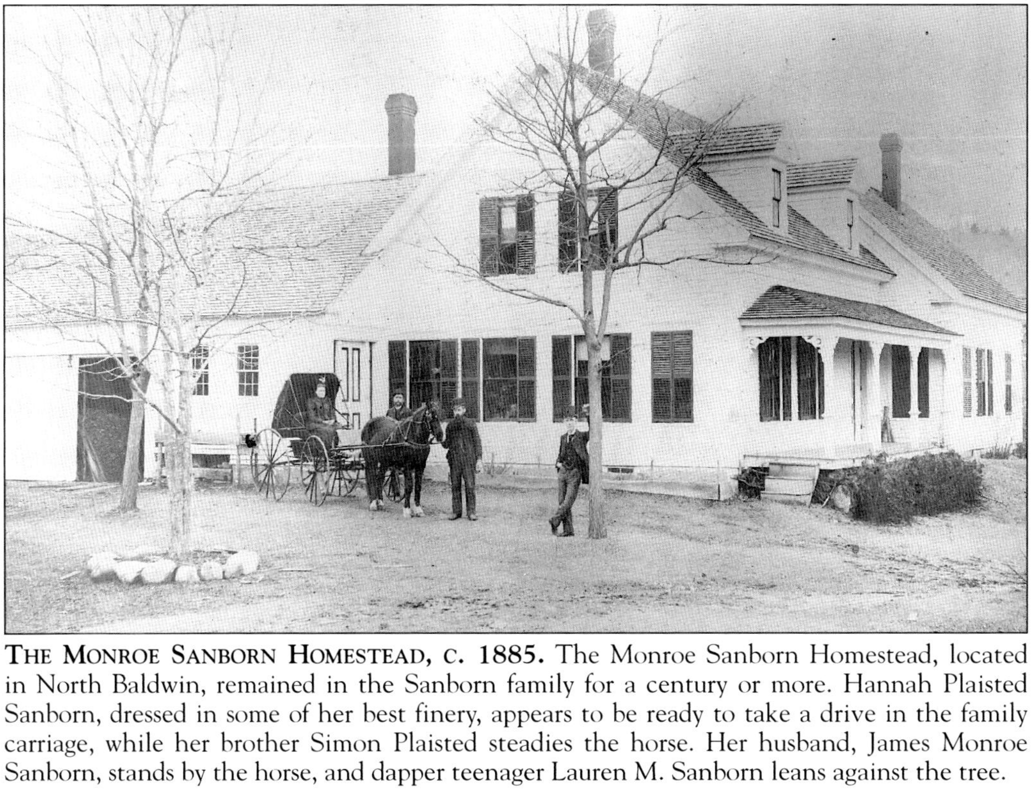

The Monroe Sanborn Homestead, c. 1885. The Monroe Sanborn Homestead, located in North Baldwin, remained in the Sanborn family for a century or more. Hannah Plaisted Sanborn, dressed in some of her best finery, appears to be ready to take a drive in the family carriage, while her brother Simon Plaisted steadies the horse. Her husband, James Monroe Sanborn, stands by the horse, and dapper teenager Lauren M. Sanborn leans against the tree.

Baldwin Old Home Day

NORTH BALDWIN GRANGE HALL

SATURDAY, AUGUST 14, 1937

9 TO 10 .... SPORTS

11 TO 11.30 .... BUSINESS MEETING

11.30 TO 12.45 .... PICNIC LUNCH

Each person please bring own lunch

COFFEE WILL BE FURNISHED

1 O'CLOCK. ENTERTAINMENT BY

CAMP O-AT-KA BOYS

STANDARD TIME

Ice Cream and Cold Drinks on Sale

BALDWIN OLD HOME DAY, AUGUST 14, 1937. Old Home Day celebrations were an annual summer event until more recent times in Baldwin. The North Baldwin (Mount Etna) Grange remains a center for social events in the area. The staff and campers at Camp O-At-Ka in East Sebago frequently participated in various summer events in Sebago and Baldwin.

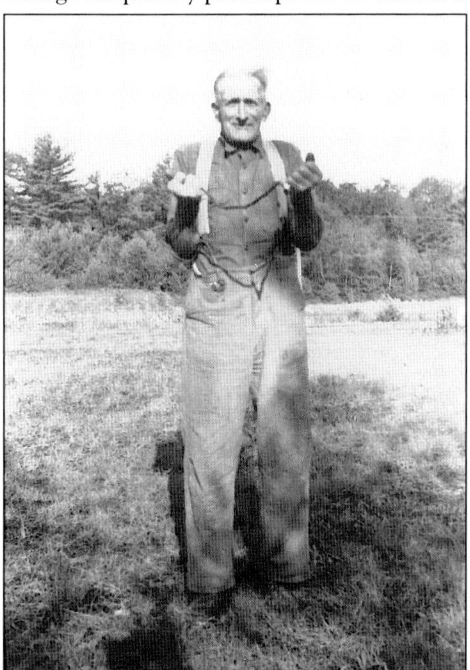

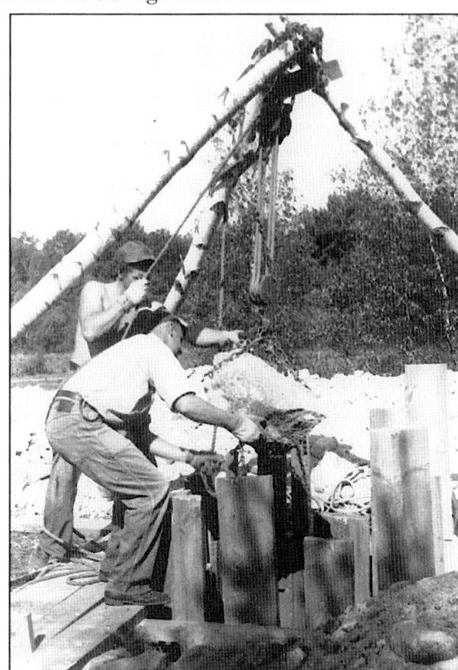

DOWSING AND DIGGING, OCTOBER 1940. H.F. Partridge, who for many years ran a store and post office at his home and farm on Wiggin Hill in North Baldwin, was also a gifted old-fashioned Yankee dowser. On the left, he has just located a good vein of water for a well at the Mount Etna Grange in North Baldwin. Shortly after Nellie Cartret—the manager, treasurer, and operator of the Baldwin-Sebago Telephone Company for 40 years—broke the soil for the new well, Prentist Wentworth and Forrest Thorne erected a tripod with a pulley and rope and began digging.

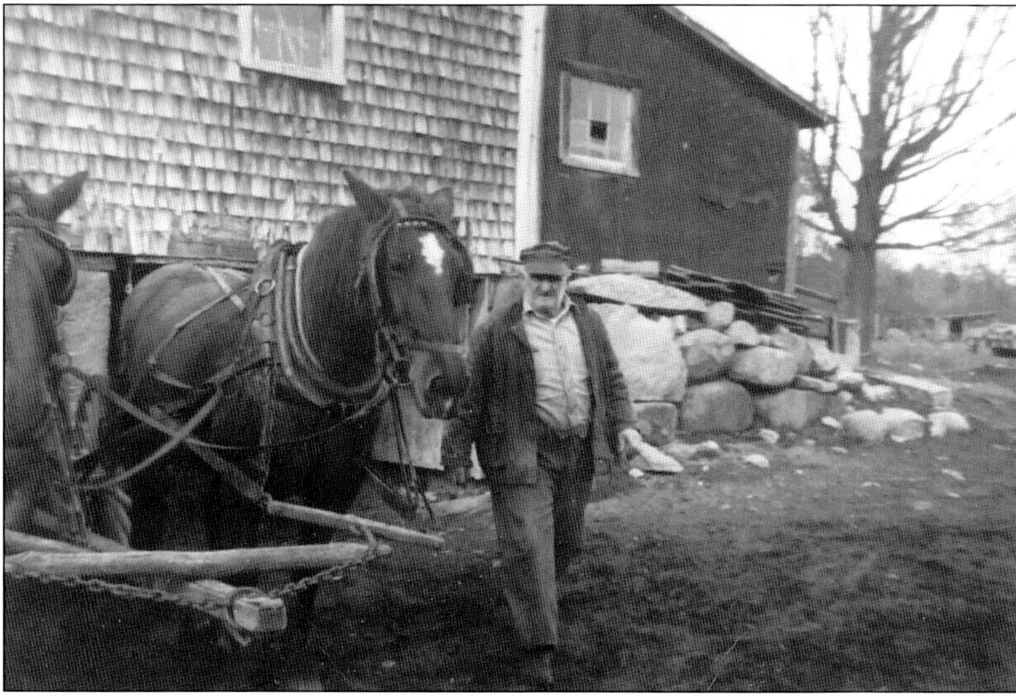

JOSES H. MURCH, 1949. Joses Murch of North Baldwin spent his entire 85 years on this 200-acre farm in North Baldwin on the Murch Road, where his grandchildren Marcia and Norman McKenney have also resided all of their lives. By 1949, most farmers in Maine were using tractors, but Murch continued to farm the traditional way. Here, his team is harnessed to a dump cart, very likely to be loaded with manure from under the dairy tie-up. For most of his life, Murch was mainly a dairy farmer with a regular year-round, house-to-house delivery, mostly to East Sebago, including Long Beach, and Wards Cove (Standish) during the summer months, when he sold fresh garden produce along with milk and cream. The Murch farm also raised and dressed broilers, roasters, and turkeys for a number of years.

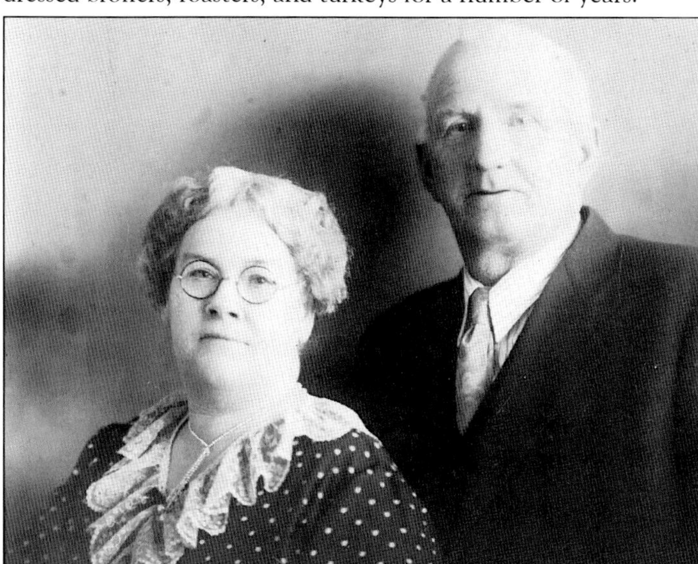

JOSES AND JULIA DOUGLAS MURCH, C. 1935. Julia (1877–1938) was born to Oliver and Laura Douglas at the family farm on Hog Fat Hill in Convene (Sebago). Joses (1879–1965) was born on the Murch farm in North Baldwin to Almon and Susan Milliken Murch. The couple is buried in the West Baldwin cemetery.

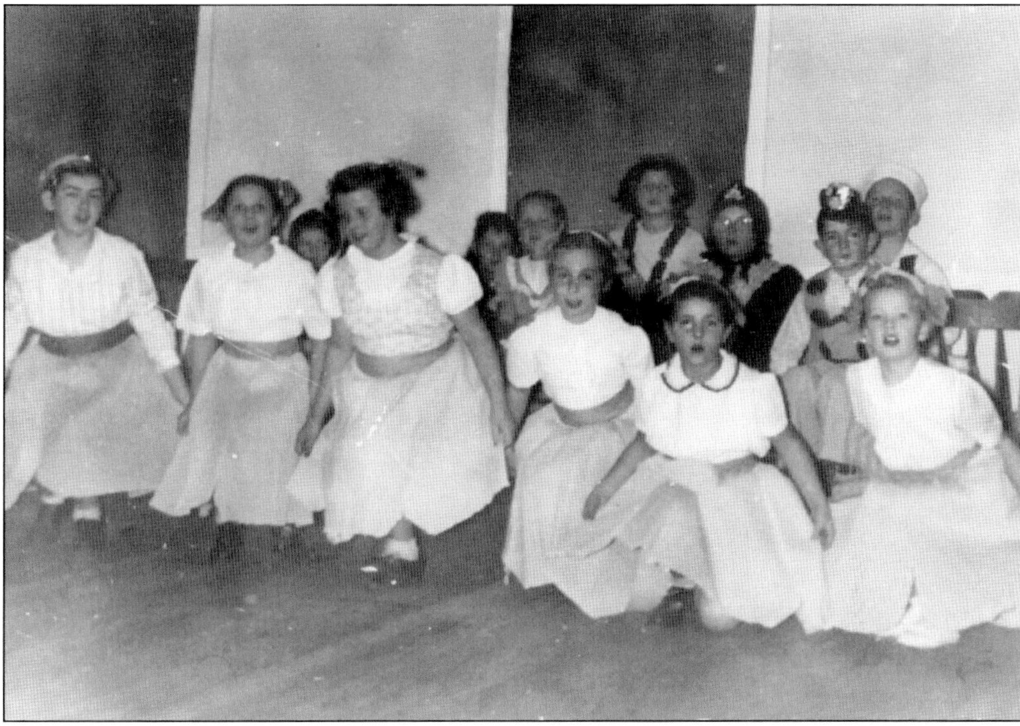

LOCAL TALENT, NOVEMBER 1949. Youngsters from North Baldwin perform in a play put on at the Mount Etna Grange in North Baldwin. Shown are, from left to right, the following: (front row) Elaine Robbins, Priscilla Muldoon, Rita Powers, Marilyn Babb, Caroline Muldoon, and Patricia Sargent; (back row) Marjorie Wiggin, Helen Crawford, Roberta Dyer, Donna Avanzato, Doris Mason, Harvey Robbins, and Phillip Babb.

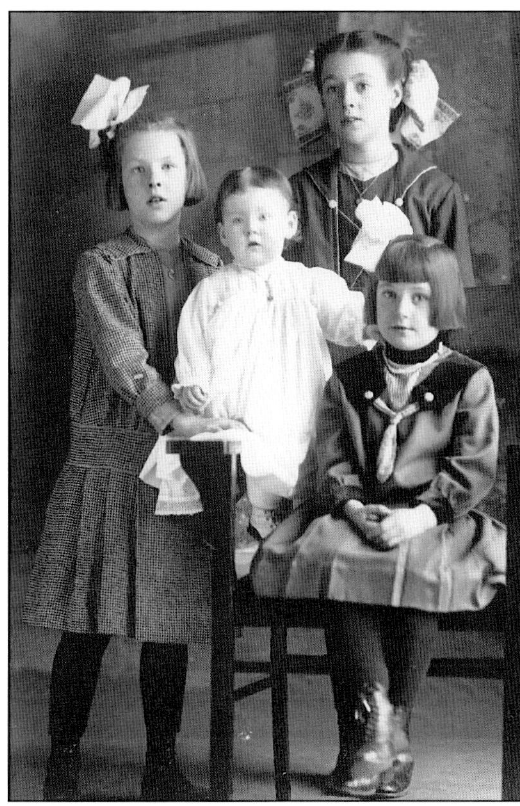

THE MURCH DAUGHTERS, C. 1916. The daughters of Joses and Julia Murch are, from left to right, Alva (1907–1986), who married Harry Sanborn and lived in West Baldwin; Genevieve (1915–1983), who married Arthur Powers and lived in North Baldwin; Ada (1905–1990), who married Dennis McKenney from Larrabee's Corner in Sebago and remained on the Murch farm in North Baldwin all her life; and Olive (1909–), who married John Orman Sanborn and resides on the Douglas Hill Road in West Baldwin.

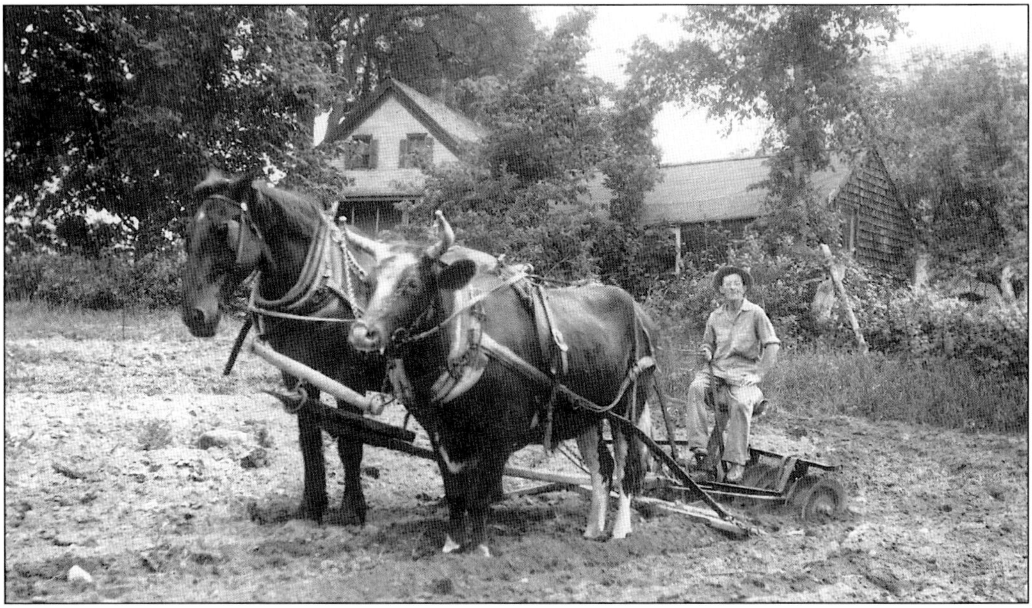

YANKEE INGENUITY, C. 1936. Before the 1940s, tractors were a rarity here in Maine. Most Maine farmers relied upon draft horses until the post-World War II era, but a few preferred to use oxen. Chester Chase, who lived on the family farm built in the early 1830s on Cross Road (Senator Black Road) in West Baldwin, may very well have been the only farmer in the state, however, to harness an ox and a horse together. Here, he is seen with his mismatched but well-trained pair harrowing a piece of land near the house. He often hitched the ox to a wagon and with whip in hand, drove it like a horse. Janet Dall and her husband, Arnold, purchased the house in 1973.

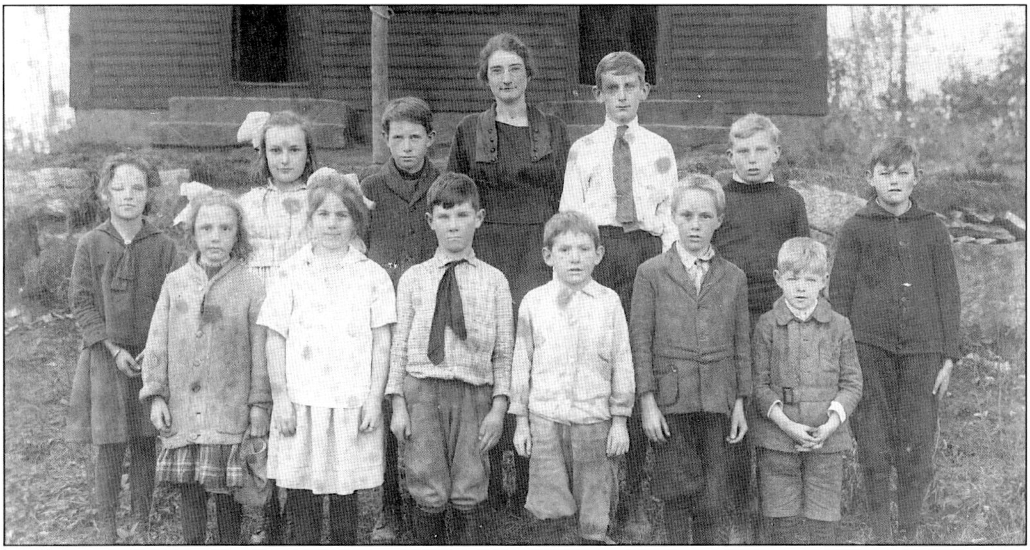

THE OLD RED SCHOOLHOUSE, C. 1921. The Old Red Schoolhouse was located in East Baldwin on the site of Arthur Jordan Jr.'s mobile home. Shown in this picture are, from left to right, the following: (front row) Eva Wood, Dorothy Sanborn, Eddy Guptill, Stanley Graffam, Gerald Wood, and Jessie Sanborn; (back row) Betty Sommers, Marion Kennard, Perry Graffam, teacher Gladys Cartret, Howard Bauckman, Harry Bauckman, and Leo Sanborn.

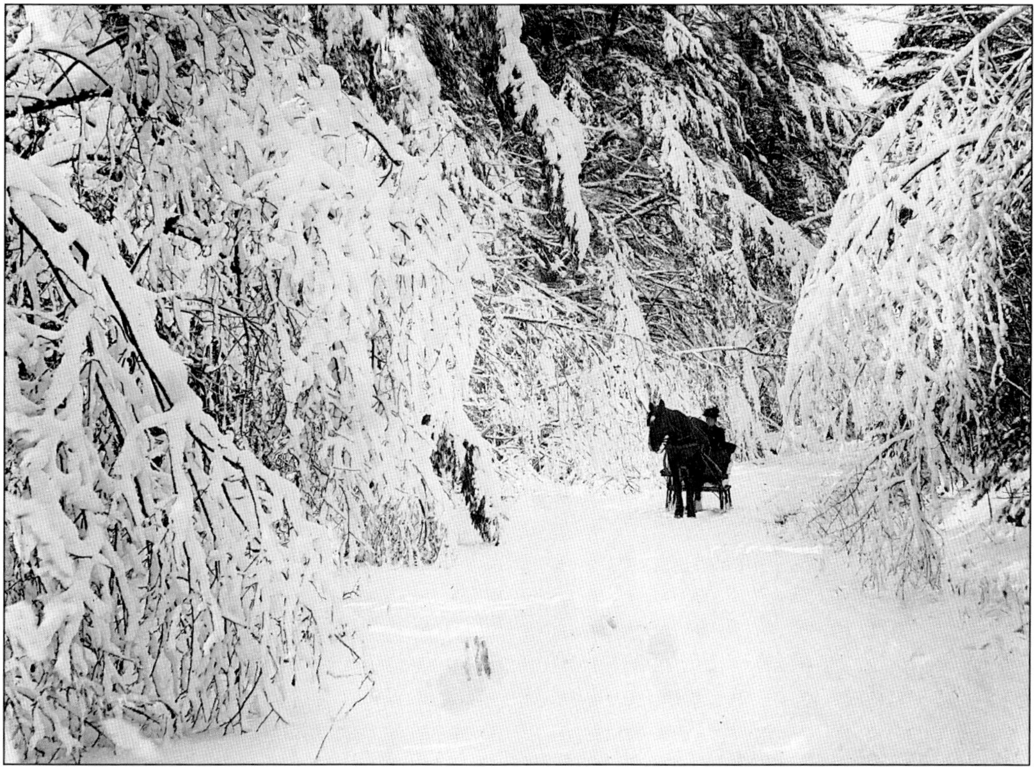

A HALCYON WINTER SCENE, C. 1937. Under the weight of a fresh winter snowfall, pine branches bow their heads and young hardwoods trail their tresses, etching designs in the soft, unsullied snow and leaving only a narrow, sinuous trail along the Douglas Hill Road for horse and driver, thought to be Roscoe Spencer, unhurriedly to follow. Although Spencer moved with the tide and acquired an automobile, he welcomed such days to hitch up his horse to a sleigh and to reconnect himself to a quieter and less stressful past.

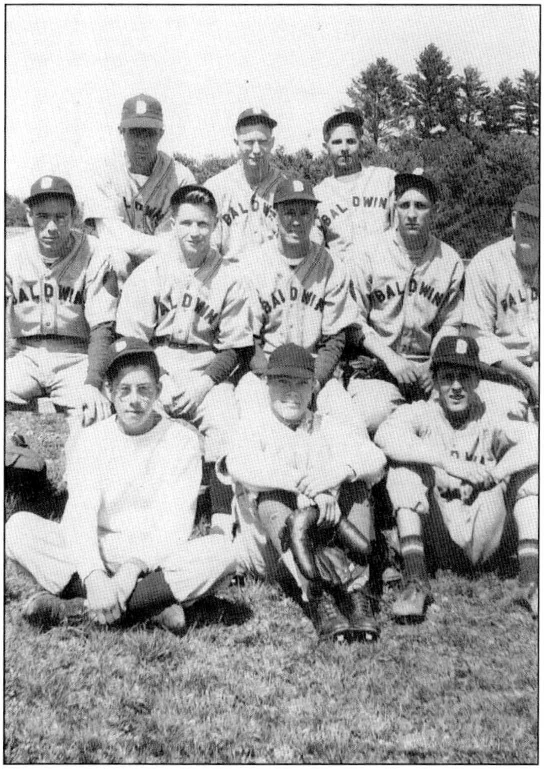

THE BALDWIN APPLES, 1947. Sunday afternoon town team baseball games were a favorite pastime throughout Maine until more recent years. Representing Baldwin here are, from left to right, the following: (front row) Mac Burnell, Bob Burnell, and Raymond Wood;. (middle row) Ralph Black, "Tinker" Day, Walter Black, Gordon Cram, and Ray Austin; (back row) Phillip Black, Clayton Wentworth and Paul Estes.

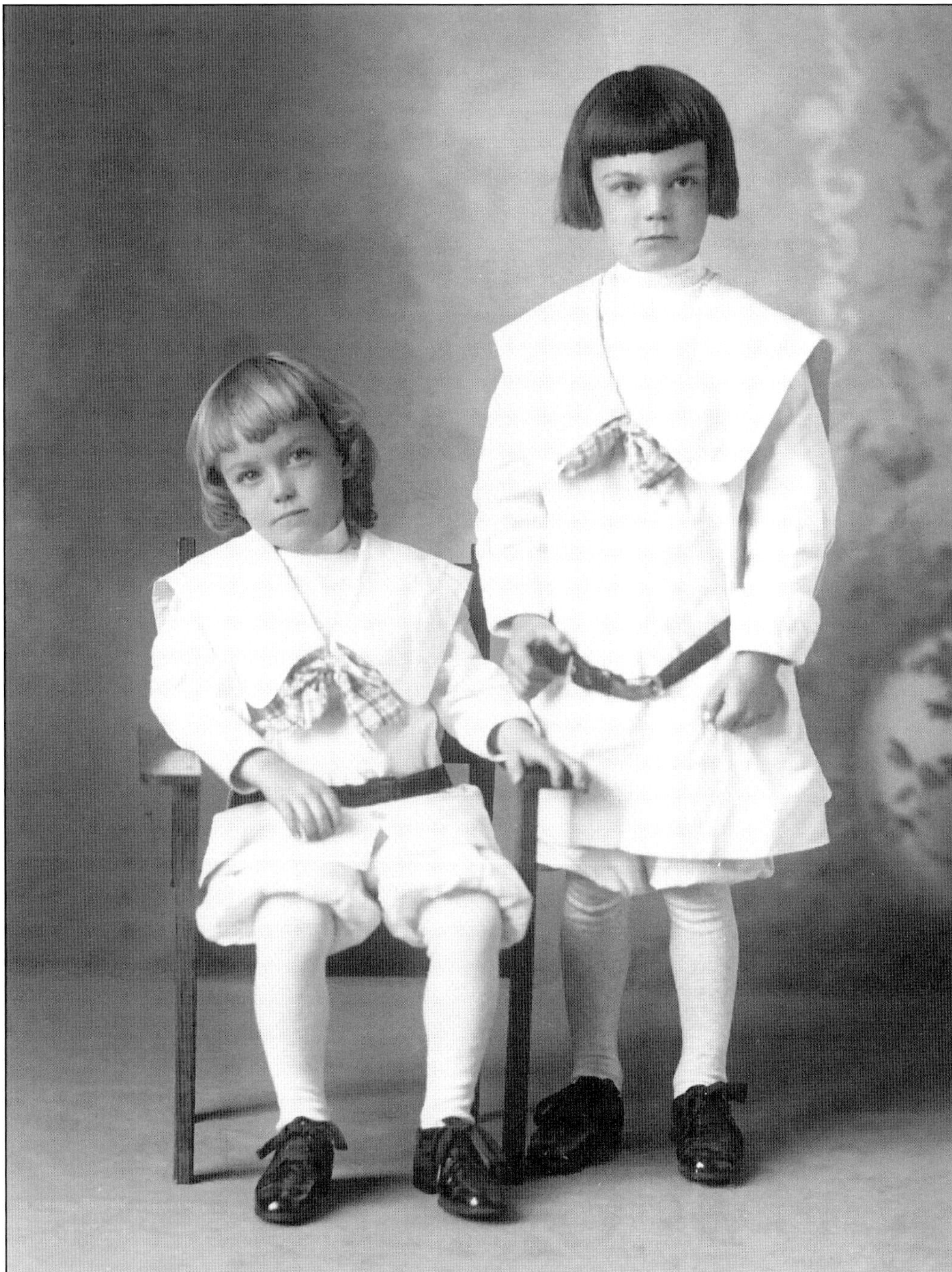

THE WOOD BROTHERS, c. 1910. Clarence, standing, born in 1904, and Clifton, born the following year, are dressed in their very best finery for this portrait taken c. 1910. They were the half brothers of Roy, Lester, and Helen Wood of East Baldwin. The two boys present an interesting study in both clothing and hairstyles in the early 1900s. Clifton and Clarence were married to the Shaw sisters, Gladys and Avis from Jim Shaw Hill in North Sebago, and lived in and ran the garage on Route 107 in East Baldwin, which is now owned by Larry Seidl.

Three

SEBAGO

First Settled: 1790
Incorporated: 1826
Population: 974
Area: 43.6 square miles
Principal Settlements: Long Beach, East Sebago, North Sebago, Sebago Center, Convene

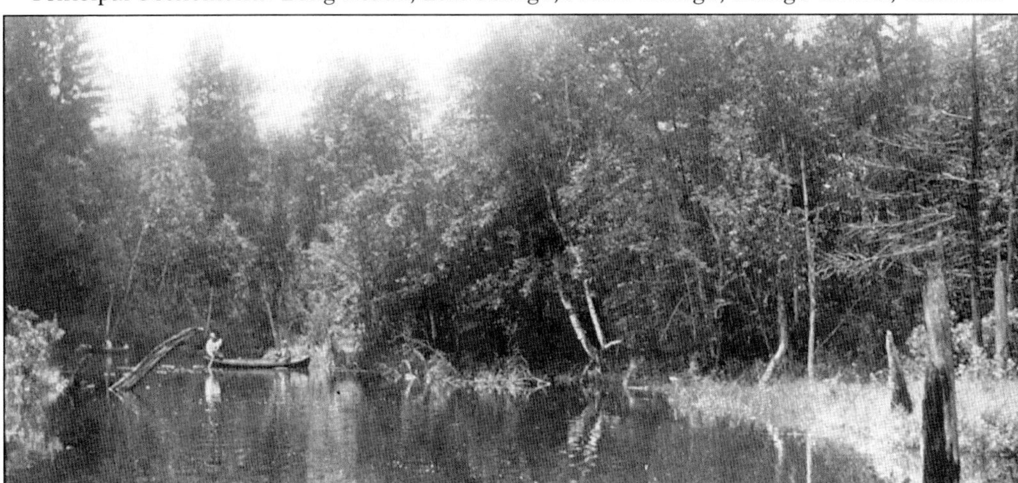

NORTHWEST RIVER, C. 1925. The Northwest River flows out of Peabody Pond in Sebago and empties into Sebago Lake at the West Shore. Before the first settlers began building their rough-hewn cabins, the sound of axes and colossal white pine trees crashing to the ground resounded throughout the hills and narrow-gauge valleys in what became Sebago in 1826. Logs were twitched by oxen to the river and driven and floated down Sebago Lake, across it, and down the Presumpscot to Portland Harbor. Shortly before 1800, dams and mills were constructed along the river, beginning with the William Fitch mill in East Sebago. Daniel McKenney Jr. and Silas McKenney built a sawmill on the river near the rustic bridge on the Folly, and Gen. Daniel Hall operated a turning mill and made furniture near his farm on the Northwest River Bog. Peter White and his son John built a dam and operated a mill just above the Mill Pond in East Sebago.

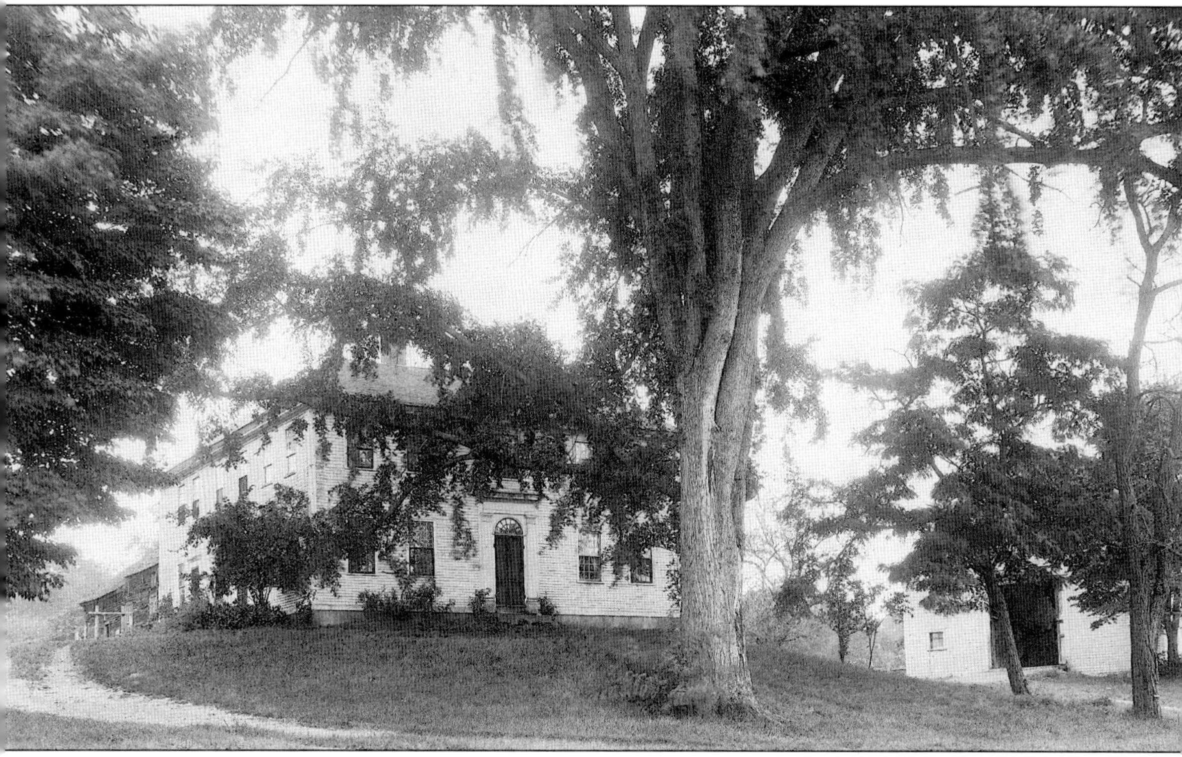

THE FITCH HOMESTEAD, C. 1930. The Fitch Homestead was built in 1811 in Sebago Village (Sebago Center) by William Fitch, when Sebago was still a part of Baldwin. Fitch was one of Sebago's first selectmen, the town's first clerk, and its first postmaster, running the post office here on the hill from 1829 to 1840. Charles E. Fitch, who was the great-grandson of William, inherited the homestead and lived here with his wife, Sarah (Sadie) Milliken from Baldwin, and their daughter Harriet and raised cattle and butchered and delivered meat. Fire destroyed this prominent landmark in 1941, but the barn was saved. Fitch's wife, daughter, son-in-law Emory Martin, and grandsons Audrey and Glenn Martin were in residence at the time of the fire. The lovely Federalist fan window, door, and Grecian pilasters were salvaged and are visible in the present dwelling built by Emory Martin and his brother Carlton Martin, a noted boat builder from East Sebago. Since Sebago originally was a part of the Flintstown Grant and remained a part of the town of Baldwin until 1826, it shares much of its early history with Baldwin. Joseph Lakin and Jacob Howe are generally credited with having pioneered the settlement of Sebago, named after the second largest lake in Maine and the third largest in all of New England. Lakin, who came from Groton, Massachusetts, built a primitive cabin at the foot of Poor's Hill near the Thomas Jackson farm, now owned by Alfred Jordan. Lakin's daughter married Deacon Daniel Hill, whose impressive Federalist dwelling remains a landmark on Route 107 near the site of Lakin's cabin. Howe served as the area's first mail carrier, making the arduous weekly trip on horseback over devious trails with the mail from Bridgton to Portland and back. Capt. Zachariah Fitch, descendent and probably the son of Flintstown Grant proprietor Benjamin Fitch, played a significant role in the early development of Baldwin and, consequently, Sebago. He was the progenitor of the Fitches in Sebago—the father of Richard, William, and Luther. A stipulation in his 1789 land grant in what became East Sebago required that he build a sawmill on the Northwest River within two years and maintain it for ten. Credit goes to James Babb, who made his way to Sebago Village in what became Sebago Center (Mud City) in 1817, for constructing the first gristmill and opening the first store. Three years after Sebago separated from Baldwin, Elija Fulton opened a store in East Sebago.

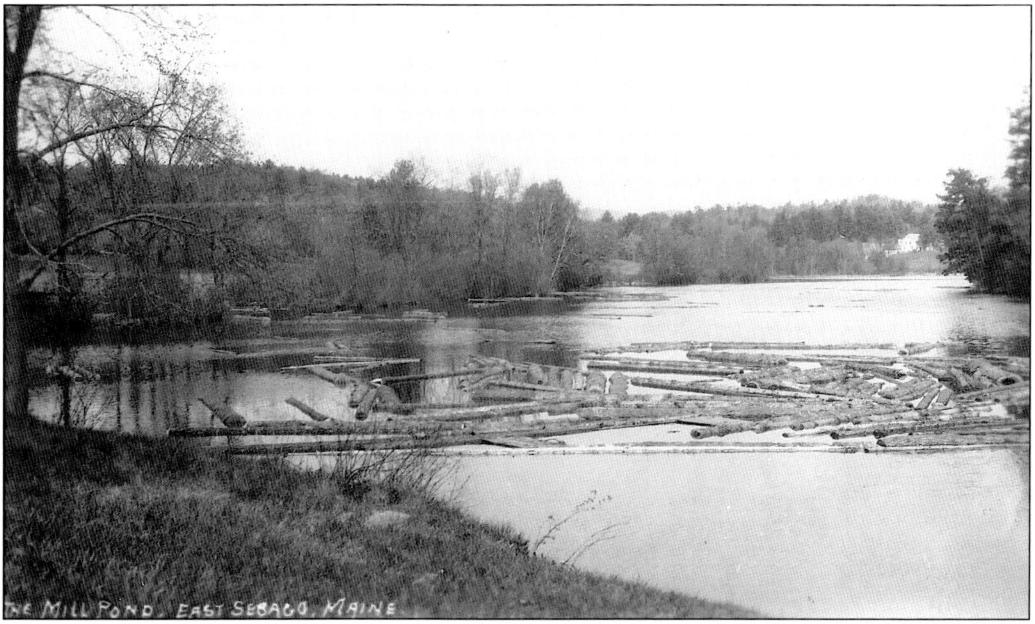

THE MILL POND, 1935. The Mill Pond was a familiar landmark and played a major role in the economy of East Sebago from the time William Fitch built a dam across the Northwest River, creating the pond, and erected a gristmill and sawmill here. In 1864, fire destroyed most of the mill and the store, then run by Fitch's son-in-law Luther H. Fitch, along with all the town records. The mill was rebuilt and was last operated by Fitch's great-grandson Harry Fitch. In winter, ice was cut from the pond to fill the icehouses in the village and at Long Beach.

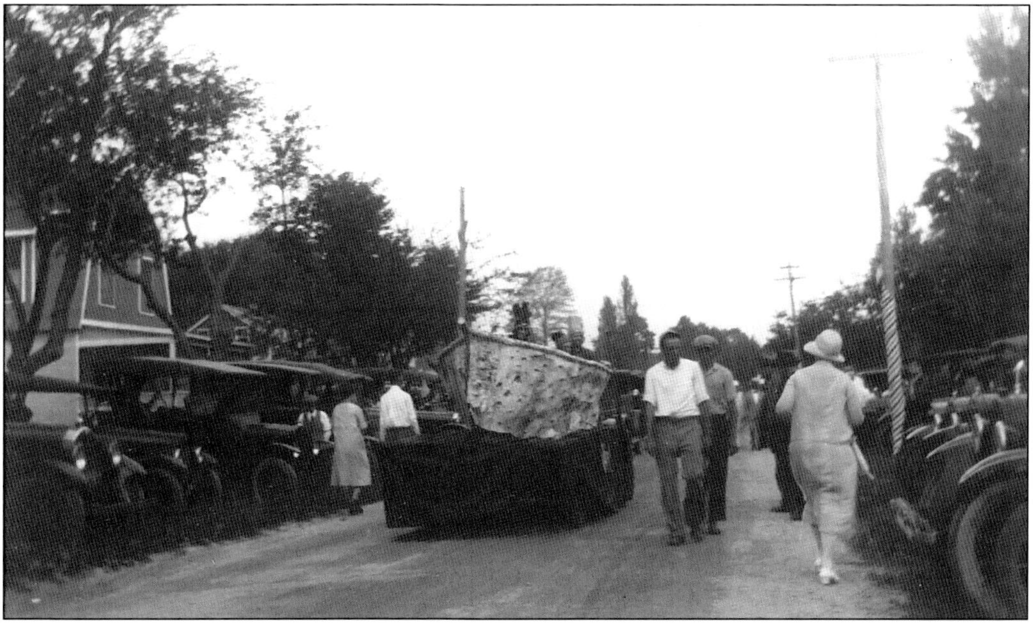

SEBAGO'S CENTENNIAL DAY PARADE, 1926. The normally halcyon little hamlet of North Sebago bristles with activity as the centennial parade edges its way down the road (Route 114) lined with automobiles, passing in front of William Brook's cottage and approaching Walter and Alice Bachelder's residence and store.

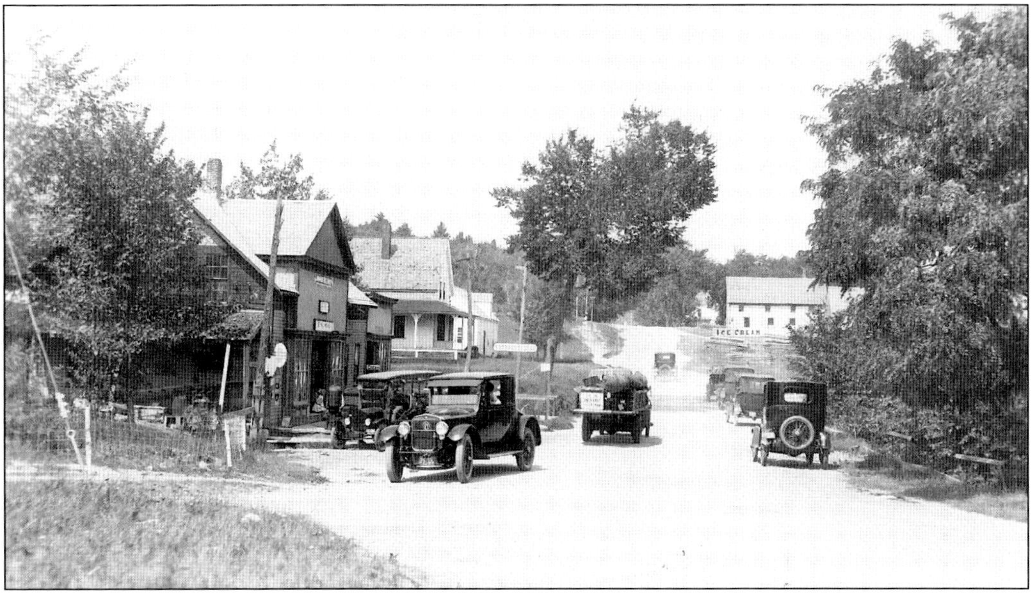

EAST SEBAGO VILLAGE, 1926. A parade of vintage automobiles stirs up a cloud of dust as it heads up the hill toward Fitch's General Store, in the distance. A nicely maintained Winton coupe appears to be heading up the Mattocks Road (Route 11). A Model T stage is parked in front of the Sanborn Store. The large building on the right just above the Fitch Brothers' lumberyard is the Red Men's Hall, where most school and community social events were held until the Community Hall was built.

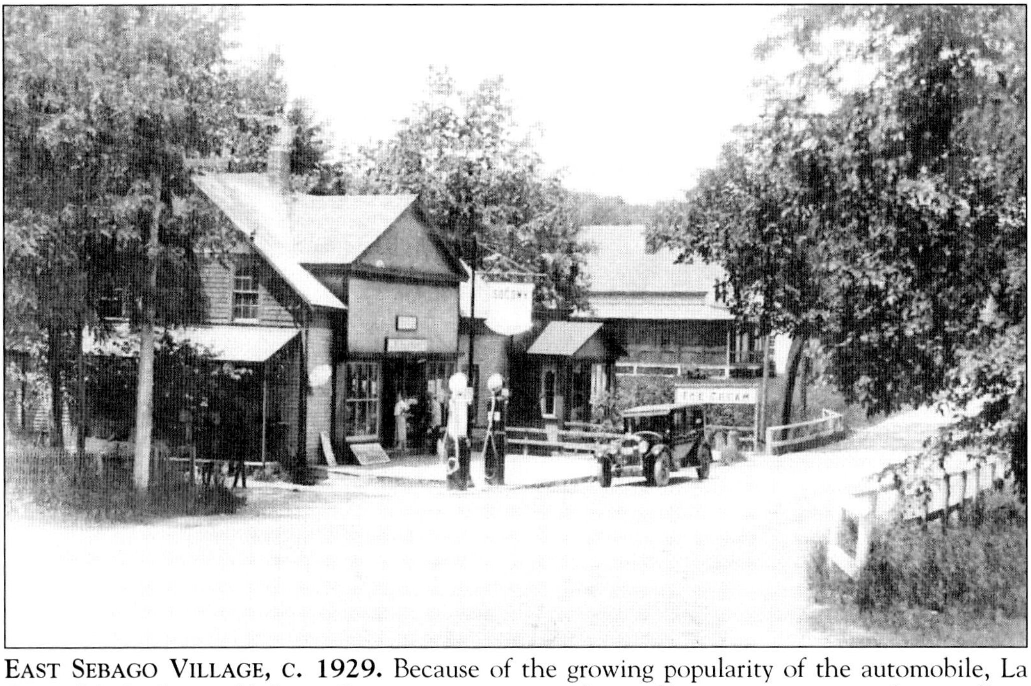

EAST SEBAGO VILLAGE, C. 1929. Because of the growing popularity of the automobile, La Grove M. Sanborn added two Socony gas pumps in front of his grocery store and post office. The automobile is a 1924 Buick.

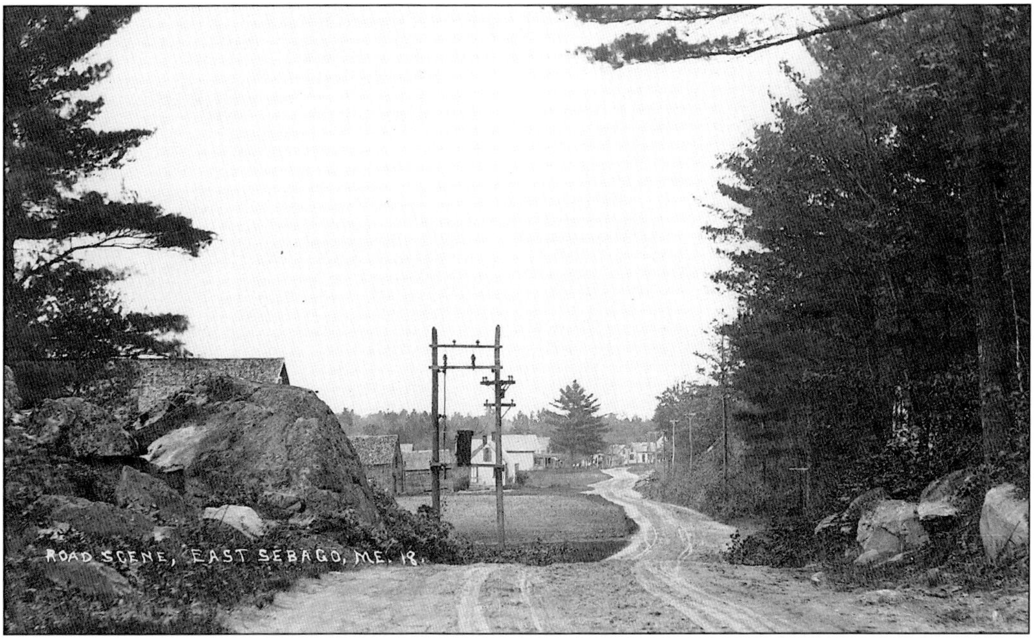

THE MATTOCKS ROAD, C. 1925. The Mattocks Road was first constructed in 1858, linking East Sebago to Mattocks (East Baldwin) and serving as a vital thoroughfare, particularly after the railroad was built through Steep Falls and Baldwin in 1870 and mail service began in 1872.

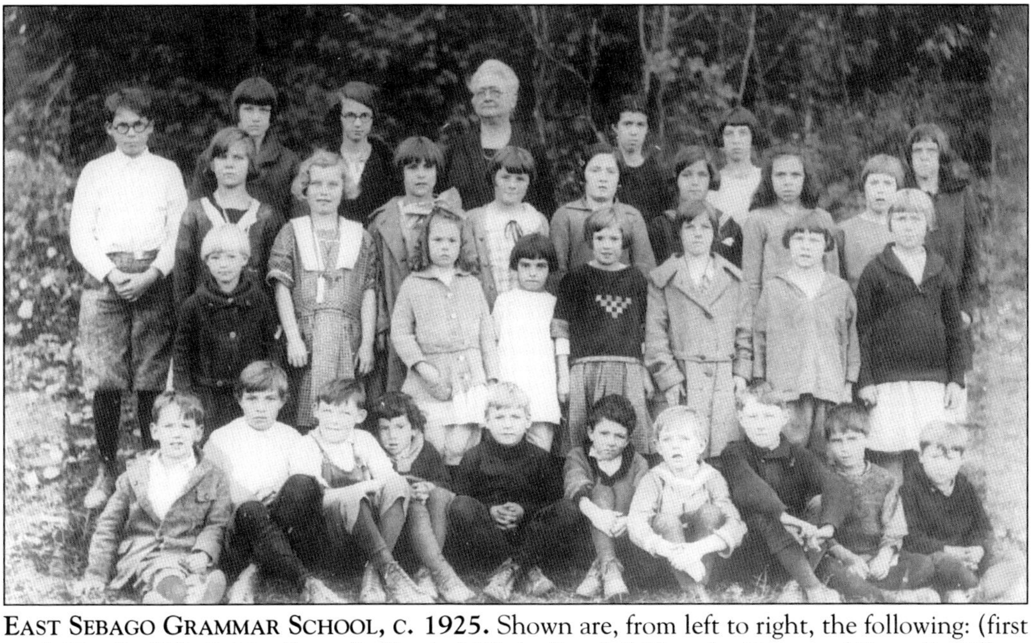

EAST SEBAGO GRAMMAR SCHOOL, C. 1925. Shown are, from left to right, the following: (first row) Charlie Hill, Bricky Burnell, "Bucky" Wade, Randall Thombs, Raymond Burnell, Gilbert Thombs, Russell Hill, Gordon Sanborn, Robert Martin, and Raymond Harmon; (second row) Elsie Burnell, Dorothy Martin, Ruth Burnell, Effie Hill, Hazel Wade, Pauline Fitch, and Eleanor Fitch; (third row) Freda Burnell, Helen Fitch, Louise Wade, Leona Johnson, Mary Shaw, Hattie Martin, Eleanor Thombs, and Grace Hill; (fourth row) Bunk Martin, Alice Wade, Hazel Sawyer, Mrs. Wadleigh, Mildred Thombs, Doris Burnell, and Blanche Wade.

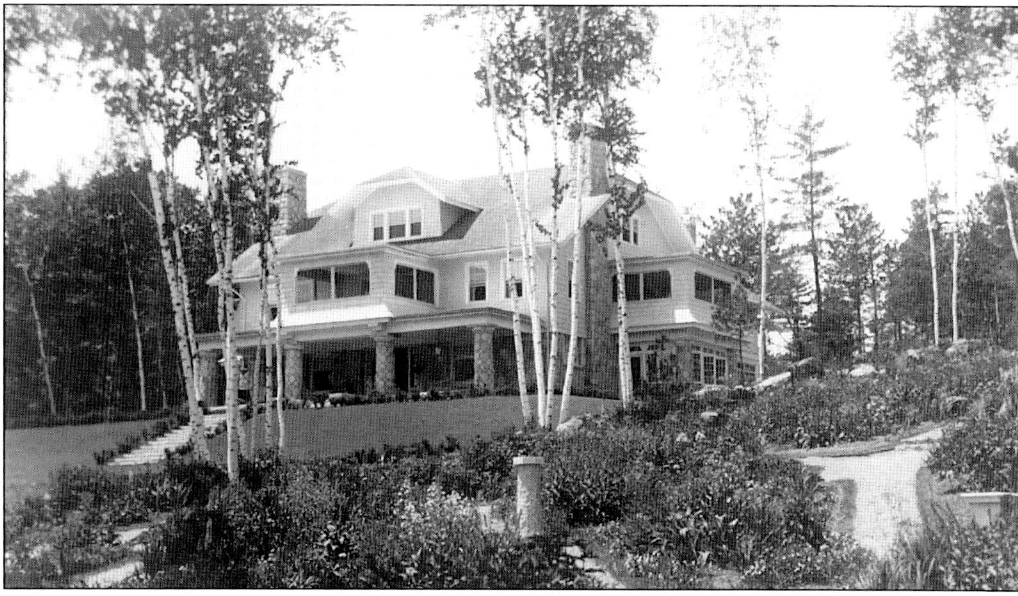

ROCKCRAFT LODGE, C. 1935. Rockcraft Lodge is located on the shore of Sebago Lake in East Sebago. Leon Spaulding (1868–1924), head of the Spaulding Fiber Company in Rochester, New Hampshire, purchased 100 acres with 850 feet of lake frontage for $100 from the Fitch brothers c. 1916 and employed local carpenters and upwards of 30 skilled Italian masons to build this imposing summer home. In later years, the home was lived in year-round by Spaulding's widow, Dorothy, who died here on October 29, 1963. Their stone mausoleum is on the estate.

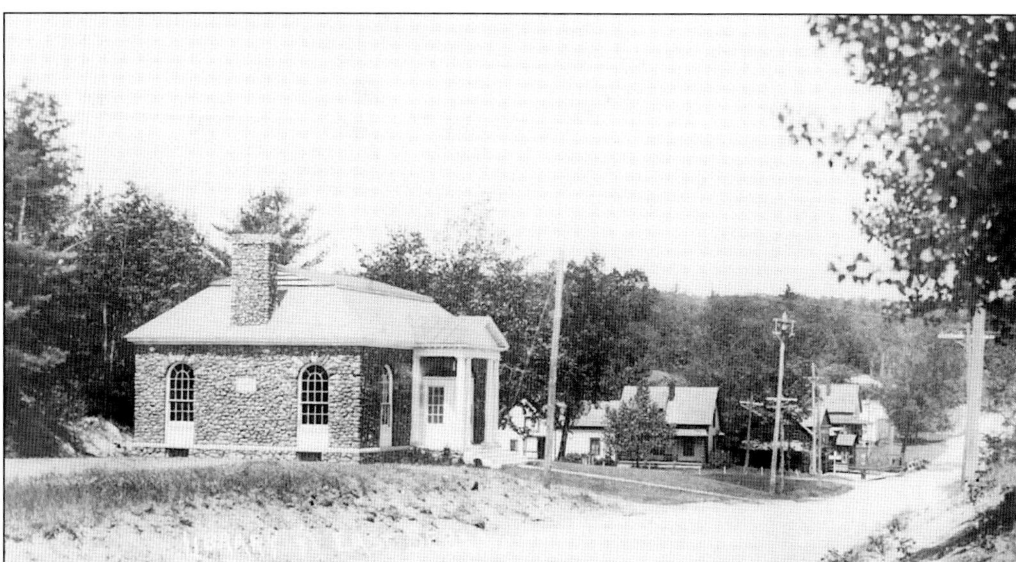

THE SPAULDING MEMORIAL LIBRARY, C. 1930. The Spaulding Memorial Library, constructed largely from local fieldstone, adds grace to East Sebago, thanks to the generosity of Leon Spaulding and Harry Fitch, who donated the land. Carlton Martin supervised its construction. The stonemasons were Charles Stewart and LeForrest Cram of Hiram. The library opened in 1925, with Lillian Smith the first to serve as librarian and Eunice Shaw the second.

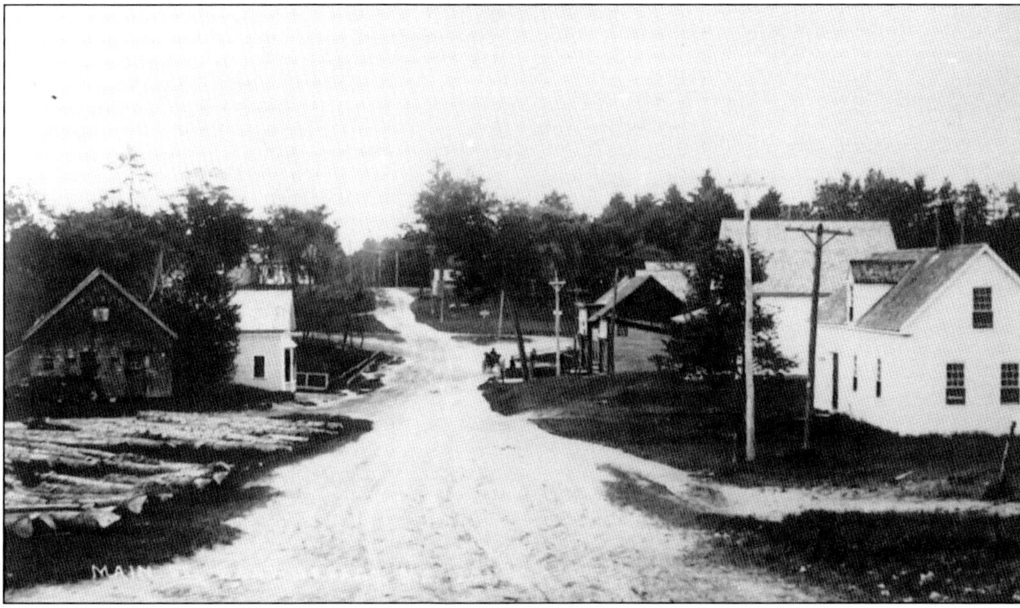

EAST SEBAGO VILLAGE, C. 1921. Highly visible in the left foreground is Fitch Brothers' sawmill, run by Harry Fitch. Below is the property of Will Martin, which in the 1930s and early 1940s was known as the Hoot Owl, a bakery and ice-cream parlor. The road below it leads to the Fitch homestead and the Lakeview Park Agricultural Association fairgrounds. In the distance is Anson Brackett's house. Opposite his house is his blacksmith shop, just beyond the lot on which the Spaulding Memorial Library was built in 1924. To the right of the Mattocks Road (Route 11) is Sanborn's Store, followed by the residences of Tom and Mandy Fitch and Henry "Sharky" Thombs.

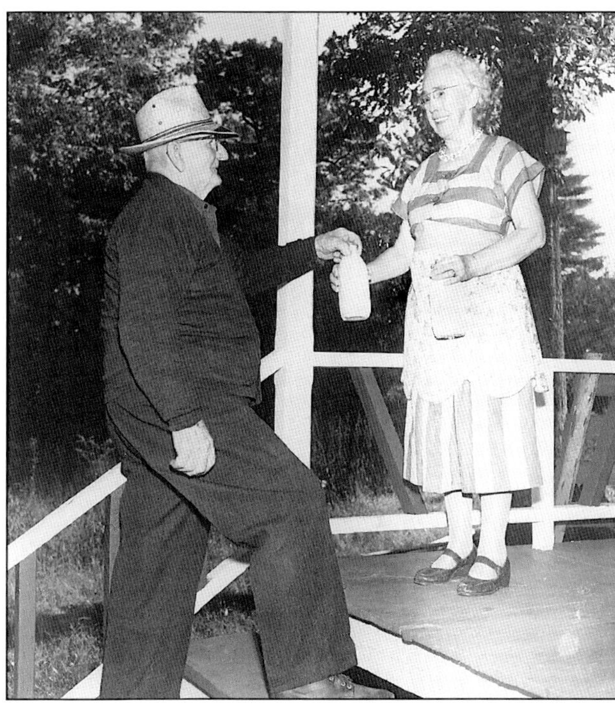

THE END OF AN ERA, 1957. O.B. Denison Jr. of Cornish captured this momentous event with his camera as Joses H. Murch, fondly called Joe by all who knew and loved him, delivers his final bottle of milk to Ida Martin in East Sebago, ending 40 years of delivering milk in the area from his farm in North Baldwin, first by horse and then by truck. In 1957, he sold his route to a Gorham dairy but continued supplying milk to the dairy for several years. Ida Dole Martin was related to the Dole pineapple people in Hawaii.

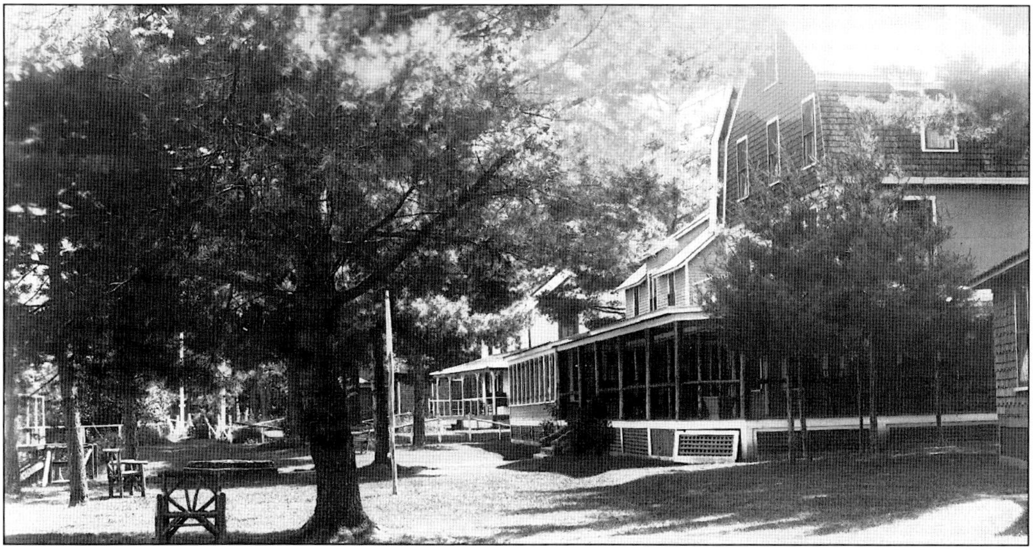

WEST SHORE HOTEL AND CAMPS, C. 1935. Soon after the advent of the automobile, Anson L. Brackett gave up blacksmithing in the village and opened a camp for sportsmen and vacationers, overlooking Sebago Lake. In 1922, he sold the camp to Frank and Ruby Kernan of Rhode Island, who greatly enlarged the main building, named it the West Shore Hotel, and added a number of cottages. The hotel closed in the early 1960s, and all the buildings are now privately owned.

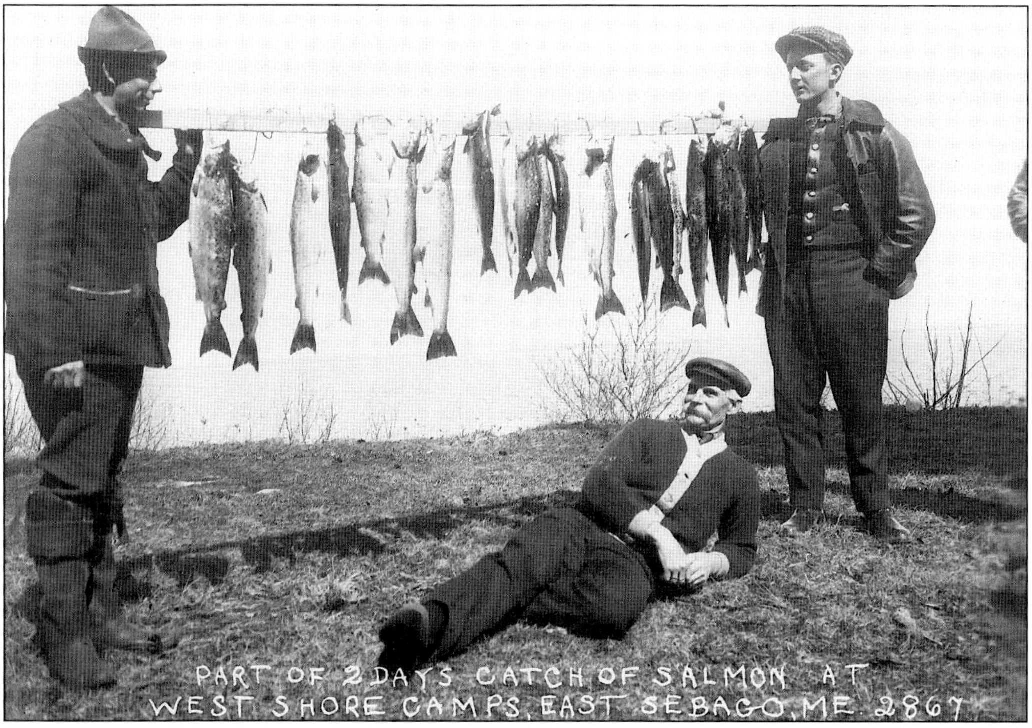

SEBAGO LAKE SALMON, C. 1920. In front of the West Shore Camps in East Sebago, Oscar Martin, left, and probably David Burnell display a string of salmon caught in Sebago Lake over a two-day period. Anson Brackett, owner of the camps, reclines on the ground.

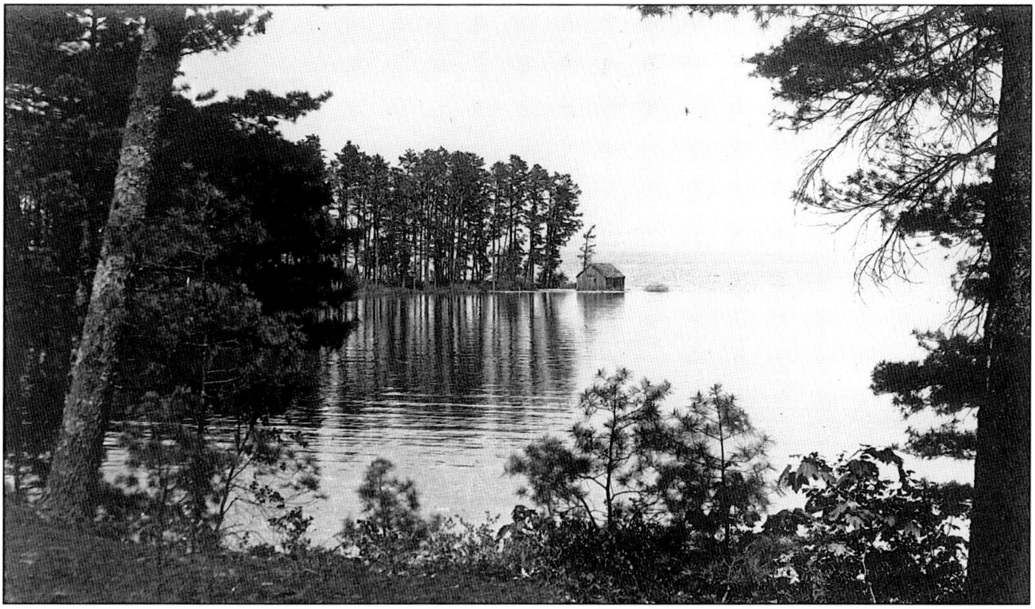

THE MOUTH OF THE RIVER, C. 1890. For at least two centuries, the quiet waters where the Northwest River empties into Sebago Lake have provided a safe haven for boaters whenever strong winds transform the Big Bay into a sea of huge waves. The long sandbar, which has been in existence for at least a century, either had not formed when this photograph was taken or had formed and been inundated after the level of the lake was raised in the 1880s. The sandbar later grew and reformed naturally. Sebago Marine gained permission from the town and state in the late 1960s to move the narrow channel from the West Shore to where it is today.

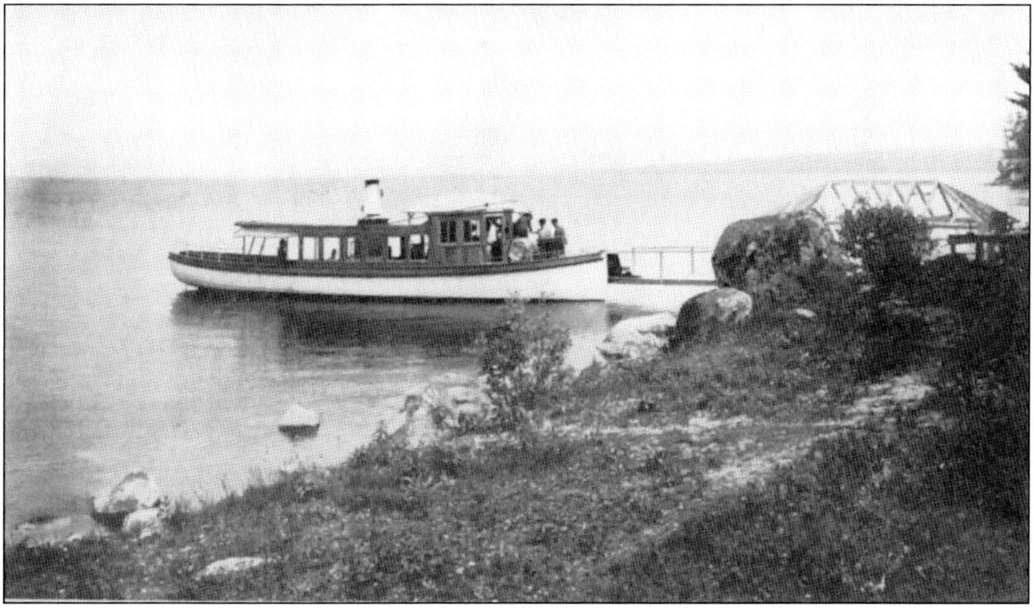

MILLIKEN'S LANDING, C. 1915. Milliken's Landing was owned by William H. Milliken and was located at the West Shore in East Sebago near the mouth of the Northwest River. Before the Cumberland & Oxford Canal was closed, supplies—especially those for Fitch's Store—were unloaded at an earlier dock in this area. The steamboat may have been Frank Sawyer's.

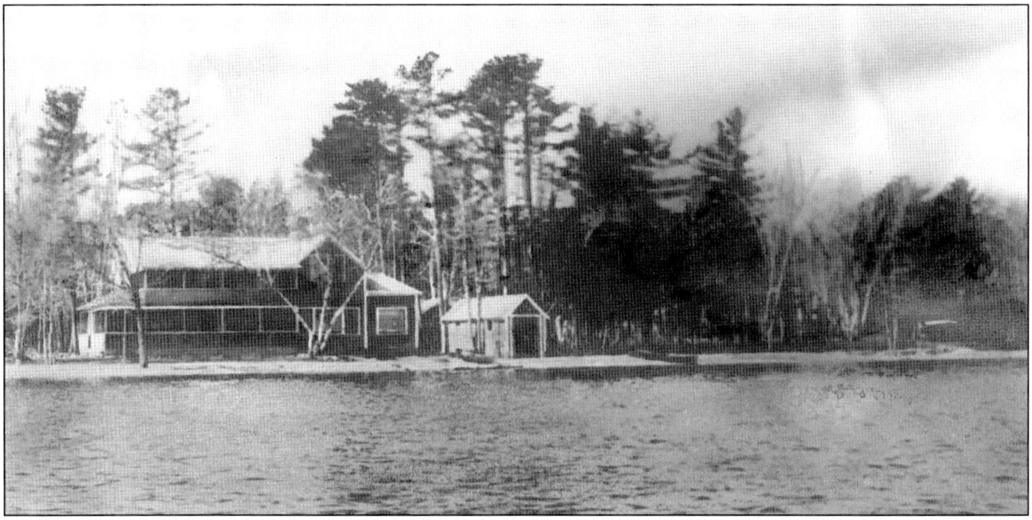

The Kakos Cottage, c. 1925. The Kakos Cottage, located between Ossipee and Naomi Streets and now the year-round home of Richard and Irene Bragdon, was one of the earliest cottages built on Long Beach. It and the Red Oak on Quest Avenue, built by Jim Williams from Douglas Hill, are the two largest cottages on Long Beach.

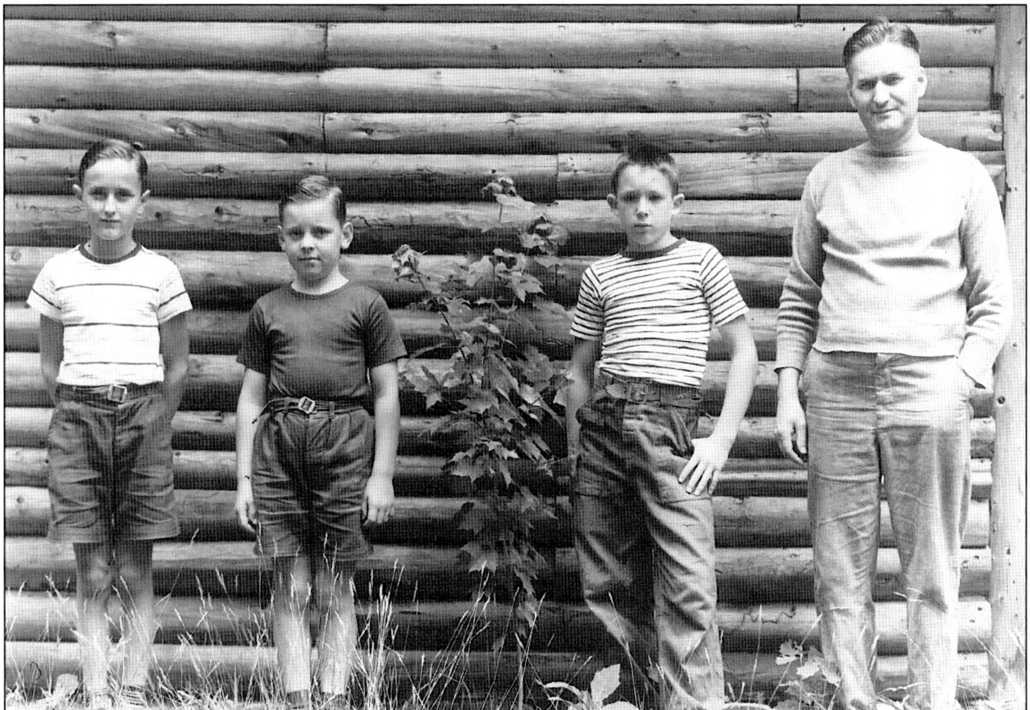

"The Way Life Used To Be," 1939. George Taylor, who owned Taylor's Pharmacy in South Portland, stands beside his log-sided cottage at Long Beach, now owned by the Doody family. Standing next to him are Francis St. Hilaire of Reading, Massachusetts; Bobby Morrison of South Portland, who became a gynecologist; and Jim Taylor, now retired after serving on the South Portland police force for 25 years.

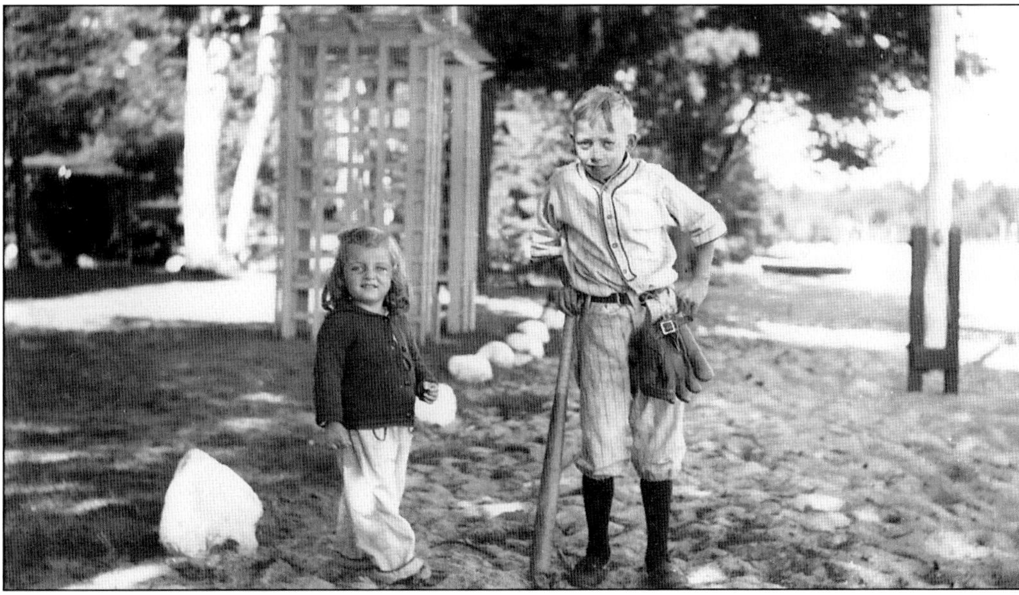

MARY AND JACK BARNES, 1936. Mary and Jack Barnes, along with their cousin Lowell "Bud" Barnes, were the only children residing year-round on Long Beach at the time this picture was taken in front of Mr. and Mrs. Walter Ray's cottage, named Richwood after their sons Woody and Richard. Mary was born in the house on Naomi Street that is now owned by the Valentinos and is the only known child ever to be born at Long Beach.

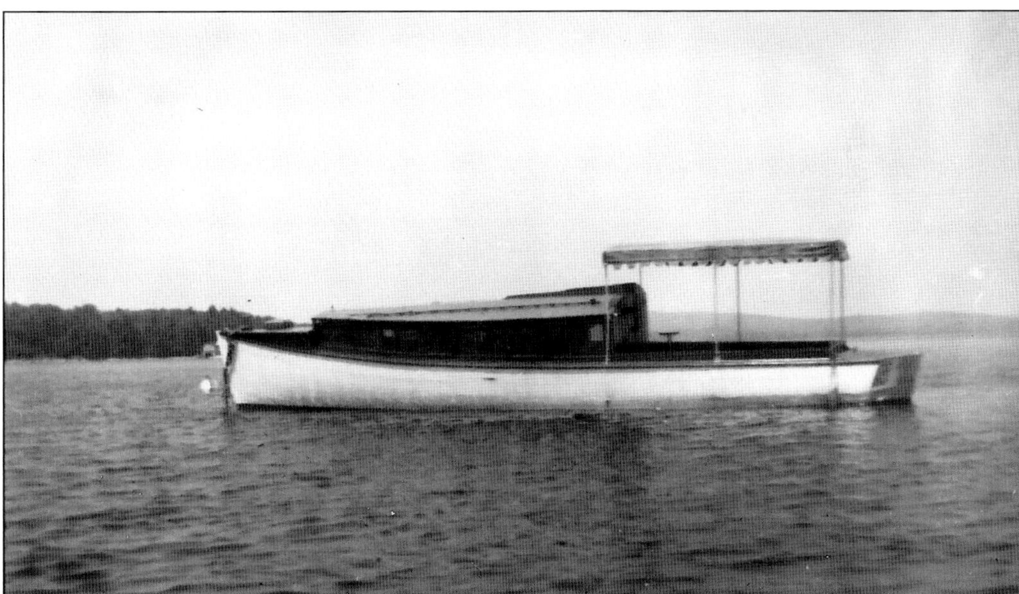

THE PRIDE FAMILY'S YACHT, C. 1937. At one time, this yacht lying at anchor off Pickering Street was the only yacht moored along Long Beach. It was owned by Merritt Pride of the B.G. Pride Coal & Fuel Oil Company in Westbrook, who owned all the lakeside property on the left side of Pickering Street. Visible off the yacht's bow is the Spaulding boathouse, where the *Ramona* was housed.

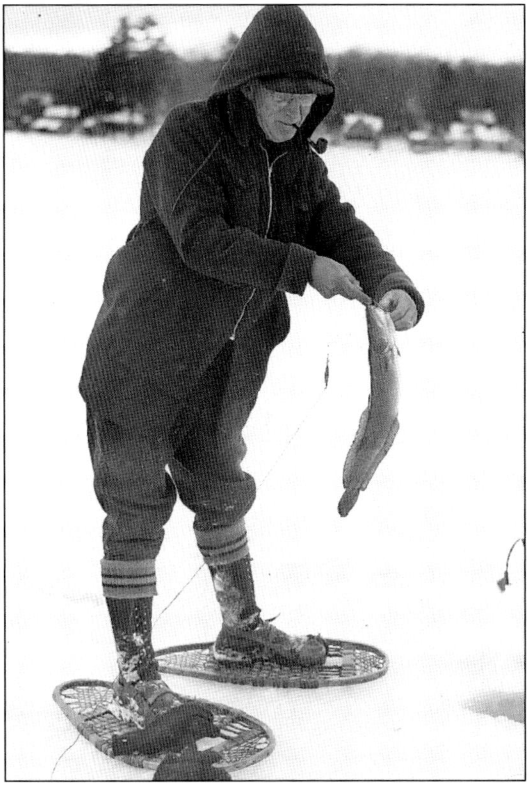

BAKED CUSK FOR SUPPER, C. 1940. C. Lowell Barnes, wearing his favorite bear-paw snowshoes, unhooks a medium-sized cusk he just caught off the West Shore on Sebago Lake. Barnes, a native of Pittsfield, married Rose Noble, granddaughter of famed fiddler and showshoe maker Mellie Dunham of Norway, Maine. The couple ran a restaurant in Norway before moving with their son "Bud" to Quest Avenue on Long Beach in the late 1920s. For many years, they rented boats and operated what later became Jordan's Store, now owned by the Cuttings. Barnes was an inveterate hunter, trapper, and fly fisherman. His Barnes Special is still a popular fly used by trout and salmon fishermen. He was planning a fall hunting expedition when he died of a heart attack on August 25, 1964.

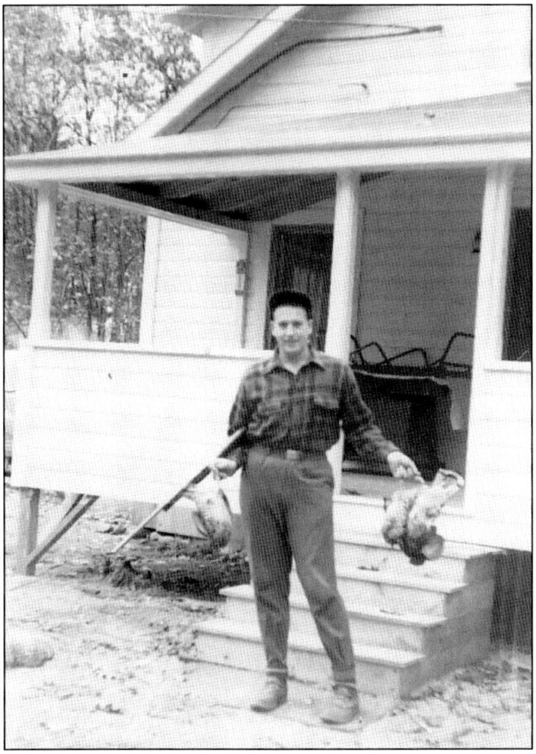

DR. LOWELL E. BARNES (1924–1995), C. 1952. Lowell "Bud" Barnes holds three ruffed grouse, which he shot with his 16-gauge shotgun in front of the house his parents built on upper Quest Avenue after they sold their store property to Jordan's. In 1956, Barnes gave up his medical practice in Akron, Ohio, moved back to his native state, and set up practice in Hiram. Over the years he became a legendary figure and a highly regarded country physician, sportsman, and conservationist. Up to the age of 8, he was taught at home by his mother, previously a teacher at the Waterford Flats school. He finished his elementary education with Mamie White at the East Sebago school and entered Fryeburg Academy at age 11. He had one year at at Hebron Academy before entering Colby College. After Pearl Harbor, he enlisted in the navy and held the rank of lieutenant. After the war, he studied at the College of Osteopathic Medicine in Des Moines, Iowa, graduating in 1951.

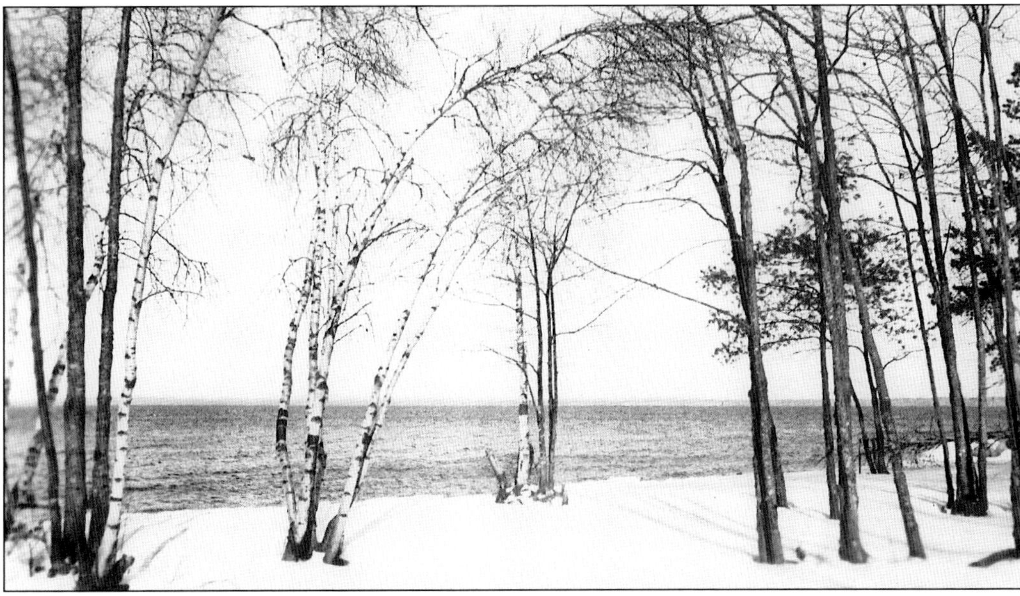

LONG BEACH IN WINTER, C. 1932. After Labor Day, most of the cottages on Long Beach were closed up for the season. In 1932, only four families—the two Barnes families, the Fitts family, and the Browns—lived here year-round. However, three consecutive winters and early springs, including the winter and spring of 1932, were made lively because of the Civilian Conservation Corps (CCC) boys, who were housed at the Red Oak on Quest Avenue and worked at eradicating the brown-tail moth.

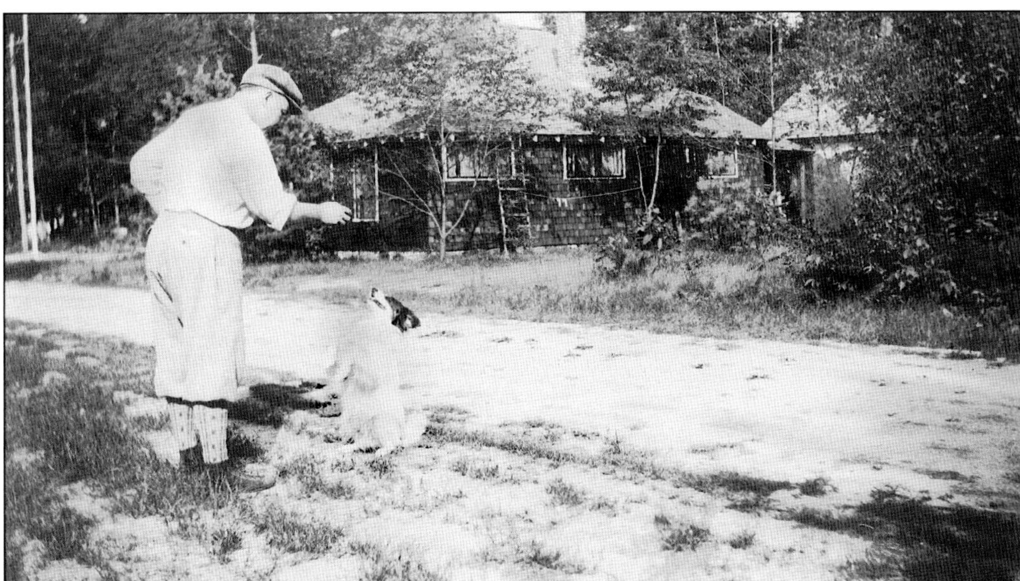

CLARENCE POTTER, C. 1932. Clarence Potter, who owned the cottage on upper Naomi Street, now the home of the Titcombs, feeds tidbits brought up from his restaurant, Potters Restaurant on Congress Street in Portland, to Spotty, owned by Clayton and Grace Barnes. Visible is the cottage then owned by the Browns of Arlington, Massachusetts. Mrs. Brown died in the cottage, c. 1934.

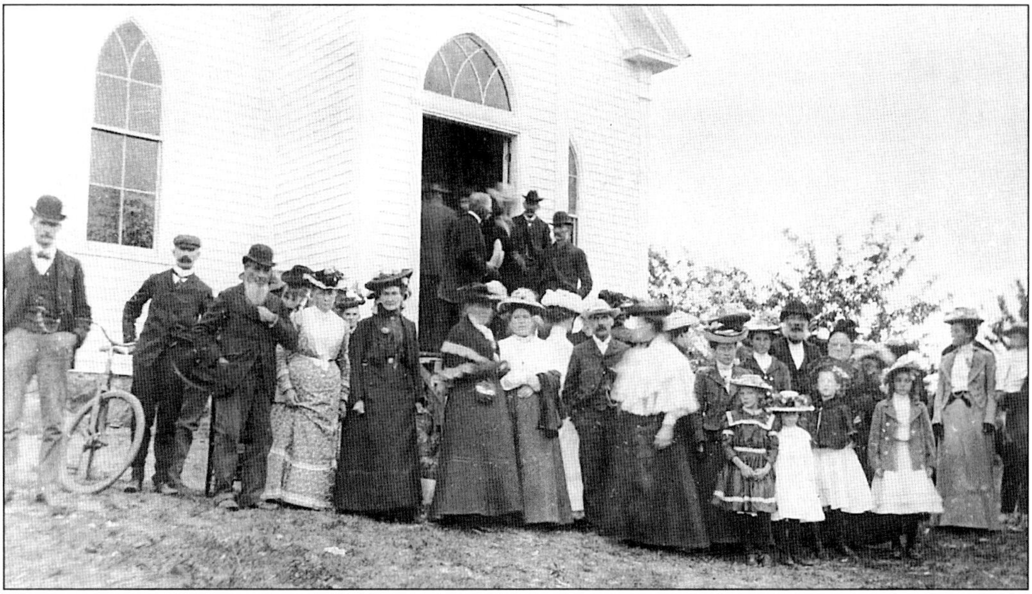

THE DEDICATION OF THE NORTH SEBAGO METHODIST CHURCH, AUGUST 30, 1903. Dressed in their best attire are, from left to right, Fred Robinson, Maurice Libby, Paris Ward, Francis Ward, Mrs. J.J. Allan, Asenall Burnell, Nellie McKenney, Mrs. Charles Jones, Julia Shaw, Carrie Bacheldor, Flora Shaw, Cora McKenney, Abram Ward, Sarah Ward, Fanny Anderson, Everette Anderson, Albert Anderson, Lila Bacheldor, Edna Bacheldor, Vera Thompson, and Mauce Bacheldor. In the doorway are Joseph Bacheldor, Reverend McFarlan, O.S. Shaw, and Bille McKenney.

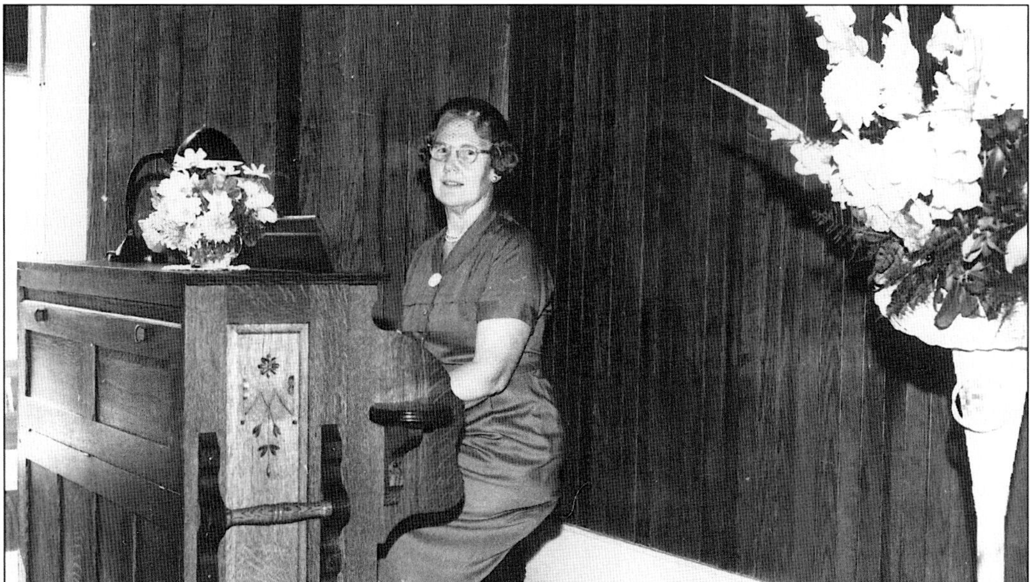

HELEN STICKNEY AT THE ORGAN, C. 1955. Helen Stickney lived at the McKenney farm on Peaked Mountain near North Sebago. For many years she taught at the one-room school near Bachelder Brook and played the organ here at the Methodist Church. She died in April 1973, four months before the church celebrated its 70th anniversary.

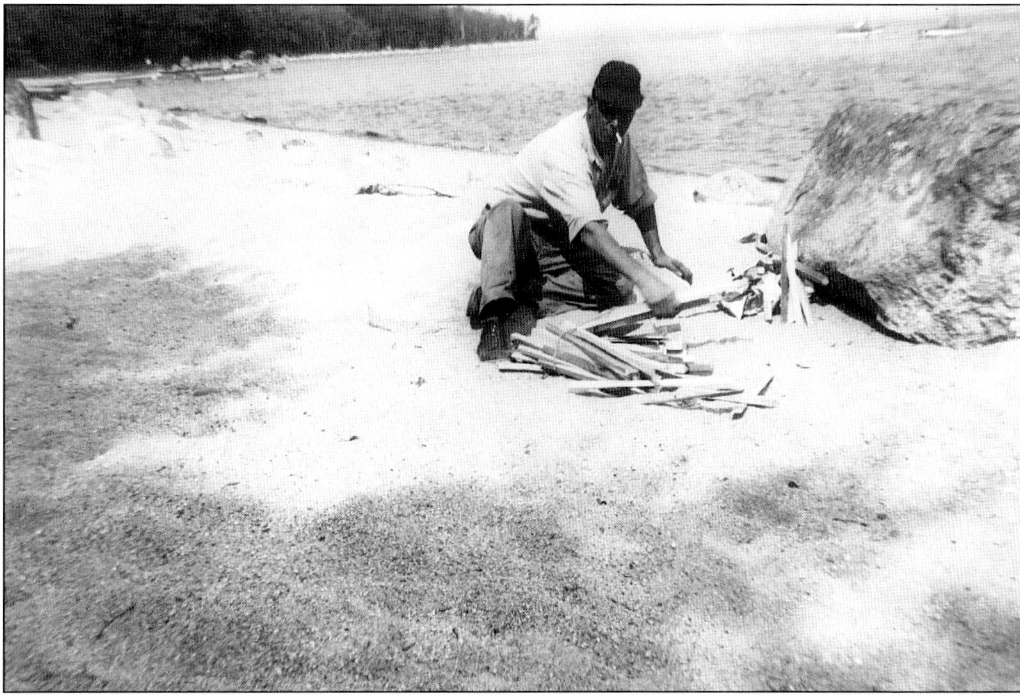

ELWYN "JIGG" SANBORN, C. 1940. Elwyn "Jigg" Sanborn prepares to light a fire for a cookout on the beach at Burnell's Corner, between East and North Sebago. Sanborn married to Doris Burnell of Burnell's Corner, lived at Sebago Center, managed the Douglas apple orchard, and plowed the roads in Sebago for several winters. The sailboats and docks in the background belong to Camp O-At-Ka.

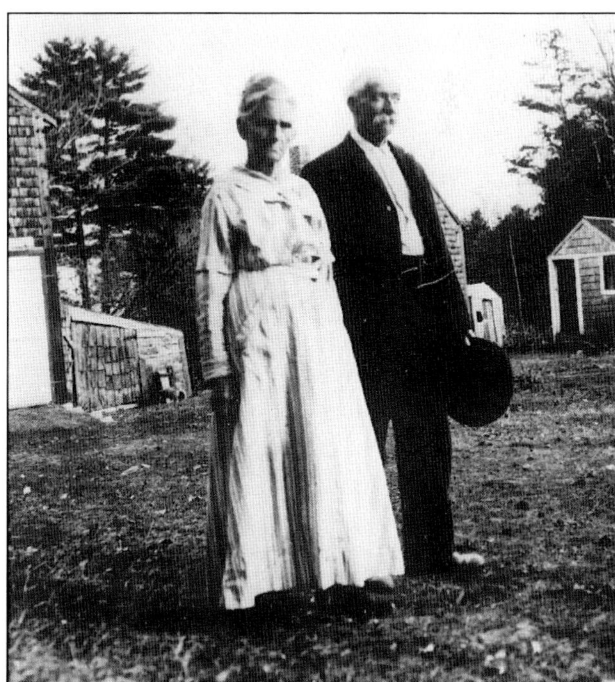

ALONZO AND FRANCENA BURNELL, C. 1925. The Burnells were the progenitors of many of the Burnells who originated at Burnell's Corner. Alonzo Burnell lived for a number of years in Lawrence, Massachusetts, before moving back to Sebago. It was here that he met and married Francena Tibbetts, his third wife, who came to Sebago from Hermon to care for her sister. The couple had 11 children.

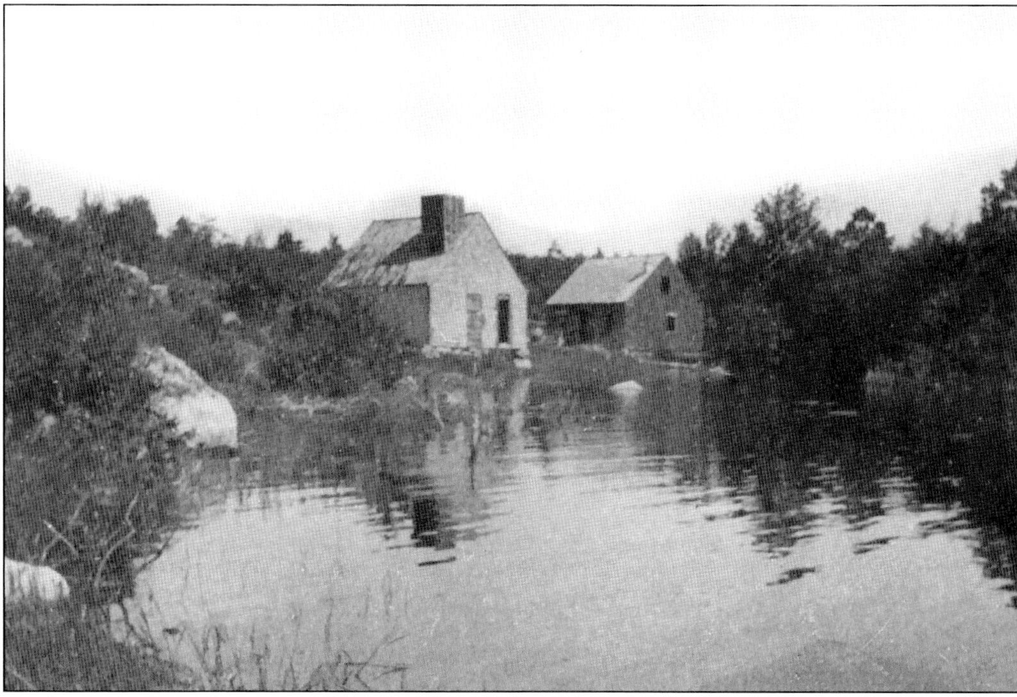

EARLY INDUSTRY AT NORTH SEBAGO, C. 1885. Although there are no sawmills operating in Sebago today, the wood products industry was once a mainstay of the town. Loren and Hannibal Bacheldor operated this sawmill and cooper shop on the west bank of Bachelder Brook near the bridge on what is now Route 114.

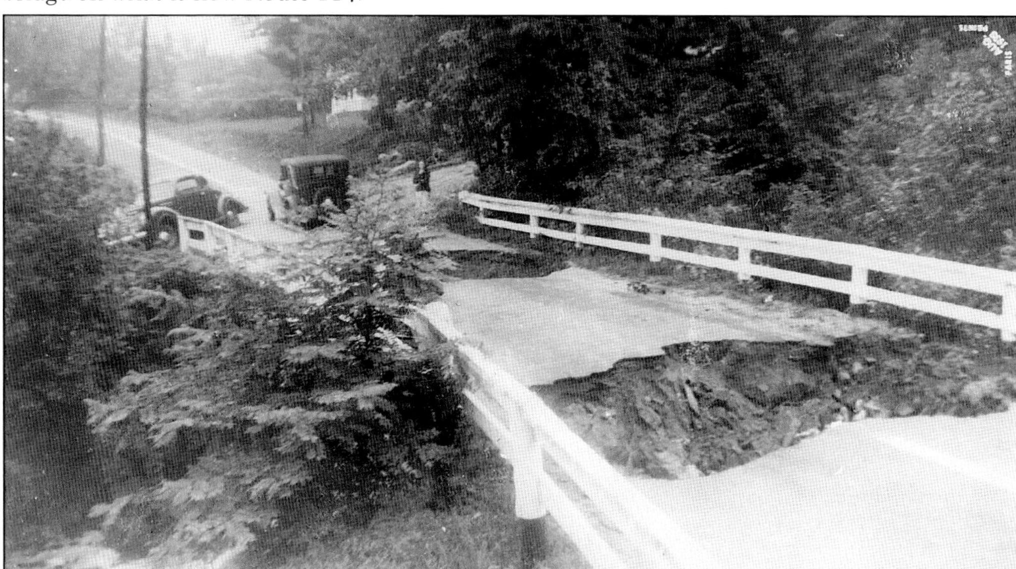

A WASHOUT, 1938. A sudden cloudburst in August washed out the bridge over Bachelder Brook in two places in North Sebago, as well as bridges and sections of roads in other parts of Sebago and Baldwin. Three people perished when the bridge over Breakneck Brook in West Baldwin was swept away. The house visible on the right belonged to Chet and Mertie Shaw, who ran Shaw's Store in North Sebago until 1951.

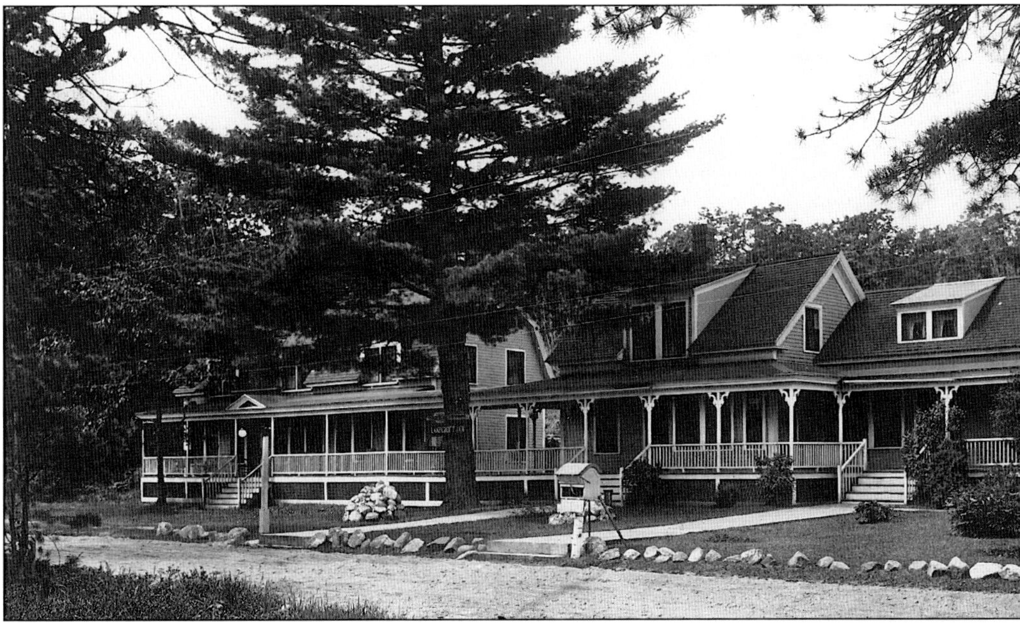

LAKECROFT, C. 1927. By the early half of the 20th century, tourism and services related to tourism had replaced agriculture and lumbering as the major source of income for the town of Sebago. Beginning in the early 1900s, Charles and Mabel Washburn operated Lakecroft in North Sebago. In 1921, Washburn departed for Texas and never returned, leaving his wife to run the establishment by herself.

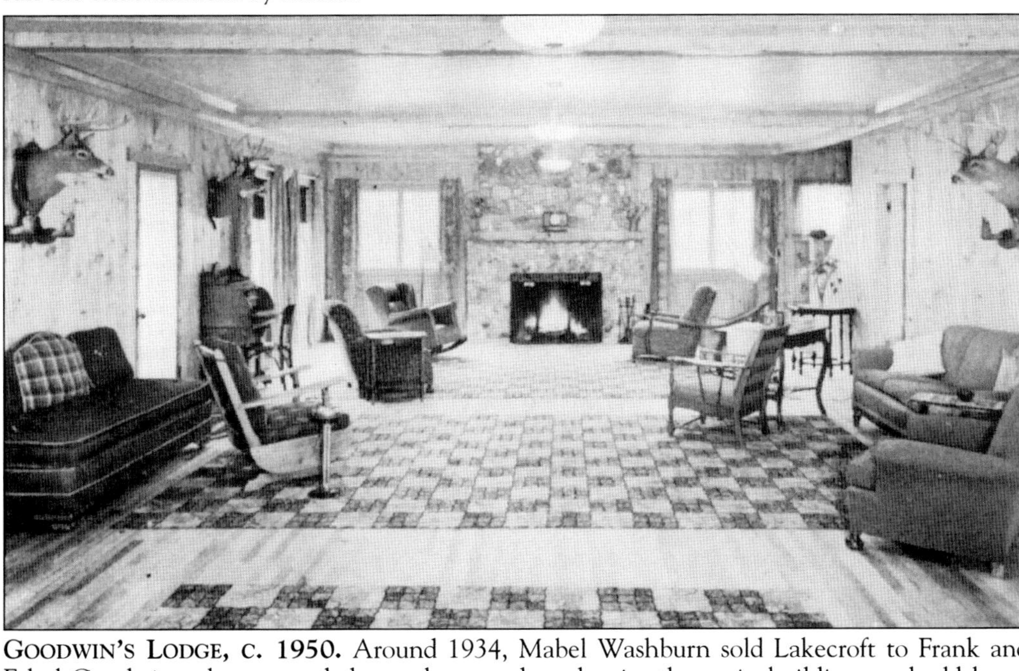

GOODWIN'S LODGE, C. 1950. Around 1934, Mabel Washburn sold Lakecroft to Frank and Ethel Goodwin, who proceeded to enlarge and modernize the main buildings and add large, modern cabins. The Goodwin's daughter Patricia ran the business for a number of years before passing it on to her son Richard, who also owns Goodwin's Food Center in Kezar Falls. The stone fireplace is one of many built in the area by Clayton E. Barnes.

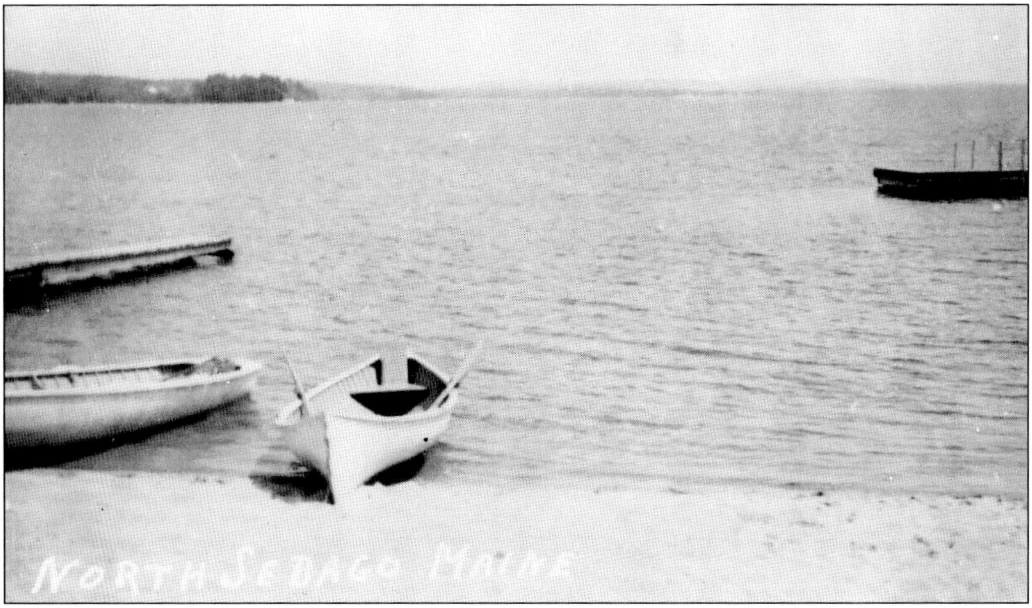

NORTH SEBAGO, C. 1935. This sandy beach to the right of Nason's Brook in front of Goodwin's Lodge and the longer Nason's Beach make up much of the shoreline of the pleasant little hamlet of North Sebago, first settled by George Ward of Scarboro in 1838. Spider Island, directly in line with the end of the pier on the left, has been owned for many years by Frank and Charlotte Schell. It is said that the island once changed ownership during a poker game being played by members of the Half Past Six Club from Portland at Sokokis Castle on Sanborn's Point, to the right of this beach.

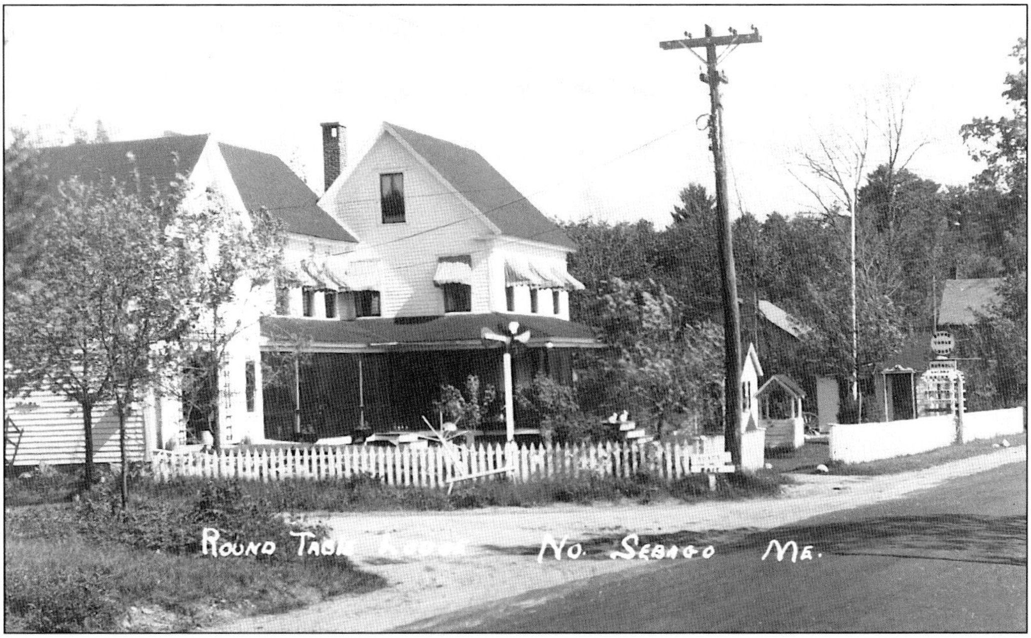

ROUND TABLE LODGE, C. 1950. The Round Table Lodge, as it became known during the years that Clarence and Etta Burnell operated it, was originally called Liberty Camp. It is now owned by the Sloan family.

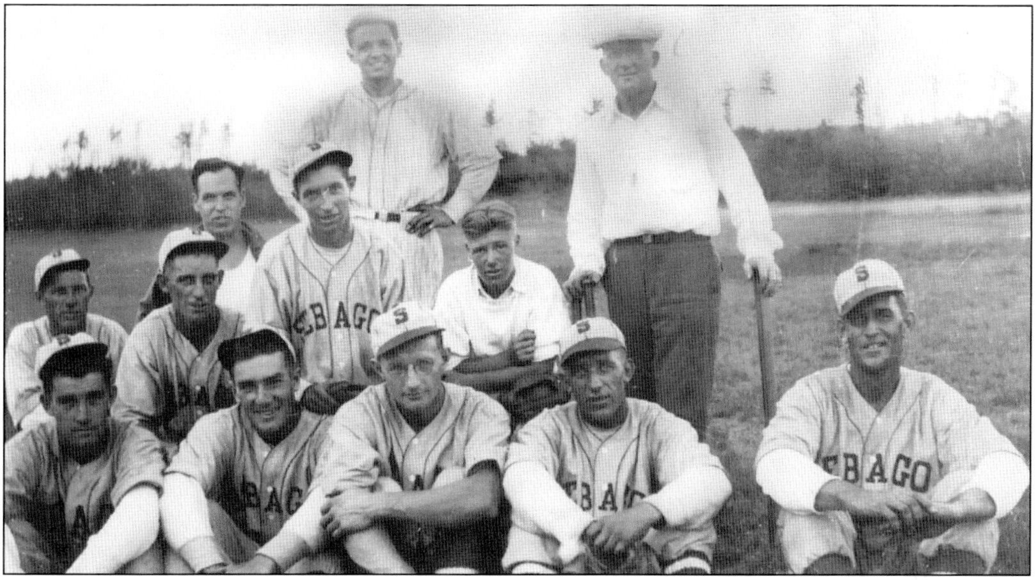

THE SEBAGO TOWN TEAM, 1935. The Sebago Town Team played its home games on the field now used as a summer trailer park at Nason's Beach. Posing for a team picture, after defeating Hiram 6-4 in Hiram, are, from left to right, as the following: (front row) Melvin Irish, Cliff Nason, Merle Durrell, Delmar Lord, and Elmer Shaw; (second row) John Lord, Franklin Irish, Bricky Burnell, and Linwood Bachelder; (back row) summer visitor and University of Pennsylvania pitcher Jack Lockwood and Percy Bachelder. Missing is Ray Burnell, who was pitching in a semipro league in eastern Maine.

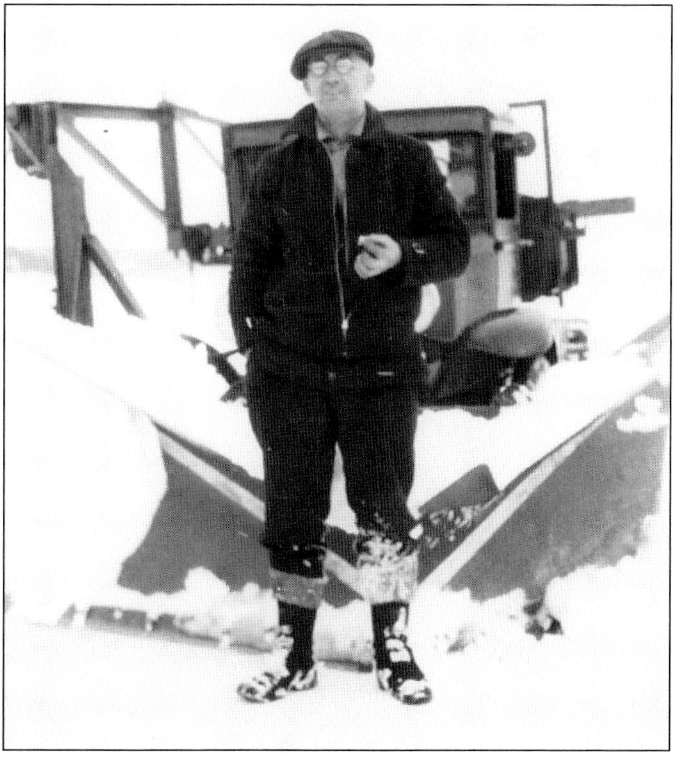

PERCY BACHELDER, 1934. Percy Bachelder, who lived on the Jim Shaw Hill Road in North Sebago, stands in front of his truck with a V-plow after clearing a road on frozen Sebago Lake from North Sebago to Muddy River in South Naples. The town owned the V-plow, with the single chain fall-operated wing, but did not acquire its own truck until 1942.

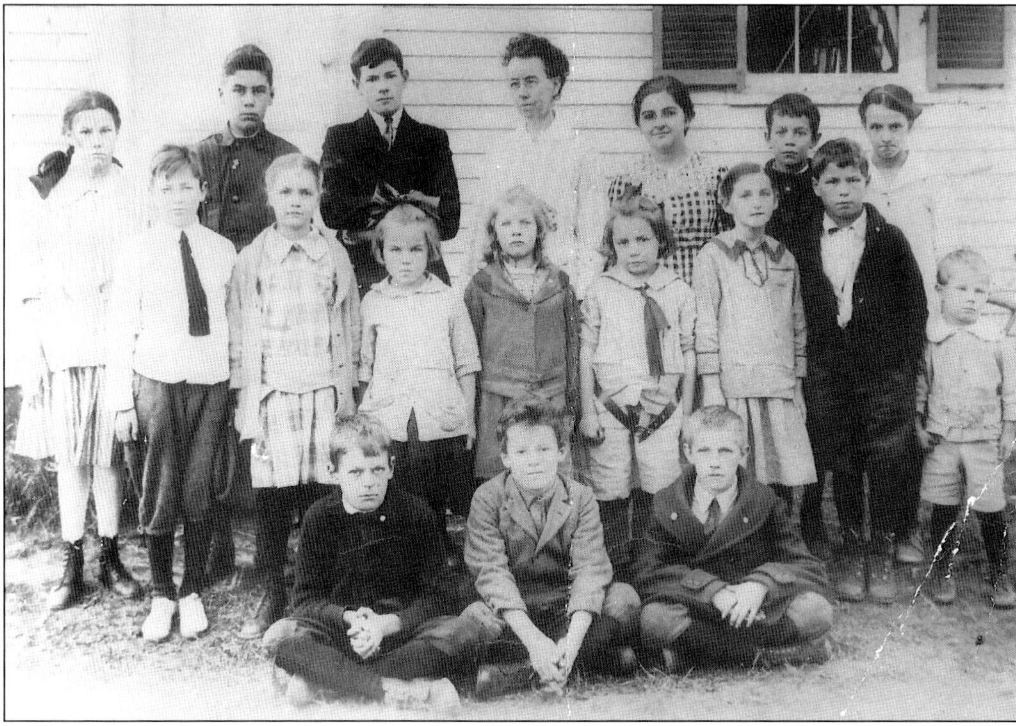

THE LARRABEE SCHOOL, C. 1921. The Larrabee School was located on the Peaked Mountain Road, a short distance from Larrabee's Corner. Shown here are, from left to right, the following: (front row) Harry McKenney, Merle Douglass, and Alton Crockett; (middle row) Howard Warren, Gladys Shunny, Marion Ward, Alice Crockett, Edna Douglass, Eulalie Larrabee, Arnold Ward, and Albert Ward; (back row) Blanche Crockett, Robert Sanborn, George Crockett, teacher Evelyn Woodman, Gertrude Johnson, Dennis McKenney, and Gladys Shaw.

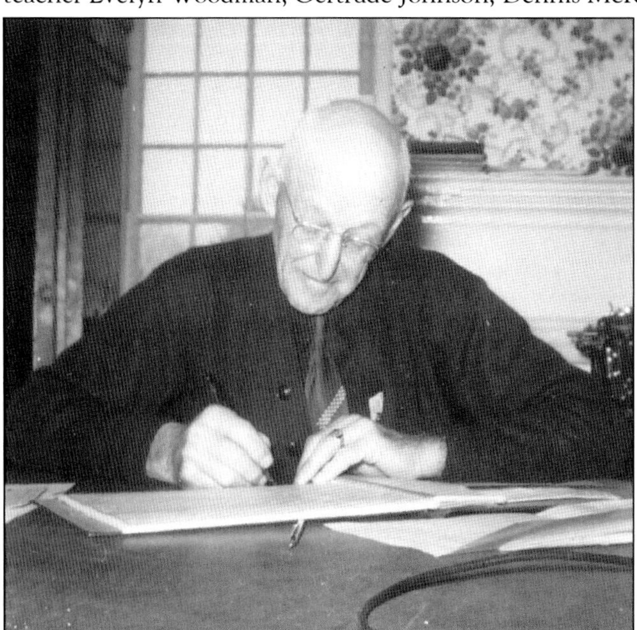

ELMER F. LARRABEE (1883 - 1969), C. 1958. Elmer Larrabee sits at his desk in his farmhouse, now owned by Robert Tiddea at Larrabee's Corner, balancing the accounts for the town of Sebago. Larrabee followed in the footsteps of his father, Plantville Larrabee, by holding at one time or another every major town office in Sebago, such as town clerk, road commissioner, and selectman. Moreover, he served in the Maine Legislature at Augusta from 1924–1927. Lawson Rowe of North Sebago stayed at the Larrabee farm during those years and took care of the livestock. Larrabee's daughter was Eulalie Lewis (1909–1999).

JOSEPH AND FLORENCE STACY LORD, C. 1940. Joseph and Florence Stacy Lord stand on the steps of their farmhouse, now owned by the Wallaces, located across from the Russo Farm on Anderson Road. For many years, Lord served as caretaker for Ciro Russo. Of the Lords ten children—Delmar, John, Edwin, Lucian, Donald, Dexter, Barbara, Edith, Eleanor, and Clara—only Eleanor and Barbara, who works at the Spaulding Memorial Library, still survive.

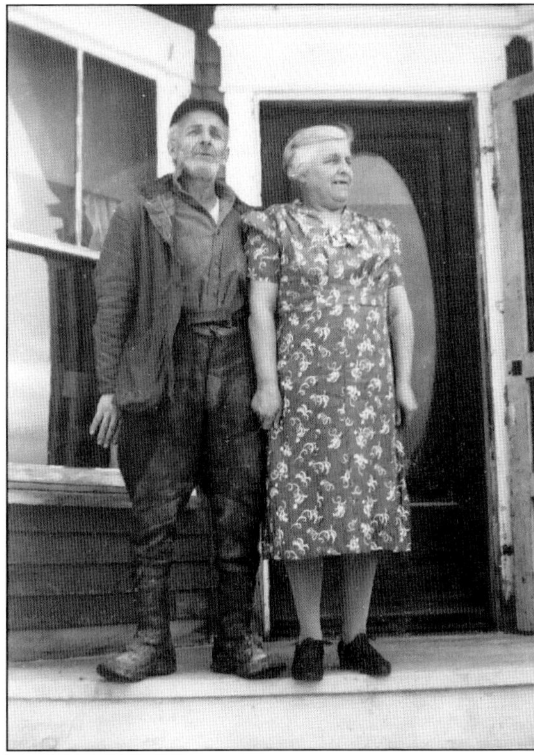

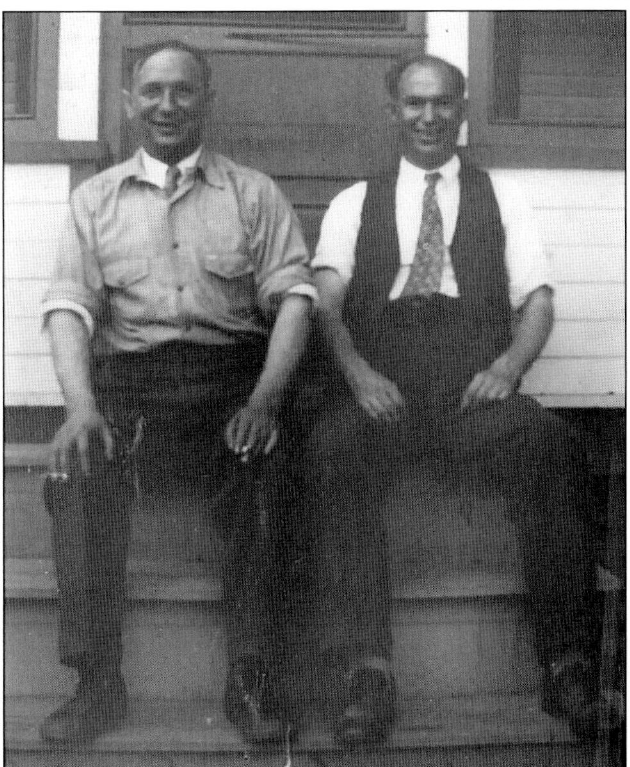

THE IMMIGRANTS, C. 1940. Vito Caggiano, left, and Ciro Russo, half brothers who emigrated from southern Italy in the early 1900s, sit on the steps of the Russo Farm, now owned by Mike Foye, located at what was then the end of Anderson Road in North Sebago. From 1927 to 1960, they owned and operated the Dirigo Bottling Company in Portland and were first attracted to the North Sebago area because of the hardwood needed to fuel their plant. They trucked wood back after delivering cases of soft drinks throughout the Lake Region. Russo's descendants reside in the area today and include his son Mose Russo Sr. and grandson Mose Russo Jr., who owns North Shore Yacht Associates and who constructed the 9-foot boat in which Bill Dunlap made his record-setting sail across the Atlantic in 1983.

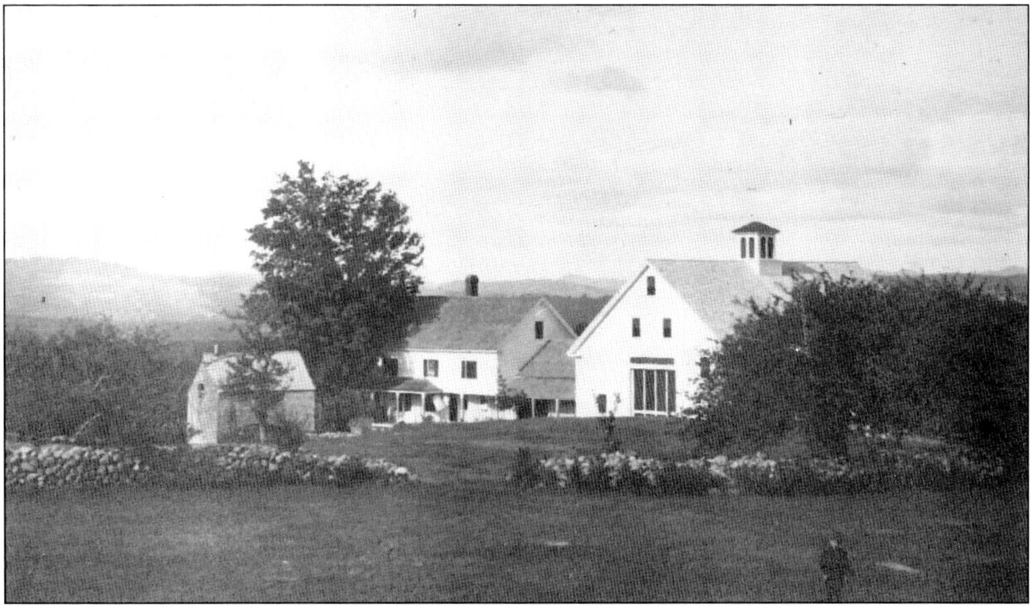

THE DOUGLASS FARM, C. 1915. This impeccably maintained farm located on the Peaked Mountain Road was built by Andrew Douglass (1810–1893) shortly after he arrived from Convene with his wife, Cassiah Irish, and their two eldest children in an ox-drawn dead-axle wagon. At the time of this photo, the Douglass's son Charles and his wife, Mary, were still living here with their son and daughter-in-law John and Madge Douglass, the parents of Merle, who is probably the one standing on the rock, and Arthur Douglass. The farm burned in 1948. Visible near the summit of Peaked Mountain is the McKenney-Clough farm.

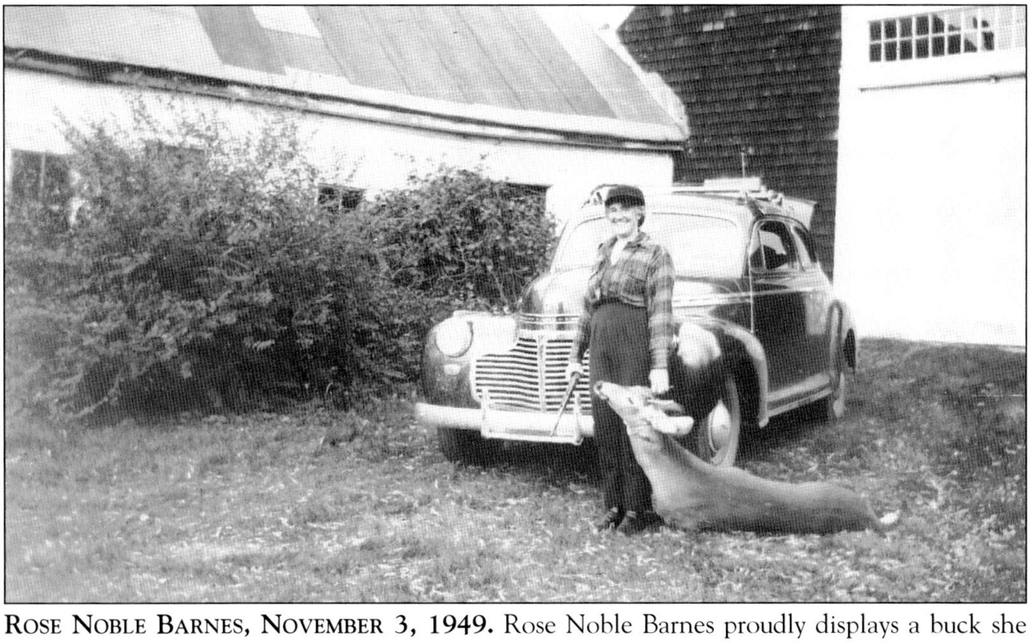

ROSE NOBLE BARNES, NOVEMBER 3, 1949. Rose Noble Barnes proudly displays a buck she just shot behind the barn of the McKenney-Clough farm. She and her husband, C.L. Barnes, acquired the farm c. 1938 from Hebron Adams of Westbrook. Adams purchased it from John Tron, a French immigrant, in 1915. The farm burned c. 1968.

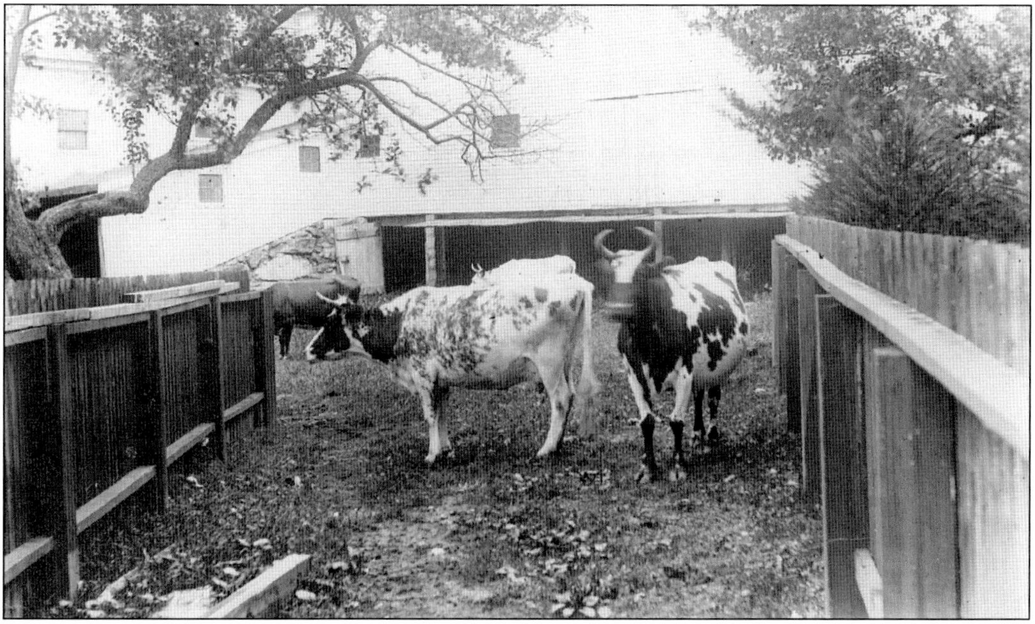

THE DYKE MOUNTAIN FARM, C. 1900. This farm owned by Oliver D. Dike was located on the opposite side of the Northwest River from Peaked Mountain, adjacent to Douglas Mountain (the Baldwin Hills). These handsome Ayrshire cows thrived on the hillside pastures.

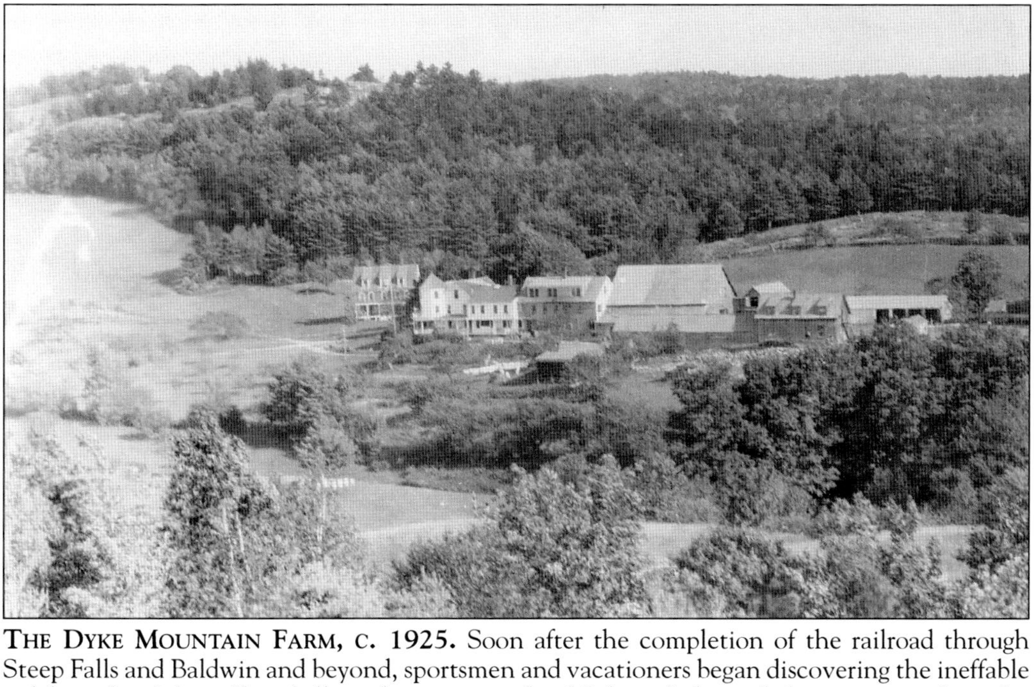

THE DYKE MOUNTAIN FARM, C. 1925. Soon after the completion of the railroad through Steep Falls and Baldwin and beyond, sportsmen and vacationers began discovering the ineffable pulchritude of the rolling hills within easy reach of Sebago Lake and the many ponds in the area. Consequently, Oliver Dyke did what many other more prosperous hill farmers did: he opened and enlarged his home to take in summer boarders. After Dyke's death in 1905, his daughter Grace continued to operate a lucrative business until all but the annex, visible on the left, went up in flames on September 11, 1927.

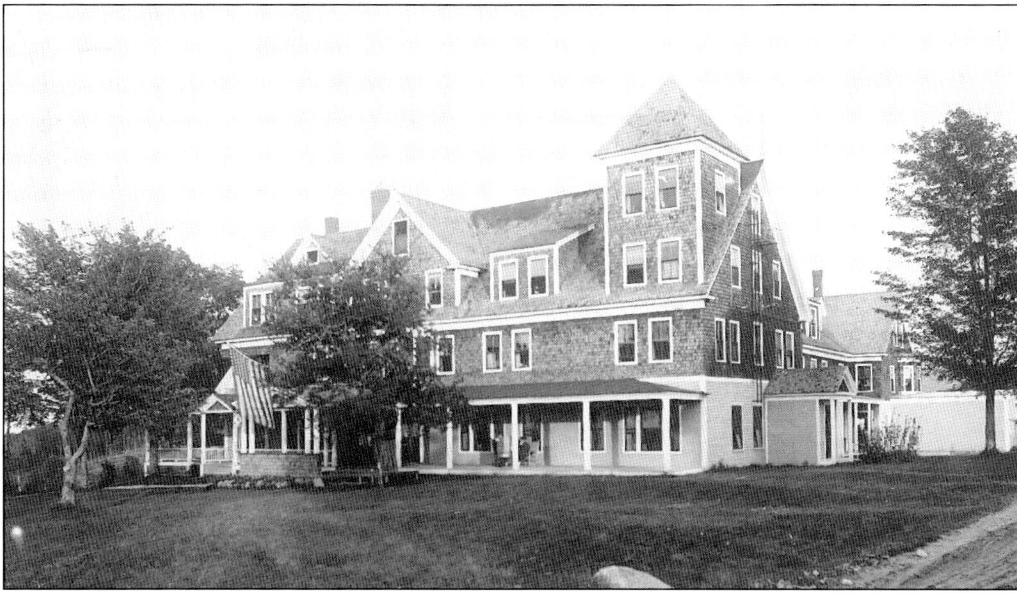

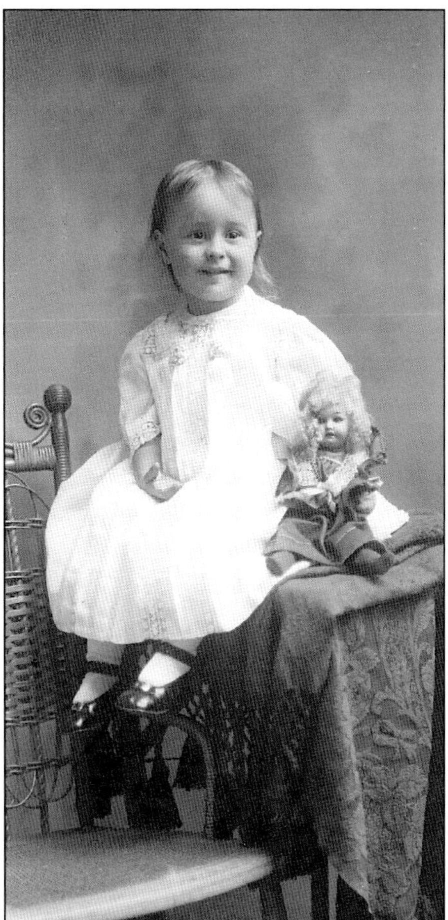

THE DOUGLAS HILL INN, C. 1915. As early as 1878, Stephen P. Douglas, who lived just a short distance from Oliver Dyke, opened his farm to summer boarders. Like the Dyke Mountain Farm, Douglas's farm, located where the Jones Museum stands today, was easily accessible by coach from the railroad and offered fresh mountain air, a magnificent view, outdoor activities, and plenty of homegrown food. In 1903, Douglas's son Edward S. Douglas built this splendid inn a short distance from his father's farm. He and his wife, Vesta Chadbourne, did a thriving business for 25 years, attracting guests from around the world and providing employment for many local people. On August 28, 1928, the inn mysteriously went up in flames. Two days later, the Douglas farm burned, destroying all but the annex. The Douglases and their daughter Helen nearly perished in the conflagration. After Edward Douglas, who set out the apple orchard on Orchard Road, sold the annex, the new owners built a bathhouse on the edge of the beach on Naomi Street at Long Beach. Around 1938, Clayton E. Barnes, who lived in the house next door, purchased the bathhouse *c.* 1938 and converted it into a cottage, which is currently owned by the Valentinos. The annex closed in the late 1940s and was demolished in 1959. It marked the end of a very colorful era.

HELEN DOUGLAS, C. 1912. Helen Douglas was born in 1910 and died in 1999. She is survived by her husband, Franklin Irish.

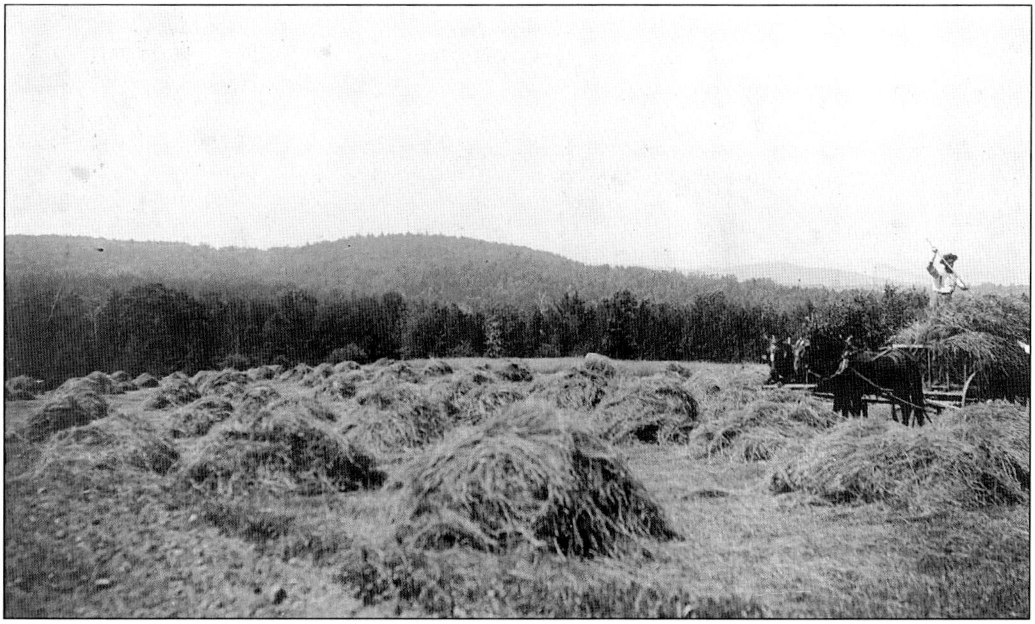

HAYING TIME, c. 1920. Henry Weed of Convene takes another forkful of hay from an unidentified helper and prepares to pack it down before trundling it up between endless mounds of hay to be carefully tagged and labeled in the lofts. Weed was one of the first residents of Sebago to own an automobile.

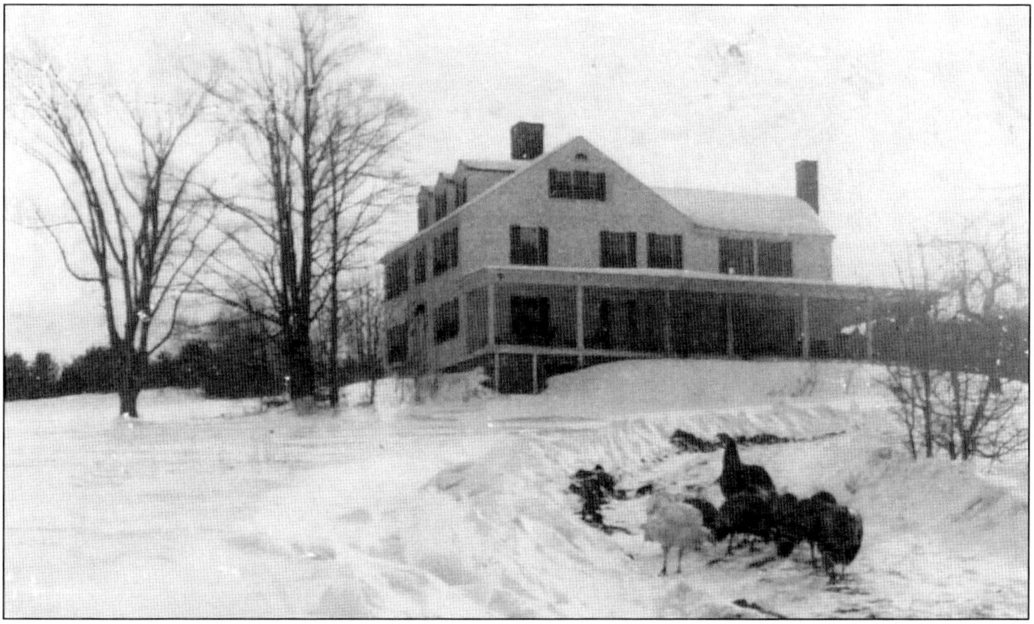

THE PIKE FARM, 1940. Oliver M. Pike trekked over from Cornish *c.* 1815, built a rude cabin, and began clearing the broad, sloping fields in Convene, which are still maintained by the Allens, who have owned the property since 1923. In 1826, Pike erected the original two-and-a-half-story Federalist section of this house. He and his wife, Sarah Page of Epping, New Hampshire, reared ten children. Besides farming, Pike was a member of the Maine Legislature, a self-styled lawyer, and a local selectman. The Pikes farmed here until 1901.

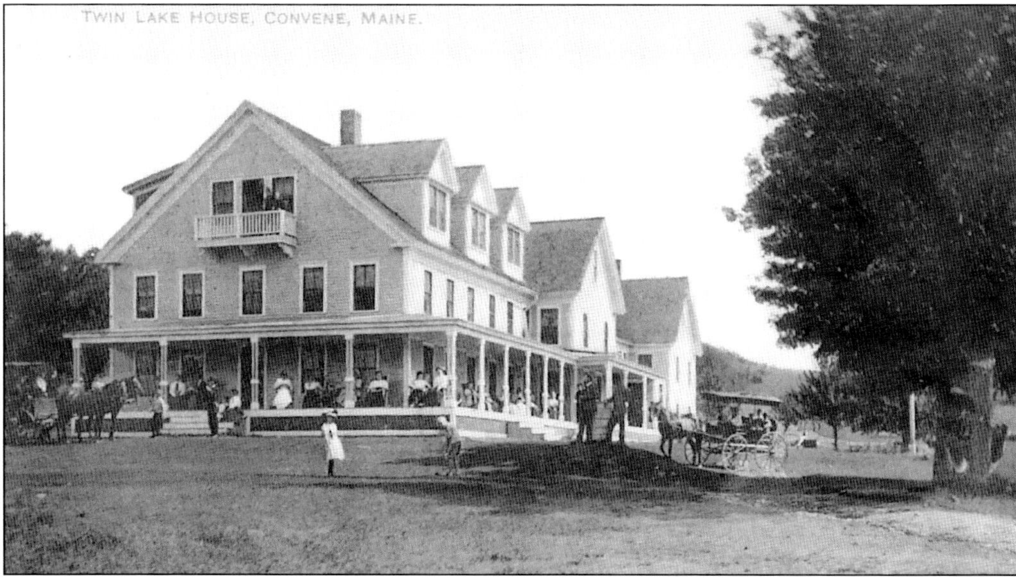

THE TWIN LAKE HOUSE, C. 1910. Located near the summit of Hog Fat Hill in Convene, the Twin Lake House was owned and run as a summer hotel by Charles and Annie Douglas Hunt from 1905 until Annie's death in 1933. In the early years, most of the guests arrived at the Bridgton Junction in Hiram via the Maine Central Railroad, transferred to the little 2-foot Bridgton & Saco Railroad, which went to the Twin Lake Station at Barker Pond, and then took the coach up the hill. Fire destroyed the complex in 1940.

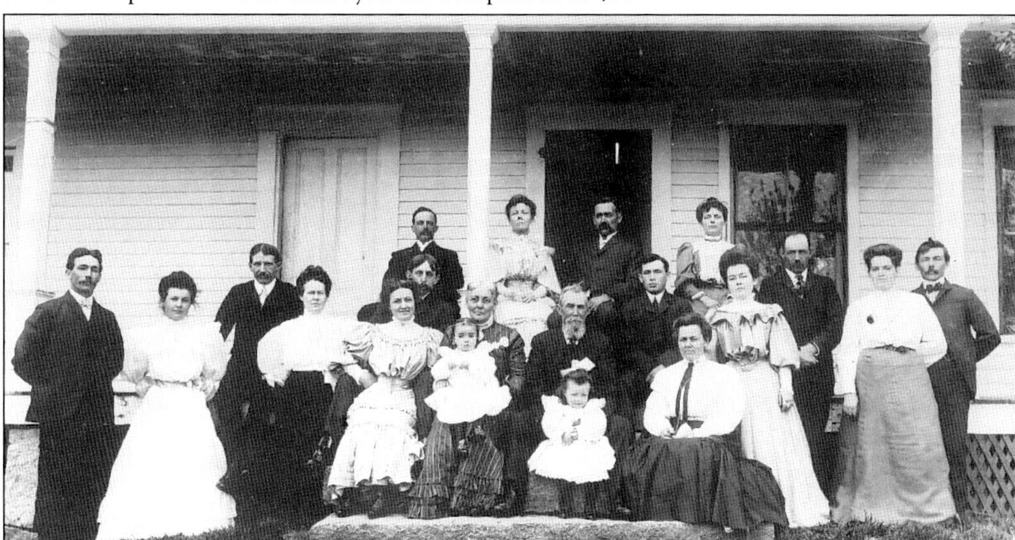

THE WEDDING OF CHARLES HUNT AND ANNIE DOUGLAS. Charles Hunt and Annie Douglas were married on June 1, 1905, at the Douglas farm, just below the Twin Lake House. Pictured, from left to right, are the following: (first row) Ethel Mae Douglas, Laura Augusta Storer holding Lillian Douglas, Oliver M. Douglas holding Laura Spencer, and Delia D. Fly; (second row) Oliver Morton Douglas, Eva Douglas Hanson, Julia D. Murch, Bertha D. Neil, Laura and Oliver Douglas, and Olive Douglas; (third row) Joses Murch, Chester Neil, Grover Douglas, Horace Spencer, and Harry Douglas; (fourth row) Ben Douglas, Annie Douglas, Charles Hunt, and Celia D. Spencer.

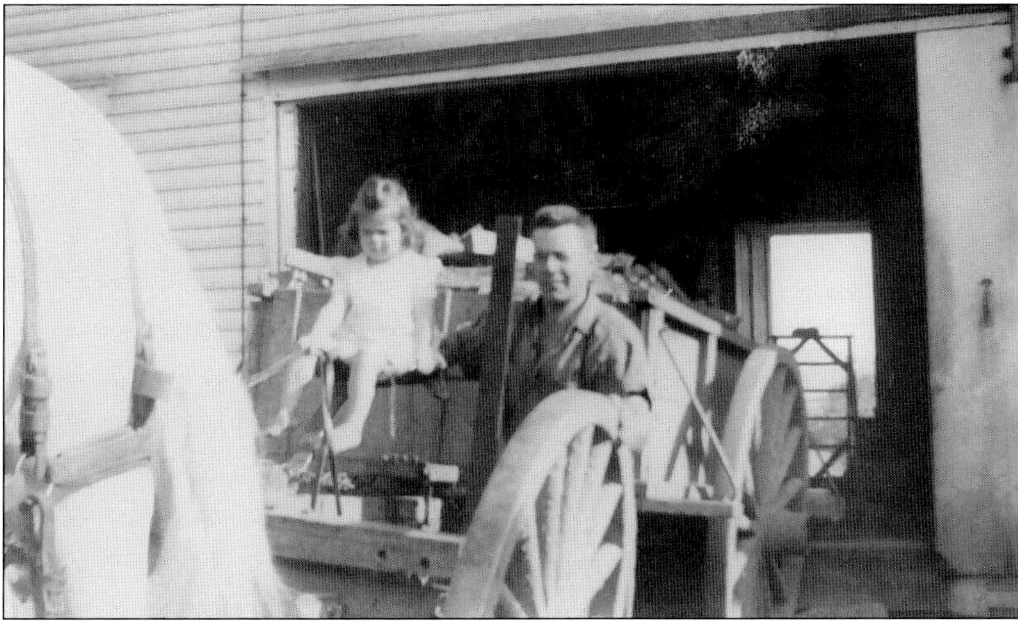

PUTTING IN THE WINTER'S WOOD, 1945. John Douglas stands beside a dump cart loaded with dry hardwood that he had cut and split the previous year to be unloaded and stacked in his shed on the family farm on Hog Fat Hill in Convene. His 2-year-old daughter Janet (Anderson) holds the reins to steady Prince and Dick. Horses were still more prevalent than tractors on hardscabble Maine farms in the mid-1940s.

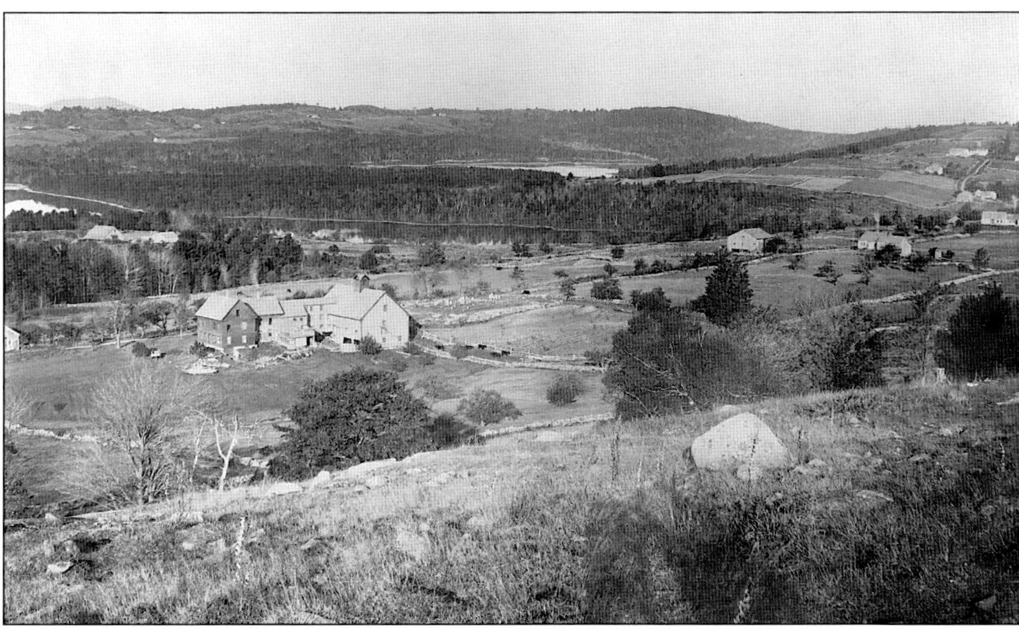

VIEW FROM A HILL, C. 1890. This splendid bucolic panorama was taken from the rocky hill above the Frank Haley farm in Convene (New Limington), looking across to Tear Cap in Hiram. On the left is Southeast Pond, and on the right is Barker Pond, with the Bridgton & Saco River Railroad tracks running parallel to the pond on the far side. On the far right is Hog Fat Hill and what in 1905 became the Twin Lake House.

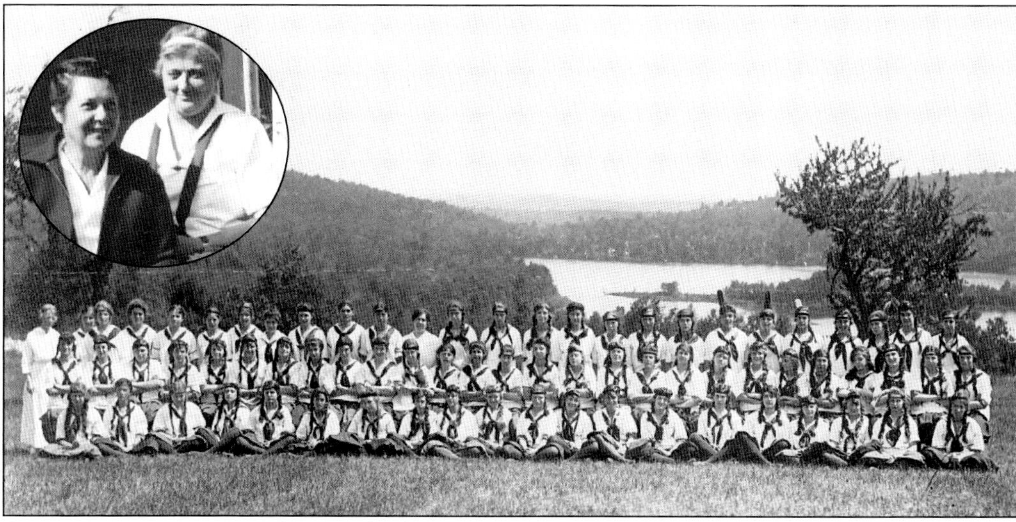

CAMP ACCOMAC. Located on Peabody Pond, Camp Accomac was founded c. 1915 by Corinne B. Arnold, who appears in this c. 1938 photograph without a headband in the middle of the top row. Note the standard attire: bloomers, headband, ankle-high stockings, and sneakers. The woman in the long dress is the camp nurse. In the inset are Alice Garson Wolf, left, who was camp director from 1930 to 1955, and Elizabeth R. Moriarty, who was assistant director from 1914 to 1952. The camp was sold in 1955 and is now Moose Cove Lodge.

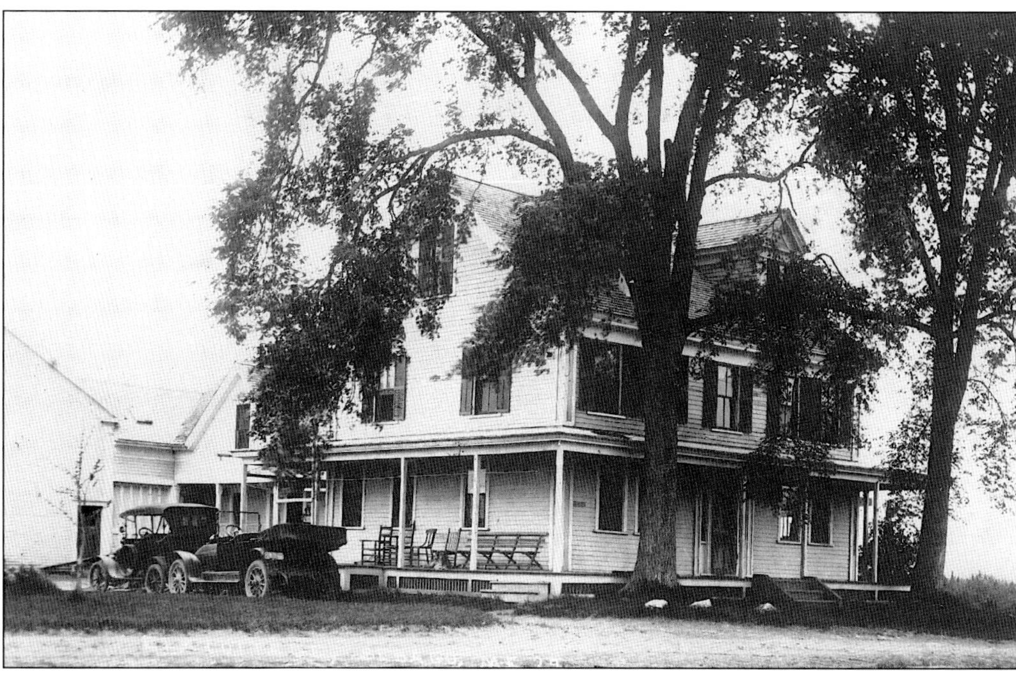

ELM COTTAGE, C. 1915. Elm Cottage, located on he Ridge Road (Hancock Pond Road) was built by Captain Babb in 1817. Over the years it underwent several remodelings, and James C. Babb is credited with being the first person in Sebago to take in summer boarders. Most of the guests arrived via the narrow gauge rail line at the West Sebago station on Hancock Pond. The property is now owned by Joanne Chessey.

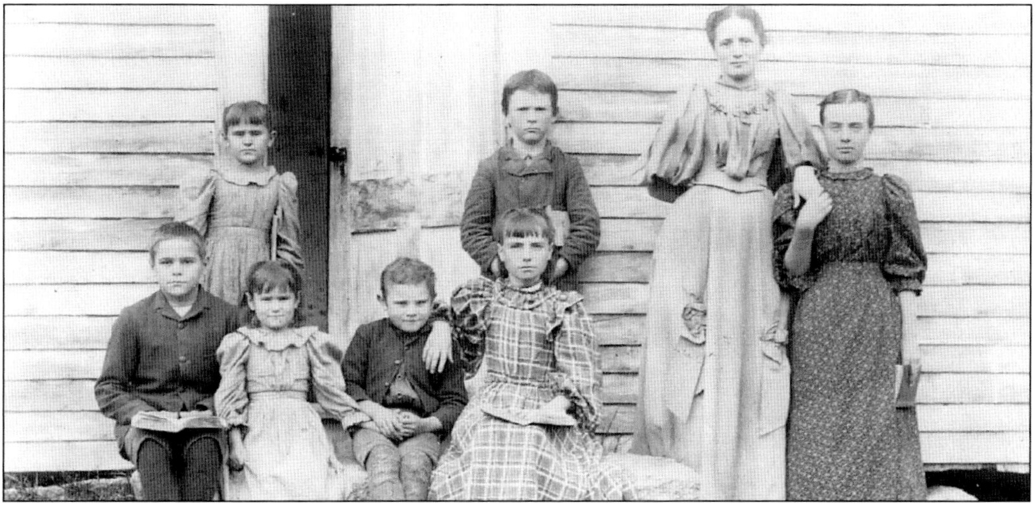

THE FOLLY SCHOOL, C. 1900. The Folly School was built in 1854 at the intersection of the Folly and Peaked Mountain Roads. From 1893 to 1934, each teacher in Sebago taught subprimary through grade eight. Students ranged in ages from 5 to 21. Those identifiable are, from left to right, the following: Leon White, Florence White Frost, and G. Cleveland White. Standing on the left is Cora White Weed. The teacher is Lunetta Poor Chessey, well-known locally for her poetry. The school closed in 1907, reflecting the rapid decline in population on the Folly Road.

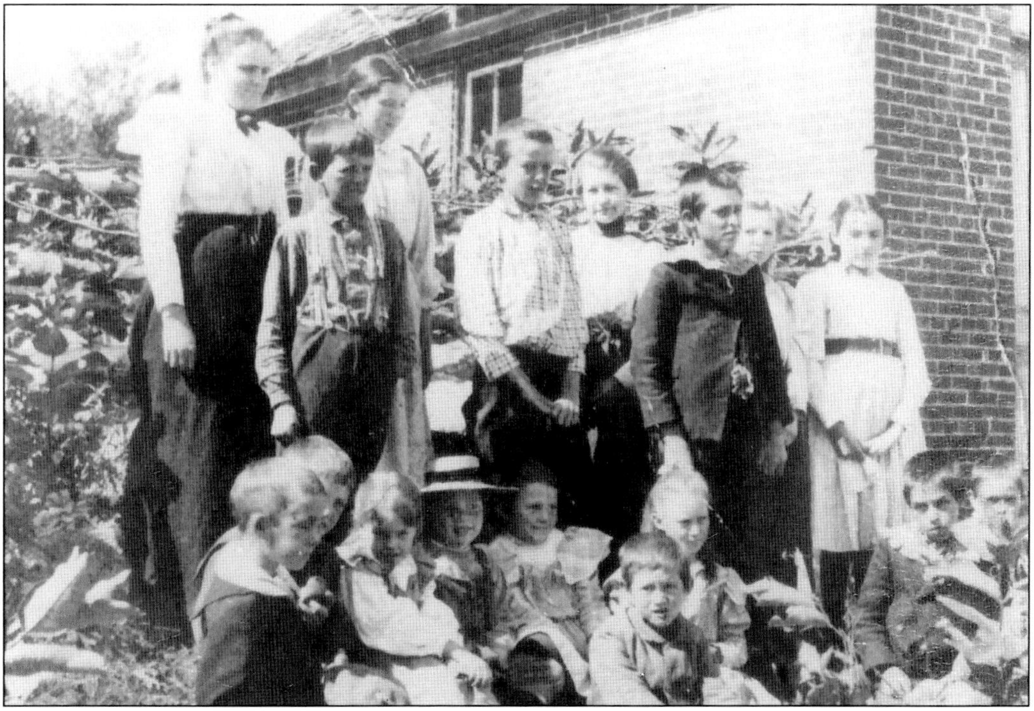

THE LITTLE BRICK SCHOOL, C. 1900. The Little Brick School, the only brick building in town, was built at Sebago Center in 1836 and closed *c.* 1901. It was used as a town office until 1951. The teacher is Mamie White, who taught most of her long career in Sebago. Several Decker children appear in the photograph.

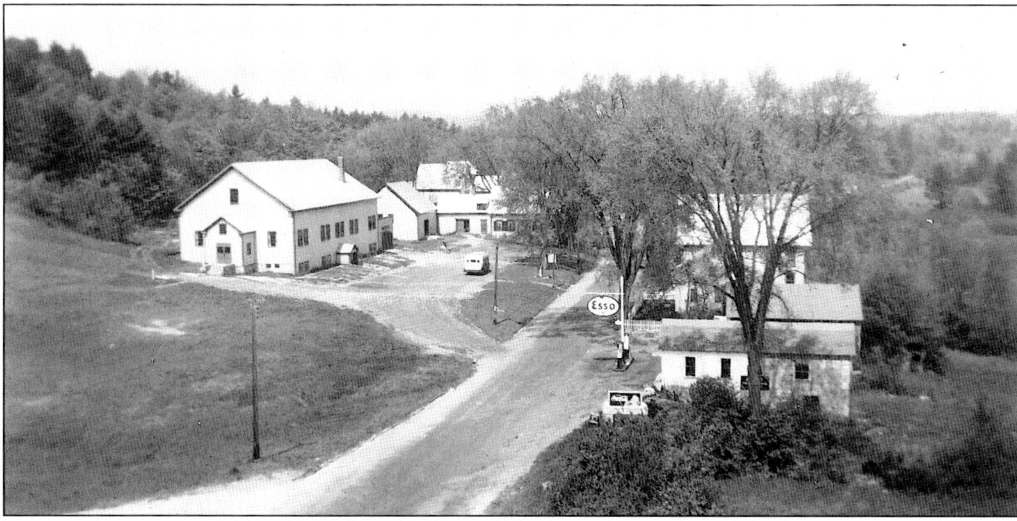

Sebago Center, 1948. Sebago Center became a vibrant little community after Potter Academy opened its doors on the hill to its first 40 students in 1895. The academy was named in honor of Sebago's native son Dr. Joseph Fitch Potter, a prominent physician in Cincinnati, Ohio, whose generosity made the school possible. Pictured on the right is Gordon Irish's garage and Esso station. The building next door was for many years the town hall and the academy gym, before it was converted into a girls' dormitory. In 1939, the ground floor became a home economics classroom. The new gymnasium was completed across the street in 1941. The ground floor became an industrial arts room.

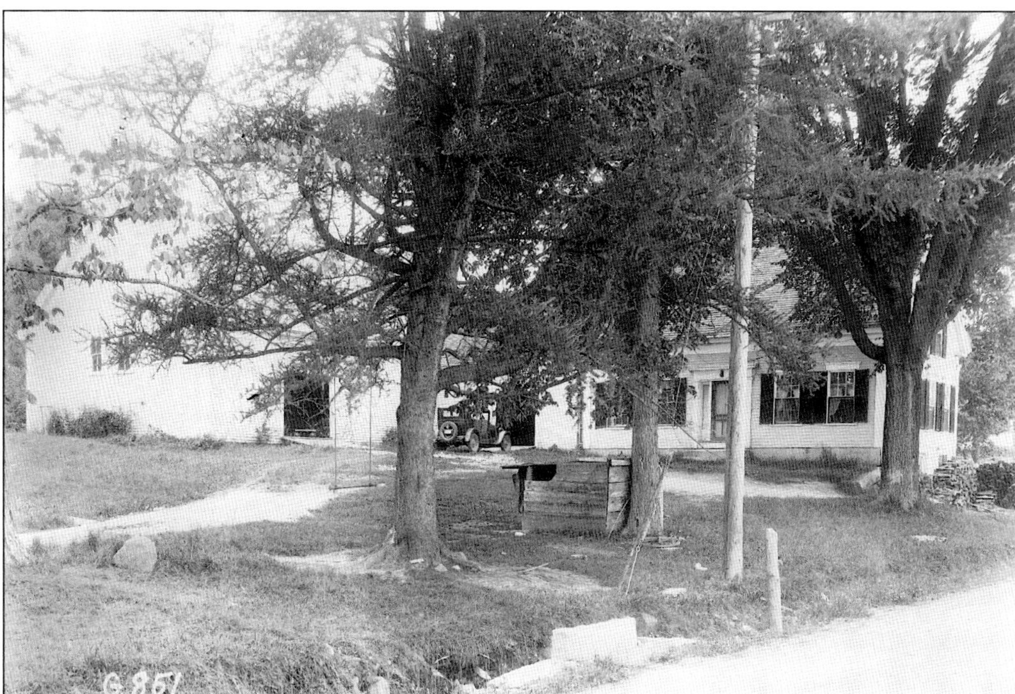

The Principal's House, c. 1928. The principal and his family lived downstairs, and the boys' dormitory was on the second floor.

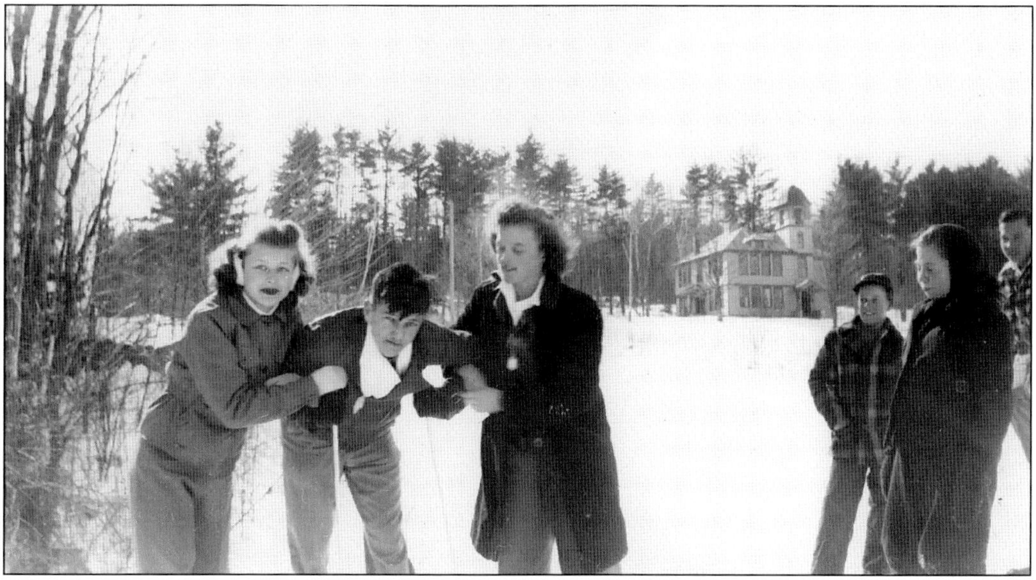

The Winter Carnival, February 1946. Edith Snow, left, and Irma Gould obviously have Joe Hutchins under control, while other Potter Academy students look on. The academy on the hill served not only the students of Sebago but also many from the adjacent towns of Denmark, Hiram, Baldwin, and some from greater distances. It closed its doors in 1967. It burned in 1974 while occupied by Elan, a rehabilitation center for troubled youth.

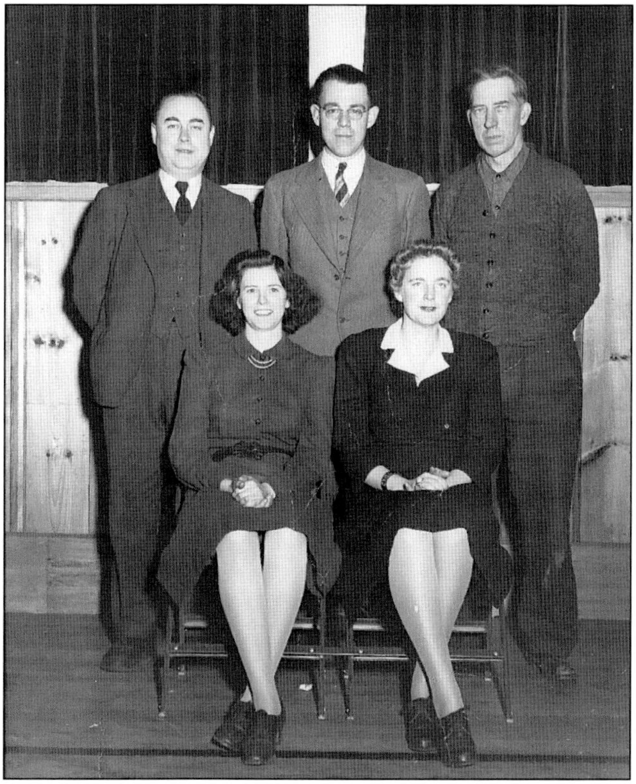

The Potter Academy Faculty, 1943–1944. Members of the Potter Academy faculty pose in front of the stage in the new academy gymnasium. They are, from left to right, as follows: (front row) Thelma King, home economics; and Gwendolyn Trefethan, English and languages; (back row) John Getchell, music, in all the Sebago schools; Walter Leach, principal; and Edson Brown, industrial arts.

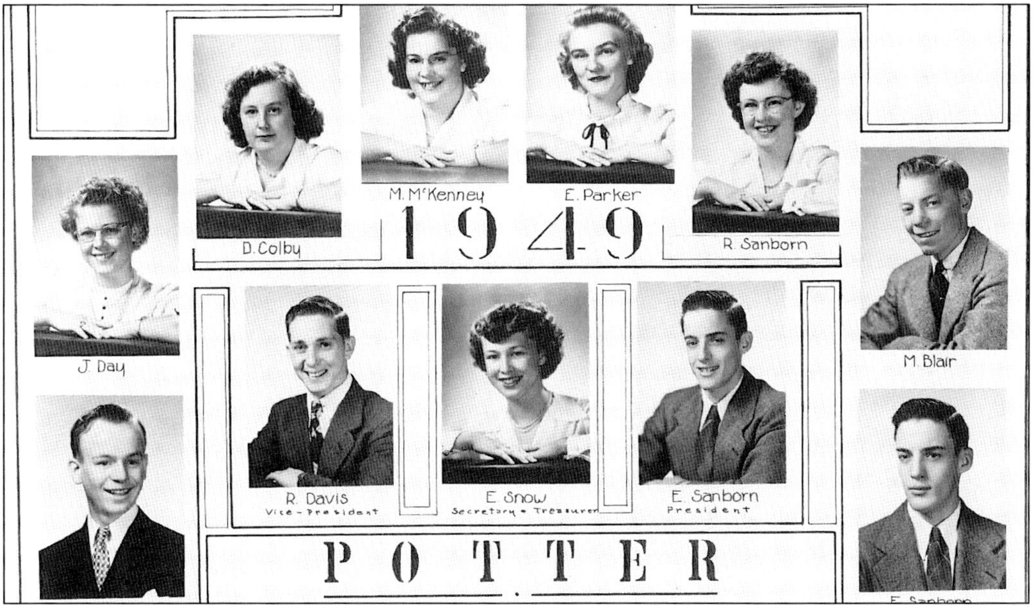

THE POTTER ACADEMY GRADUATING CLASS OF 1949. The Class of 1949 entered the academy on a happy and carefree note. World War II had ended. Veterans were returning. The young men did not have hanging over them the dark cloud of knowing they were going to war soon after graduation. Unfortunately, shortly after graduation the Korean War broke out.

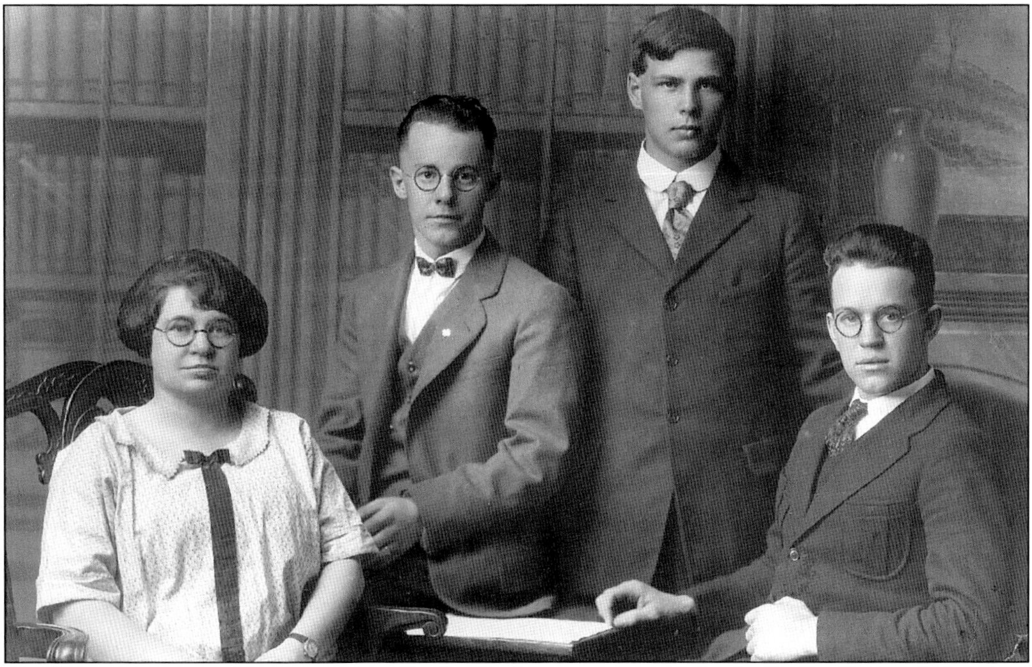

THE CLASS OF 1925. Classes were never large at Potter Academy; only four scholars were in the graduating Class of 1925. The students and faculty at Potter Academy were like an extended family, similar to that which the vast majority of students were accustomed, living on farms on the back roads in Sebago and neighboring towns. Shown here, from left to right, are Martha Robinson, Merle Douglass, Arnold Ward, and Dennis McKenney.

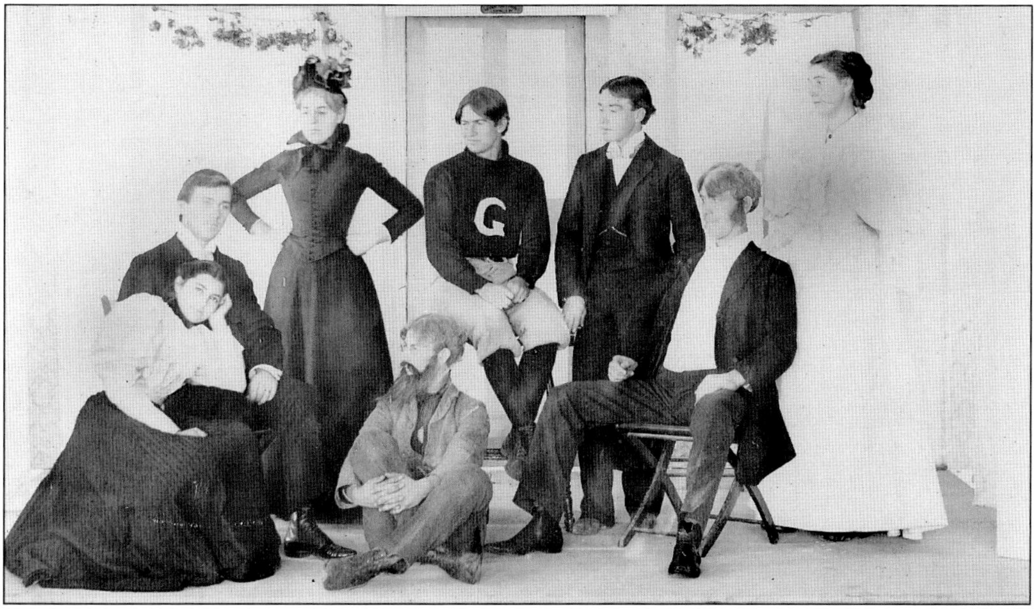

MY *BROTHER'S KEEPER*, POTTER ACADEMY, FALL 1896. Starring in Potter Academy's production of My *Brother's Keeper* are George Rounds as Abel Benton, Lizzie Jewell as Aunt Betsey, Lemuel Rich as Charley, Emma Clough as Grace, Will Rand as Richard Carner, Montford Fitch as Mathew Allen, Edna Dyer as Rachel, and Herbert Thompson as Old Scraps. (Photograph by J.F. Haley of Convene.)

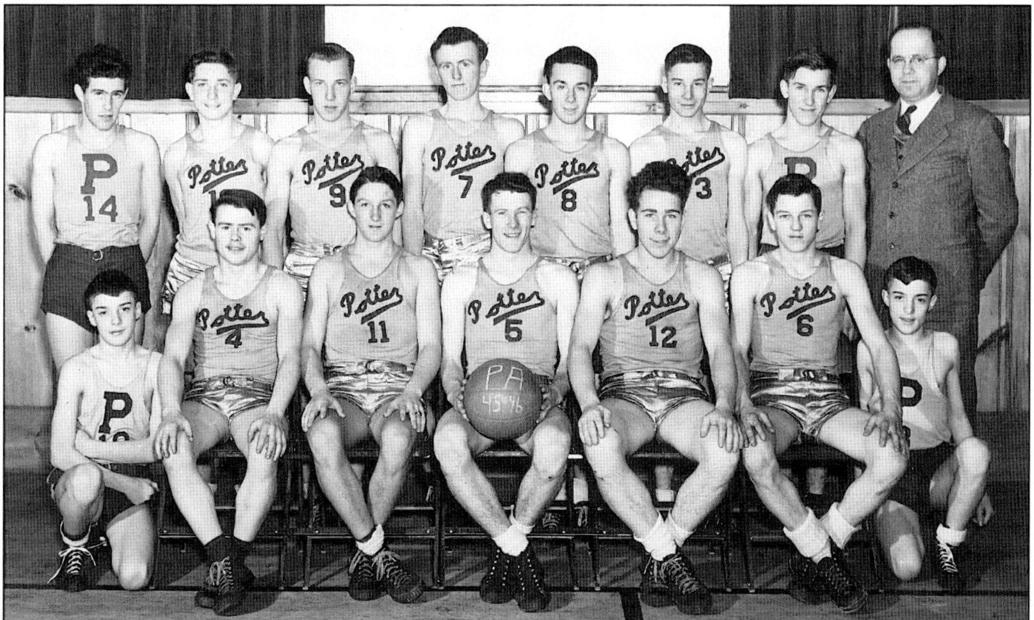

THE PANTHERS, 1945–1946. Shown are, from left to right, as follows: (front row) Erwin Sanborn; Ellis Nason; Laurie Sweeney; Alden Bachelder, captain; "Buddy" Howard; Joe Hutchins; and Elwin Sanborn; (back row) Pete Webb; Bobby Davis; Arthur Howard; Billy Guptill; Norman McKenney; Clayton Douglass; Eben Harmon; and Joseph Roy, coach. This was a large squad for a small school.

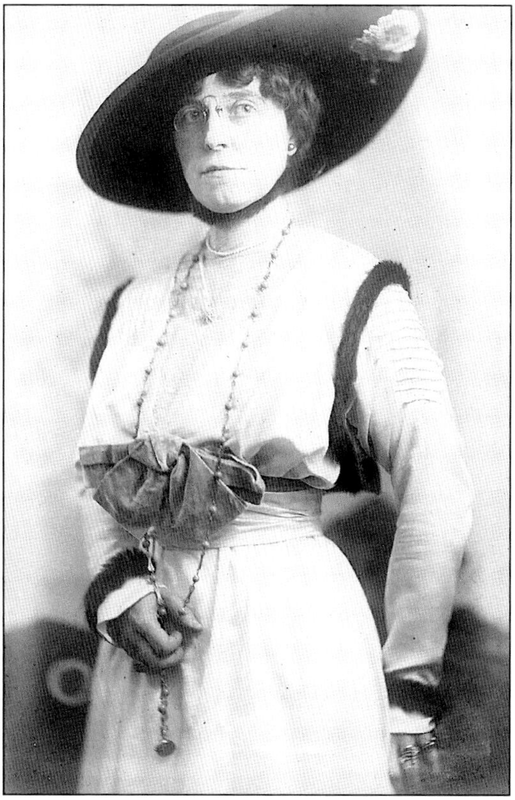

ALICE DYER BALDASSERONI, C. 1925. Alice Dyer was born to Arthur and Alice Hustler Dyer in 1874 in the Sebago House, one of the town's oldest dwellings, at Mac's Corner, where her niece Leona Greene currently resides. She attended the little brick school on the edge of Sebago Center and graduated from Bridgton Academy. In 1902, she married John Mussey Plummer of Portland, who died two years later. Before World War I, she did secretarial work in Boston; when the United States entered the war in 1917, she joined the Red Cross and served with distinction in Europe. She crossed the Atlantic 16 times during and after the war. During the war she met Francisco Baldasseroni, who served in the Italian army. She married him in 1922 and spent some time at the Dyer home. After his death in 1949, she lived in the family home with her sister Ada. She died on January 9, 1962.

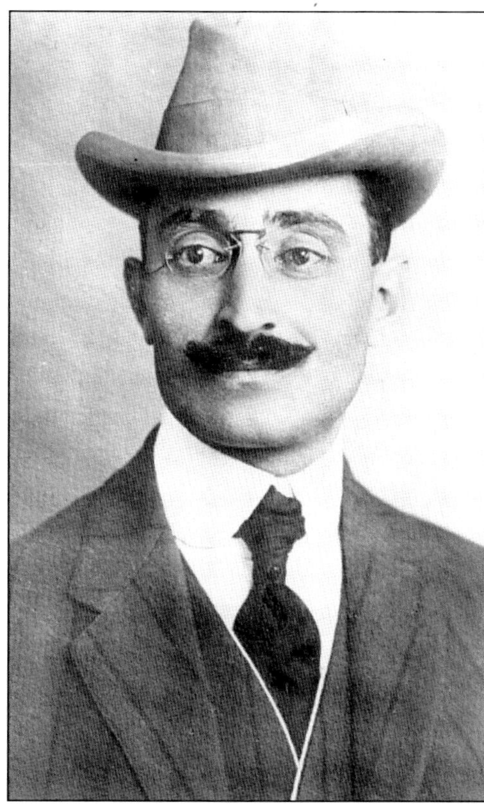

FRANCISCO BALDASSERONI, C. 1925. Professor Baldasseroni was born in Florence, Italy. At the age of 12, he was sent to a military school where he apparently received most of his education. After World War I, he immigrated to the United States, and for a number of years he and his sister ran a finishing school for girls in Boston. Alice Dyer, who became his wife in 1922, was also involved in the school. Besides teaching, he did some interpreting, translating, and writing. Locally, he was known as "the Count." Although he never felt really comfortable here in Sebago, both he and his wife are buried in the Dyer family plot in nearby North Baldwin.

Four

NAPLES

First Settled: 1774
Incorporated: 1834
Population: 3,000
Area: 31.25 square miles
Principal Settlements: Naples Village, Edes' Falls

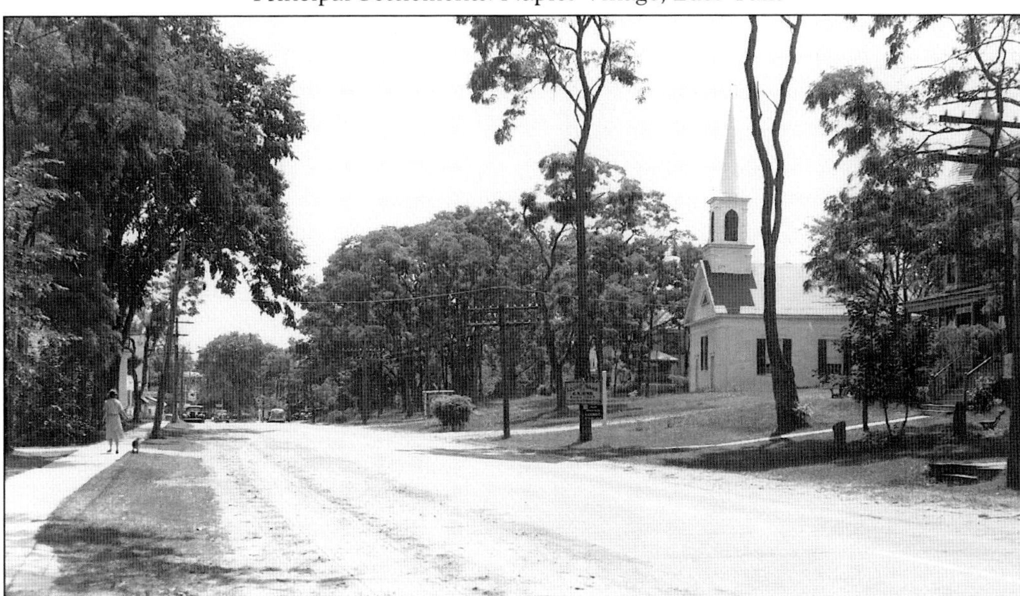

VILLAGE STREET, NAPLES, C. 1937. Village Street lacked the steady stream of traffic that now passes through here daily on the Roosevelt Trail (Route 302), which ever since it was laid out in 1784, has played a vital role in the economic and social development of the area, linking Naples and areas beyond with Portland. Prominent in the photograph is the Union Church, erected in 1857 by the union committee of two Freewill Baptist churches and the Congregational church. It is said that the little church was packed during the dedication ceremony on January 26, 1857. It is now on the National Register of Historic Places.

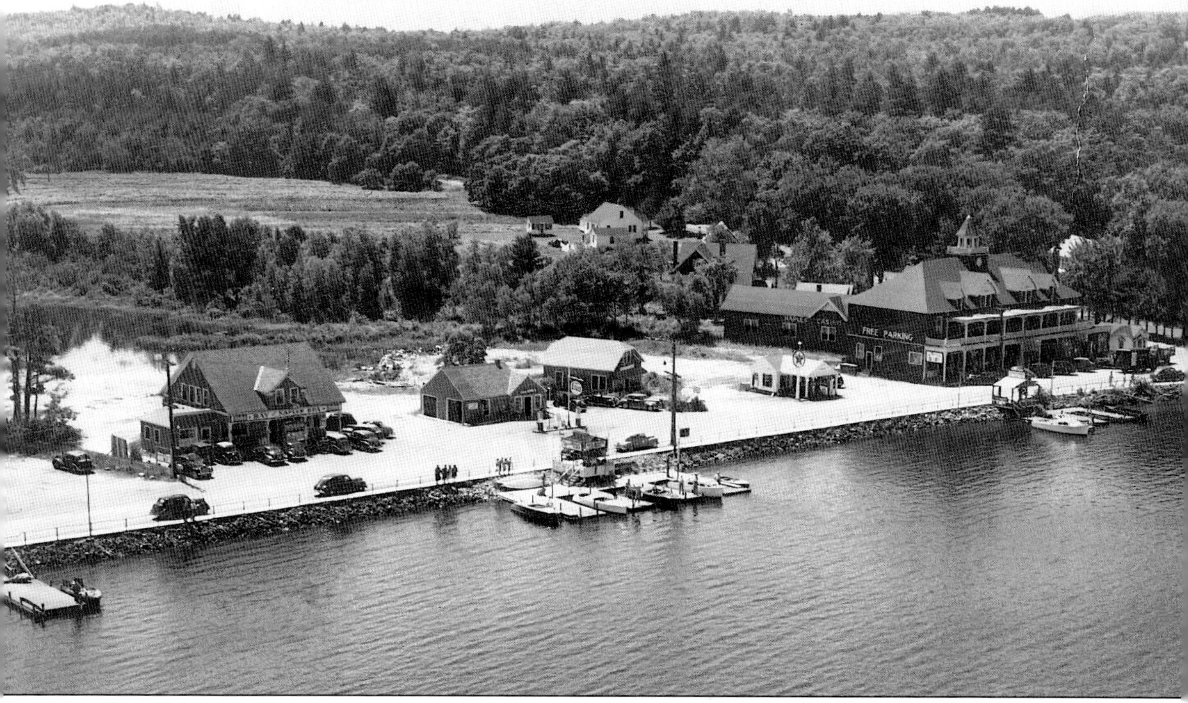

THE NAPLES CAUSEWAY, C. 1940. Even before the advent of the automobile, the Naples Causeway was a mecca for sportsmen and vacationers. The commercial buildings facing Long Lake and to the rear Brandy Pond are, from left to right, the central office of the Poland Telephone Company, an extension of the Bay of Naples Spa built by Gus Bove around 1930; Chester and Elwin Burnham's Esso Station; a gift shop; the Casino Filling Station; and the Casino, built in 1901, with a bowling alley attached to the rear. The town of Naples was created from portions of Bridgton, Harrison, Otisfield, Raymond, and Sebago and was incorporated on March 4, 1834. Located at a central link in an extensive chain of waterways, the town has been blessed by geography as few other towns in the hinterland of Maine have. Early adventurers and settlers who came into the area had an alternative to a long, arduous trek through a vast wilderness with only devious deer and Indian trails to follow. They could make their way inland from Falmouth (Portland) by poling their way up the Presumpscot River, as Thomas Chute did *c.* 1737, to the Lower Basin of Sebago Lake. From there they could paddle across mighty Sebago Lake to the mouth of the Songo and up the sinuous river. Just before the rapids (Songo Locks), they could choose to head up Crooked River—as Squire George Pierce did in 1774 to reach the falls, which that originally bore his name, where he built a rude log cabin, a sawmill, and a gristmill. Later, the falls became Edes' Falls, named in honor of Thomas Edes, who settled there in 1837, long after Pierce had abruptly vacated the falls, moved up to the foot of Skid Hill, and began building the Manor in 1799. Others could choose to continue over the Songo rapids and head up to Brandy Pond, through Chute's River, and up Long Pond (Lake) all the way to what became Harrison. Skid Hill and Mast Cove on Long Lake are reminders that the pristine forests in the area were harvested early, and prime logs and masts reached Portland either by being poled and floated down the open waters in spring and summer or transported by ox teams over the frozen waterways in winter. What a boon the Cumberland & Oxford Canal was to the area: although an average trip by canal boat from Long Lake to Portland took three days, a boat loaded with apples from Sam Perley's farm at Mast Cove made it in a day. It was a slow, bone-rattling trek to Portland by road until the advent of the automobile and the road (Roosevelt Trail) was improved.

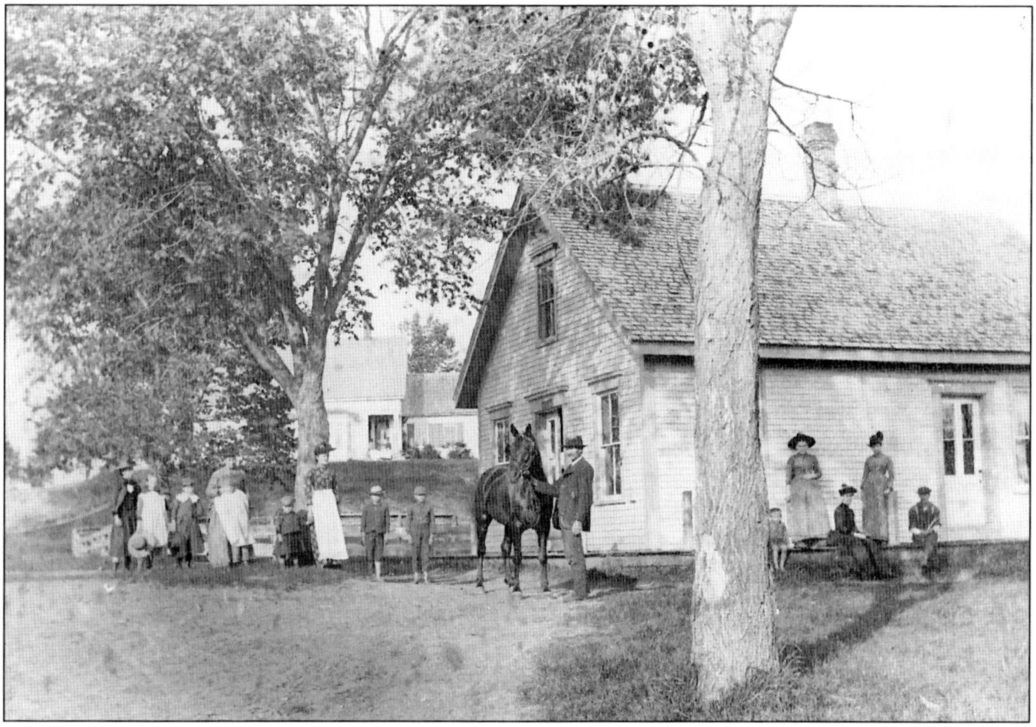

EDES' FALLS, 1895. Edes' Falls was once a thriving community, which at its apex supported six stores, a pants shop, a milling company, two sawmills, and a wool-carding plant built by Joseph Hall in 1832, when the settlement on Crooked River was still a part of Otisfield. In the foreground is the Leo Hall house and store. Beyond is the James Flagg residence.

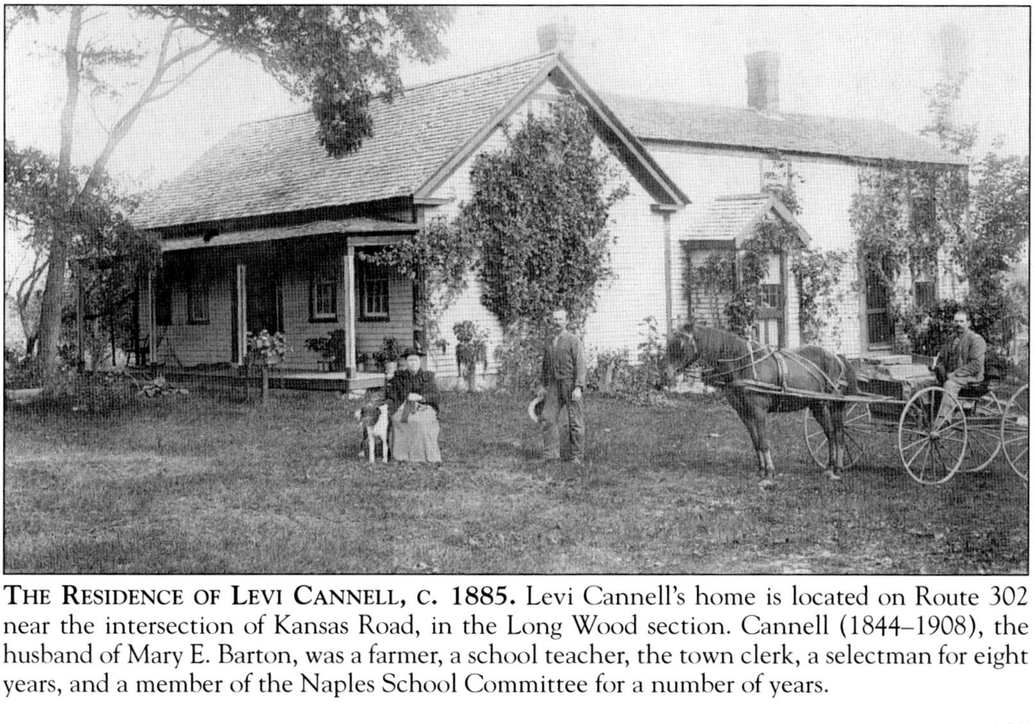

THE RESIDENCE OF LEVI CANNELL, C. 1885. Levi Cannell's home is located on Route 302 near the intersection of Kansas Road, in the Long Wood section. Cannell (1844–1908), the husband of Mary E. Barton, was a farmer, a school teacher, the town clerk, a selectman for eight years, and a member of the Naples School Committee for a number of years.

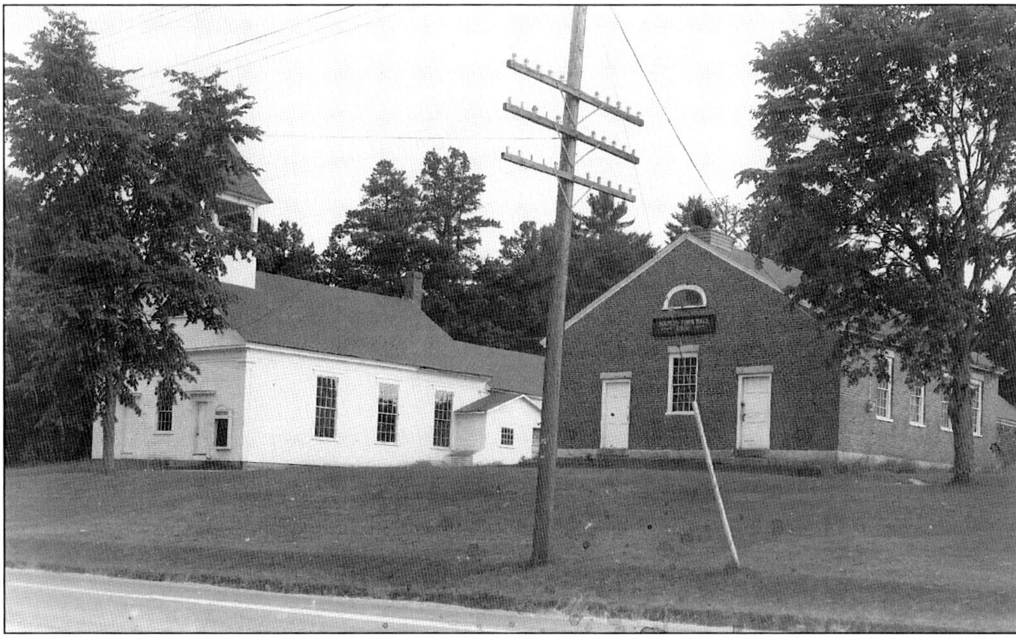

THE TOWN GROUNDS, C. 1960. The Town Grounds, now called the Town Green, was a center of community activity even before Naples was incorporated. Rev. Sargent S. Gray was instrumental in promoting the building of the Methodist church in 1857. The little brick school, now the Naples Historical Society and for many years the Naples house of pure democracy, was built *c.* 1831. Enoch Gammon and Benjamin Goodrich donated the land to the town.

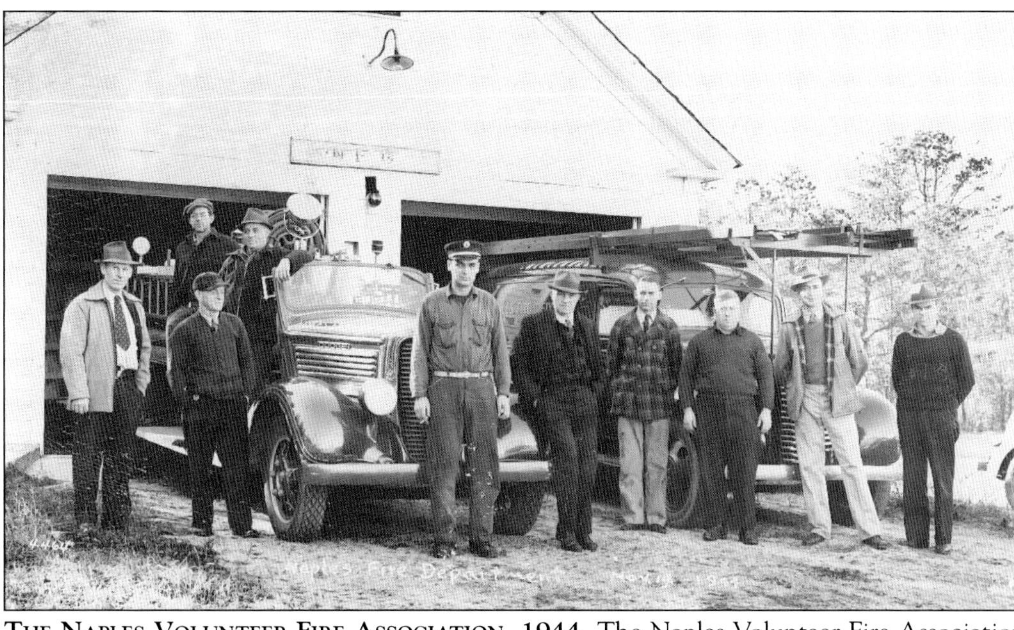

THE NAPLES VOLUNTEER FIRE ASSOCIATION, 1944. The Naples Volunteer Fire Association held its first meeting on April 26, 1938. Volunteers are, from left to right, as follows: (front row) Carroll Mayo, Harold Welch, Elmer Plummer, Al Ridlon, Chester Burnham, James Build, Freelon Knight, and Edwin Burnham; (back row) Thomas Mains and Howard Dearborn.

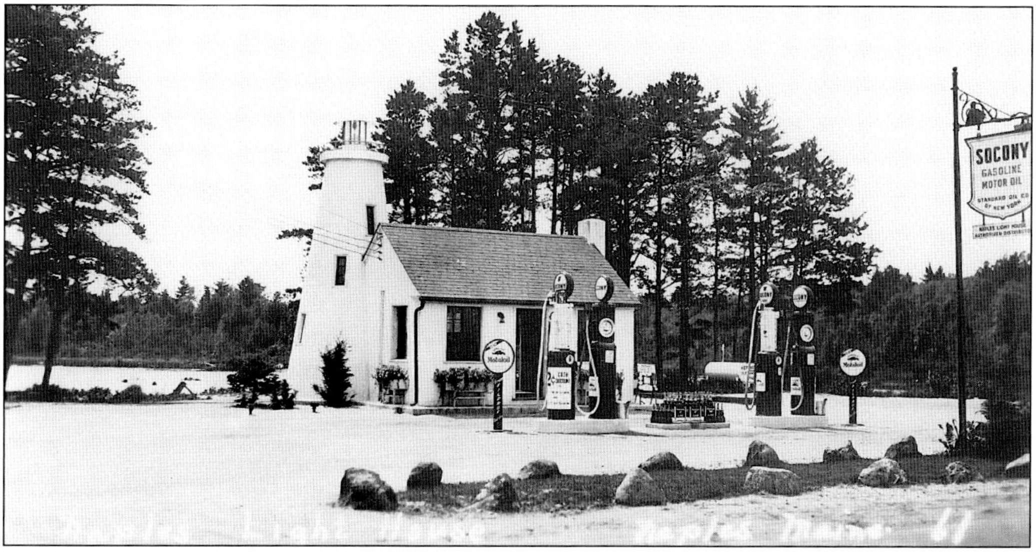

THE LIGHTHOUSE, C. 1940. The Lighthouse is one of the landmarks on the Causeway. At the time of this photograph, the gas station was owned and operated by Mr. Dockum, who also ran Howard Johnson's. Later, Gilbert Knight operated it before it became a real estate office. Today, it is occupied by Nancy Knight Hanson, a descendent of Louis Knight, who is owner and broker of DeWolfe Lakes Region Properties.

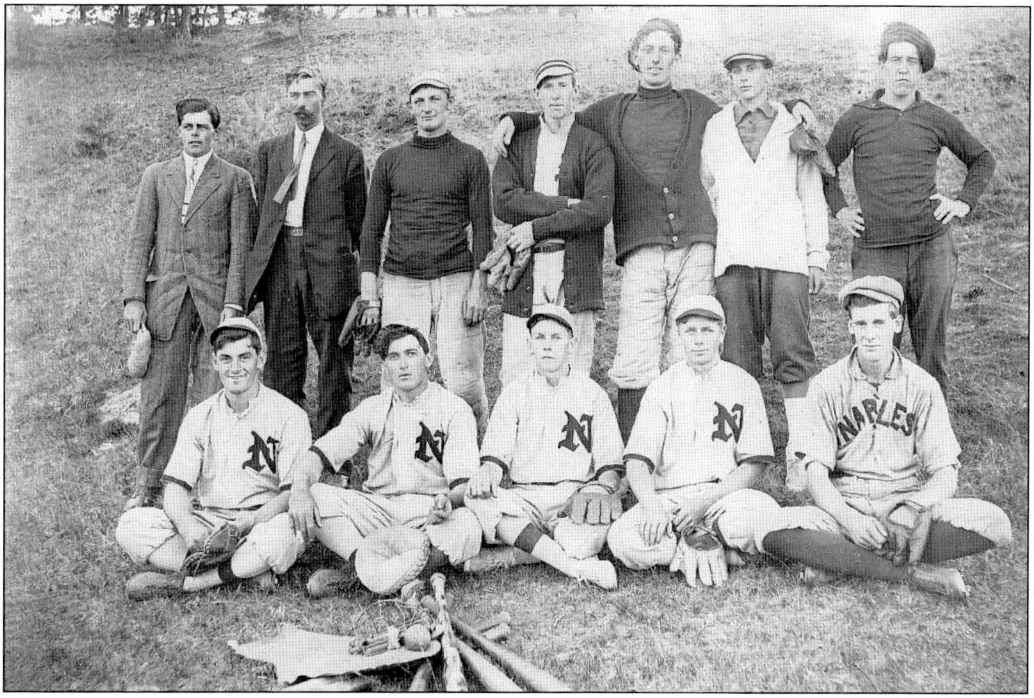

THE NAPLES TOWNIES, 1910. The Townies traveled either by horse and wagon or boat whenever they played rival teams at away games. Obviously baseball equipment has improved immensely since the early 20th century. Among those pictured are the following: (front row) Frank Davis, Earl Kilburn, Robert Edes, and Frank Brown; (back row) Charles Jones, Asa Folsom, Ed Barker, Charlie Bartlett, Ansel Morton, and Carl Green.

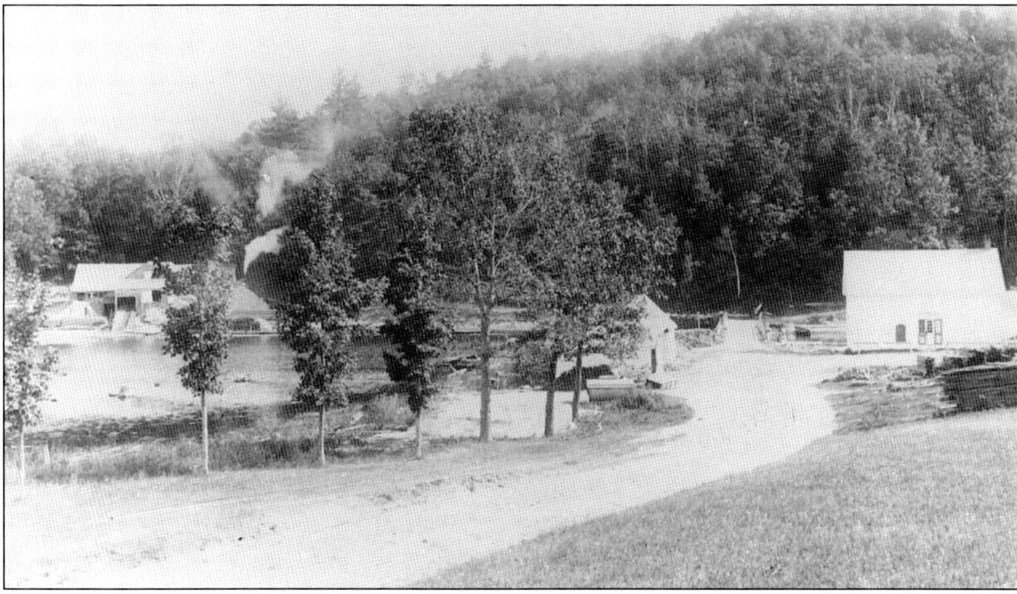

SOUTH NAPLES, c. 1915. For more than a century, South Naples resounded with the buzzing of saws here at Lewis Crockett's mill (earlier Benjamin Mitchell's), where Muddy River flows into Sebago Lake. Mitchell constructed a dam at the north end and created the little pond—still visible today beside the old Deacon Mitchell house—from which a penstock conveyed the water to the waterwheel 80 feet below. There were several other early mills farther up Muddy River, beginning at the outlet of Holt's Pond. Note that what is now Route 114 once followed the east bank of Muddy River instead of going straight up Crockett's Hill.

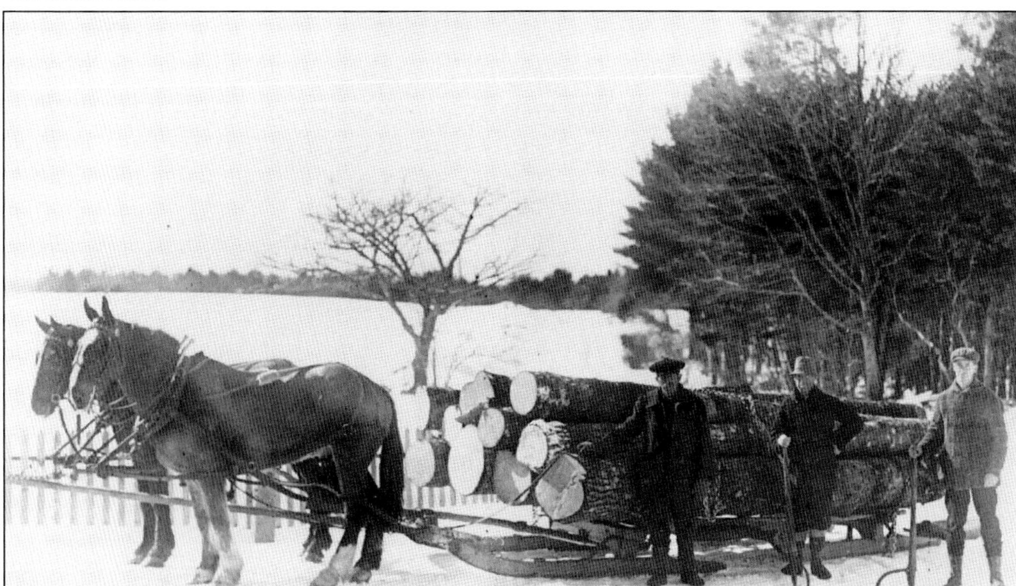

LOGGING, c. 1920. Frank Lamb, standing nearest to the horses, has his bobsled loaded with choice white pine, very likely to be unloaded on ice-covered Long Lake. Loton Rogers and Fred Brown are standing next to him with cant dogs (peaveys).

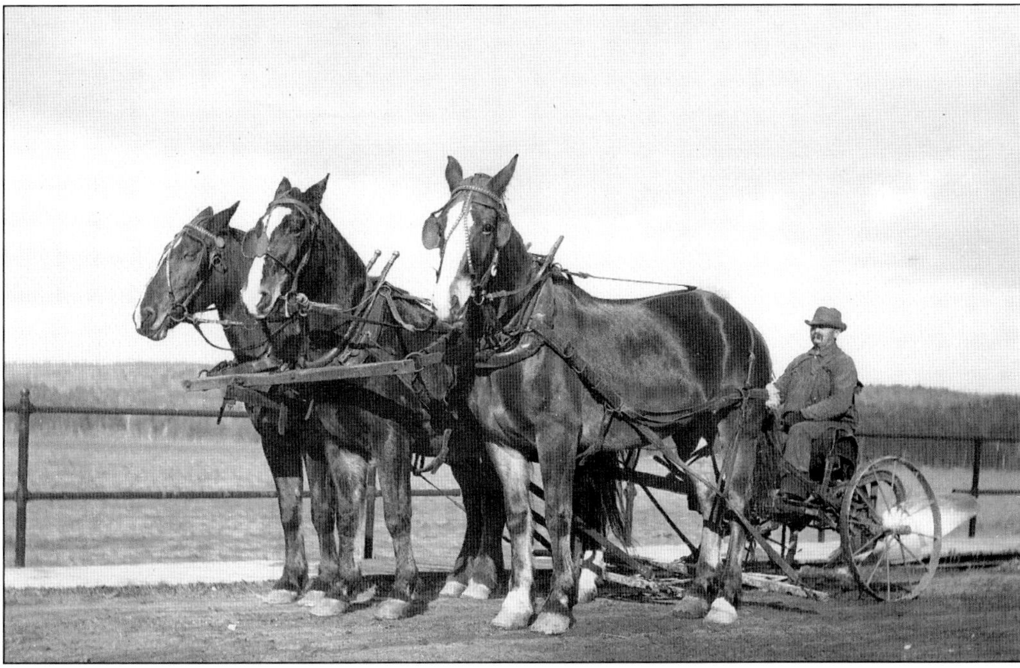

LOTON D. ROGERS, C. 1935. Loton Rogers, seated on a sulky plow, drives his team of three horses across the Bay of Naples Causeway. Loton, who was born in 1877 and resided in the village opposite the Union Church, earlier had been frequently in charge of driving immense rafts of logs from Long Lake down Crooked and Songo Rivers and Sebago Lake to the E.I. Dupont de Nemours Company at Smith Mills in Standish. There, the logs were sawed into boards and made into wooden boxes for munitions. Rafts of logs destined for the Diamond Match Company were floated to Sebago Lake Station and shipped by rail to the mill in Biddeford.

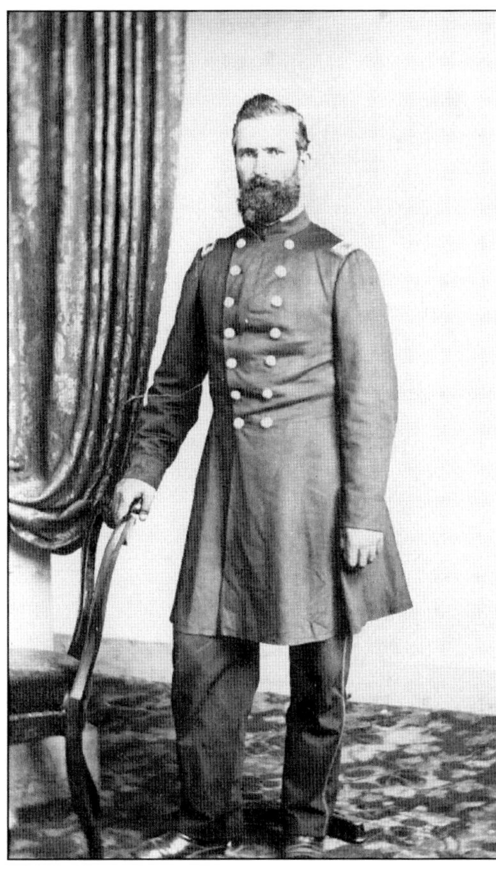

COL. DANIEL CHAPLIN, C. 1863. Colonel Chaplin was born in 1820, three years before his parents, Benjamin and Jane Welch Chaplin, moved to Naples with his two older brothers and his younger sister from New Brunswick and settled on Plaisted Hill on the Harrison Road. He enlisted in the Civil War as a captain in the 2nd Maine Infantry, which later became the 1st Maine Heavy Artillery. He was commissioned colonel of the 18th Maine and was killed by a sniper while leading his division into the Battle of Weldon Woods in 1864.

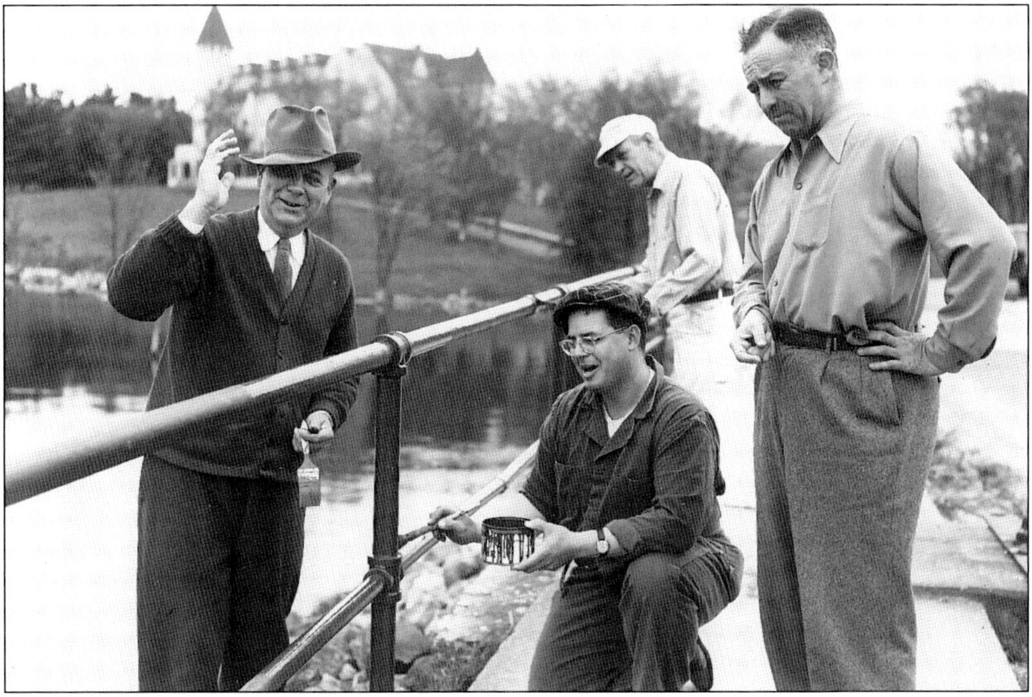

REFURBISHING THE CAUSEWAY, MAY, 1952. Lions Club members, from left to right, Lou Fickett, Phil Chute, and Urban Cannell, administer a fresh coat of paint to the 1500-foot Causeway railing, while an onlooker scrutinizes the job.

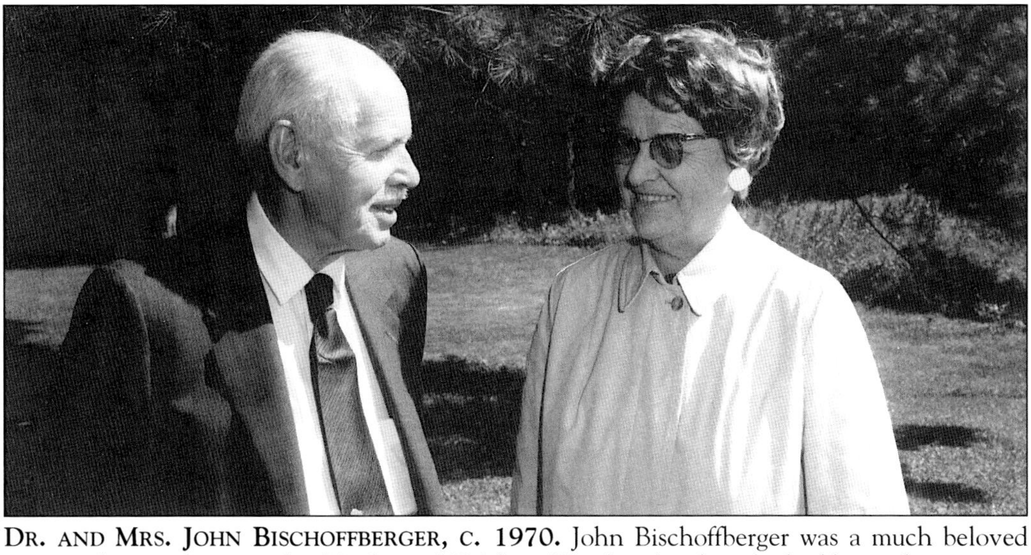

DR. AND MRS. JOHN BISCHOFFBERGER, C. 1970. John Bischoffberger was a much beloved country doctor who moved to Naples in 1926 from Westbrook, where he had begun his practice and married Rosamond Chaplin of Naples on June 29, 1927. A native of Freedom, Pennsylvania, and a World War I veteran, he practiced medicine—often using homeopathic approaches—in the area until shortly before his death in 1988 at age 87. For many years he was a state medical examiner and served on the staff of the Northern Cumberland Memorial Hospital in Bridgton, the Mercy Hospital and Maine Medical Center in Portland, and the Maine Eye and Ear Infirmary.

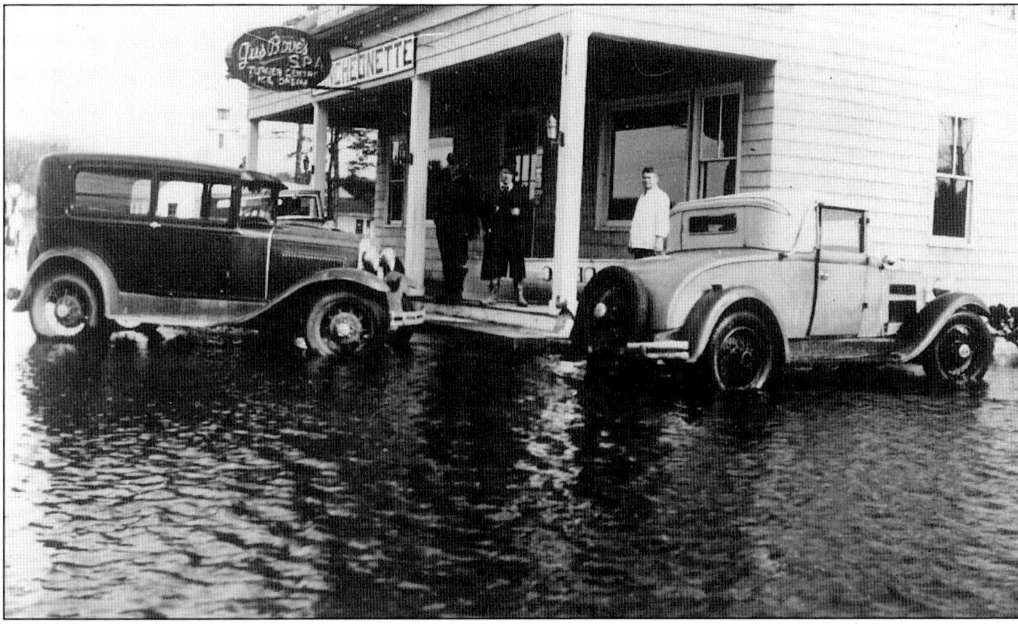

FLOOD ON THE CAUSEWAY, 1936. The water was so high in the spring of 1936 from melting snow that Long Lake inundated the Causeway and the covered bridge over Crooked River at Edes Falls was swept away. This *c.* 1930 Model A sedan and Cabriolet are parked in several inches of water in front of Gus Bove's Spa.

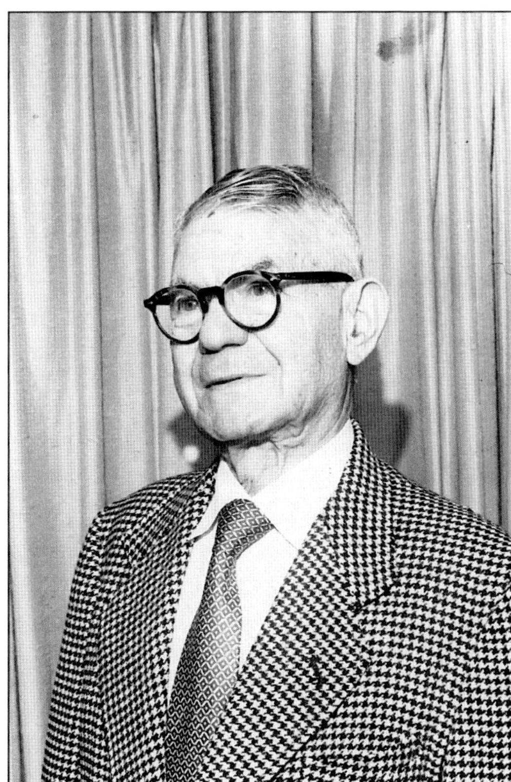

GUS BOVE, C. 1950. Gus Bove, like Ciro Russo and Vito Caggiano in North Sebago, was an Italian immigrant who distinguished himself here in the Sebago Lake area. Shortly after his arrival in America as a young man, he opened a barbershop in Farmington and later operated one summers at the Naples Casino. Soon he decided to make Naples his home. He was a charter member of the Naples Lions Club and is credited with transforming the Causeway into the mecca it became for tourists. In addition to his barber shop, he ran the Spa and the gasoline station next to it and acquired considerable real estate. Late in life he made the historical old brick Naples Hotel opposite Dr. Bischoffberger's home and office his retirement home. A few years before his death in 1967 at the age of 85, the selectmen named him honorary mayor of Naples.

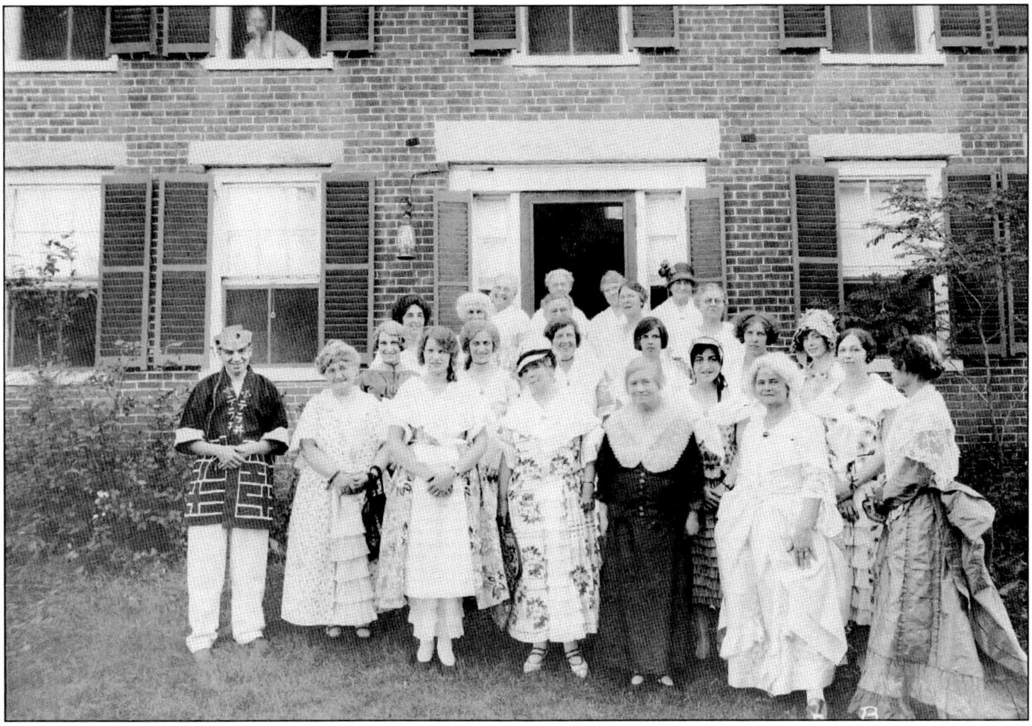

A Society Function at Louisa Robinson's, c. 1925. For many summers following the inception of the Library Association in Naples in 1907, Louisa Robinson held an annual lawn party and other social functions at her capacious brick home opposite the Lake House on Lake House Road to raise funds for the association. From 1909 to 1914, a room in her home served as the public library.

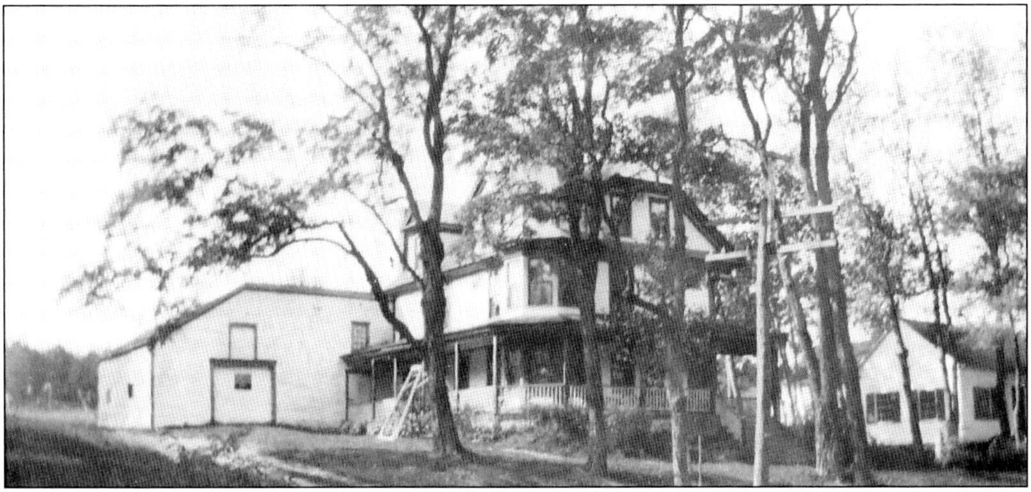

The Locust House, c. 1938. George Mann, a blacksmith by trade, opened this large Victorian home to summer boarders in 1901, charging $1 a day for lodging and meals. With the advent of the automobile and consequently tourism, his son Norman Mann became the first in the area to build overnight cabins. Eventually, George Mann's grandson Fred Mann Dodge took over the business and ran it for a number of years before giving the property to the Naples Public Library in 1984. It is claimed that Pres. William Howard Taft once stayed here.

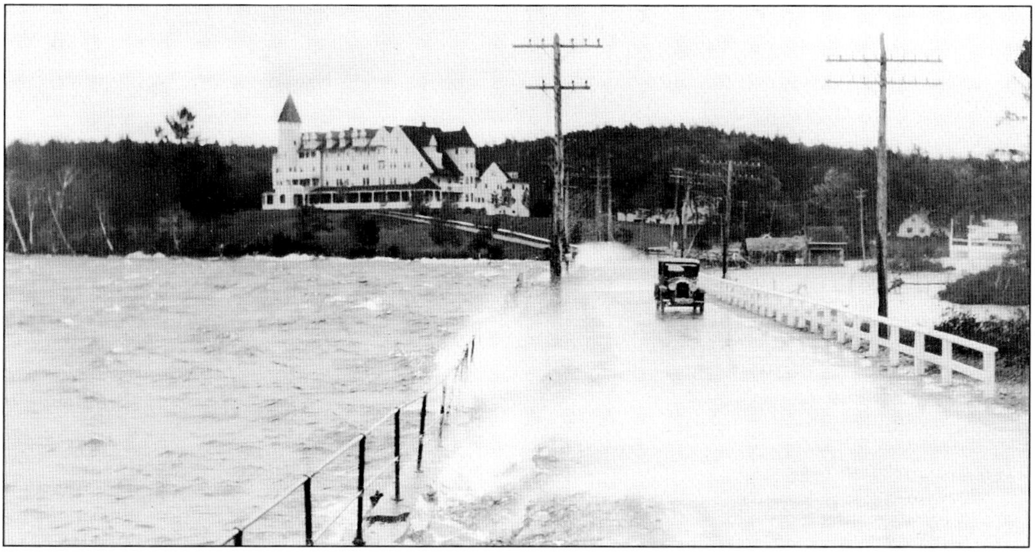

CROSSING THE CAUSEWAY, C. 1929. A solitary Buick edges its way across the Causeway as the normally placid Long Lake sends wind-tossed whitecaps crashing over the railing. Prominent is the 102-room Bay of Naples Inn, built by Charles Goodridge. The inn, one of Naples's great landmarks, first opened its doors in 1899 to vacationers drawn to the area because of its extraordinary scenery and variety of activities. The inn closed in 1951 and was demolished in 1964, marking the end of an era.

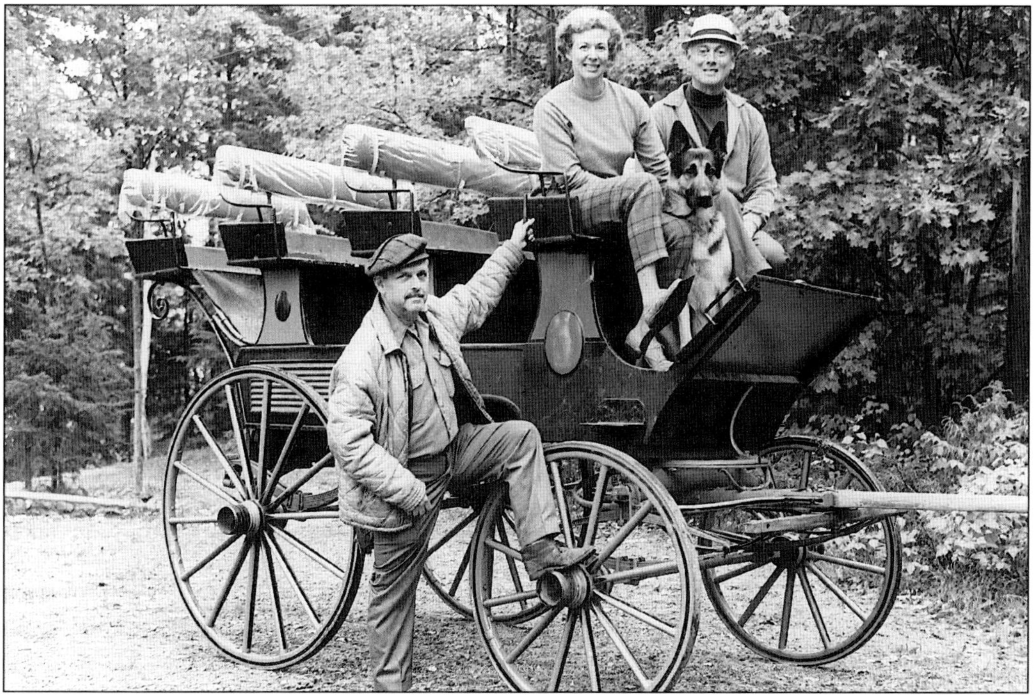

A PRECIOUS GIFT, 1967. This luxurious roof-seat brake was made by the F.O. Bailey Company of Portland, used by the Bay of Naples Inn, and later sold to Cobb's Camps of Brighton and Denmark. Here, Naples Historical Society President Bob Dingley, left, accepts the brake as a gift to the society from Margaret and Ed Siegers, who purchased it at the Cobb's auction.

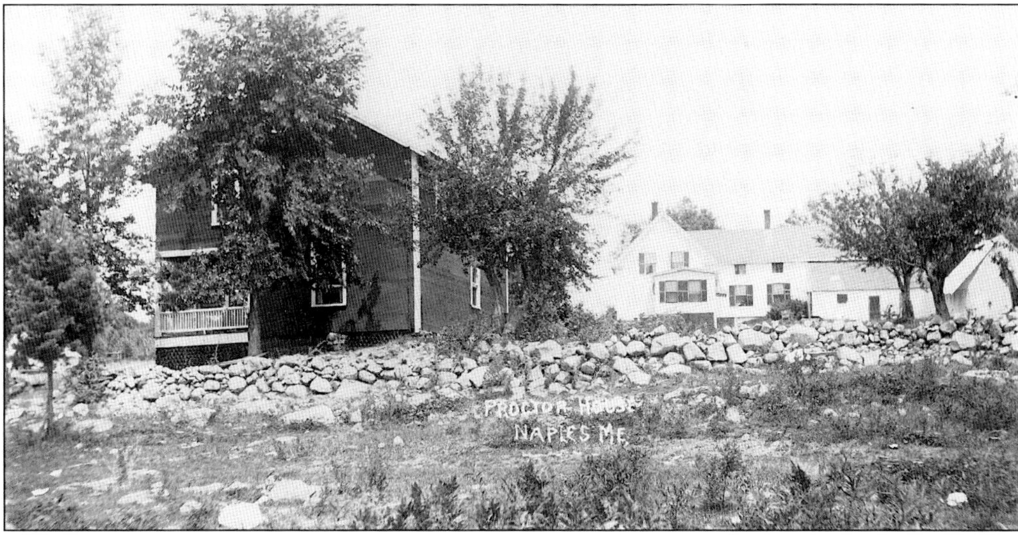

THE PROCTOR HOUSE, c. 1940. The Proctor House was one of Naples's best-known resorts. Like so many other early resorts in the area, it was for many years a prosperous farm. Charles Proctor, one of eight children born in Naples to William Proctor Jr. and Matilda Allen Proctor, raised cattle and apples, and tilled several of the broad, sweeping acres that run down to the sandy beach on Brandy Pond and planted corn for the local canning factory built in 1872. In 1910, however, he and his wife, Bessie Savory, who was born in Somerville, Massachusetts, began taking in summer boarders and eventually added another house and ten cabins. The original rambling farmhouse was later used by Sandhurst, a private summer school, and then by Elan, a treatment center for troubled youth. It was torn down in 1977.

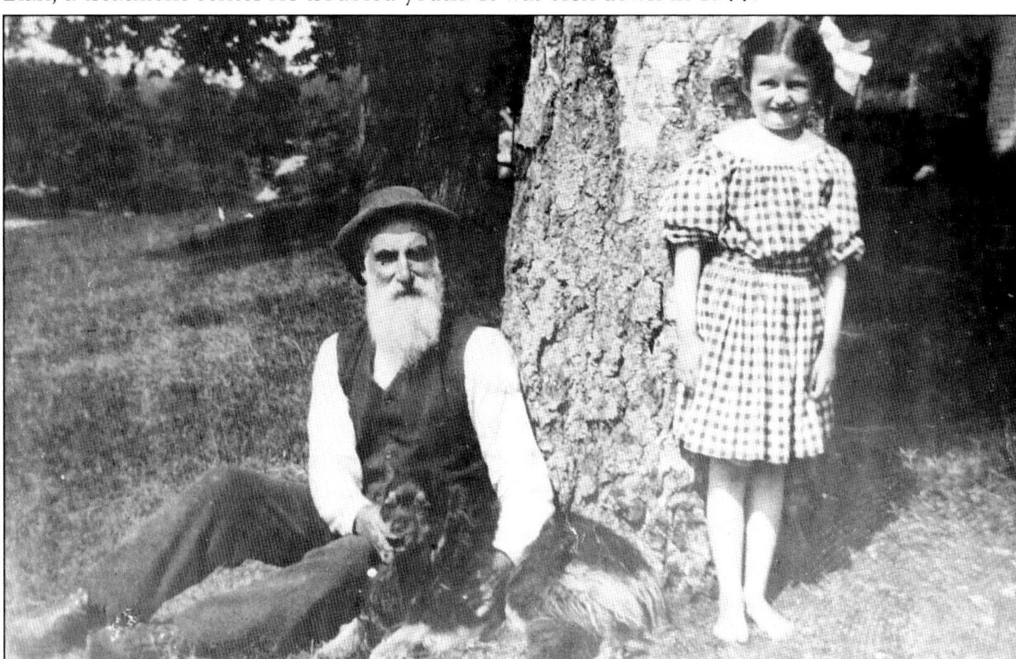

ANTHONY PROCTOR, c. 1920. Anthony Proctor, left, was the son of William Proctor Sr., one of 65 petitioners for the incorporation of Naples in 1834.

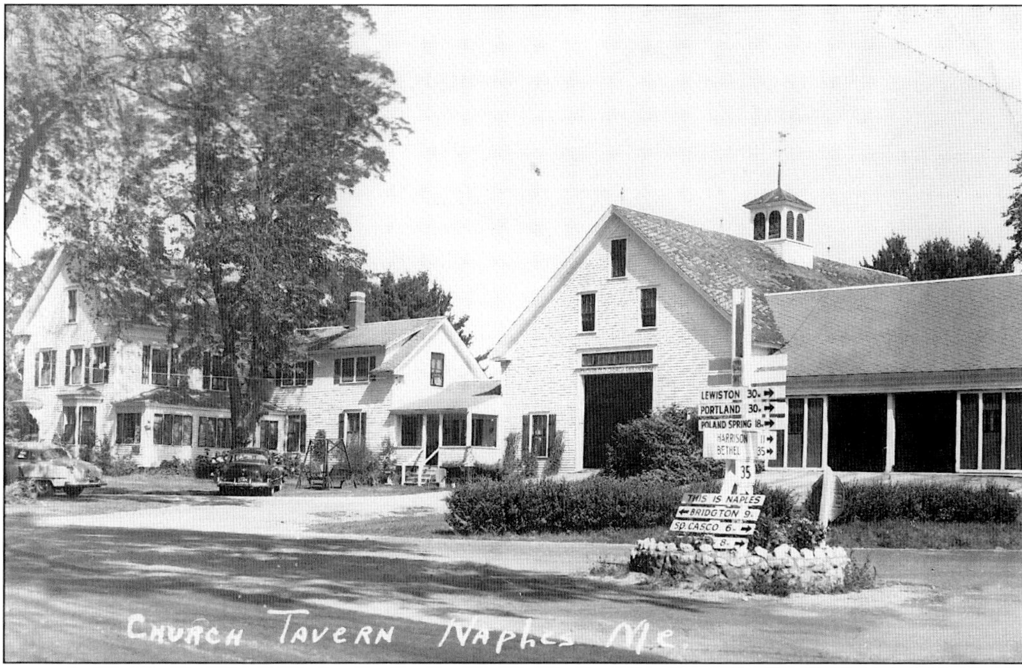

KNIGHT'S OLD CHURCH TAVERN, C. 1950. The original Old Church Tavern was built by Elliot Staples and Nathan Gerry *c.* 1790 near here. In 1816, John Chute bought it and changed the name to the Elm House. It burned in 1822 and was rebuilt in 1825. After Chute's death, his son-in-law Nathan Church and later Church's son Nathan A. Church operated it until it burned in 1876. The present structure was built by Lewis Knight and was the residence of his son Charles Knight at the time of this photograph.

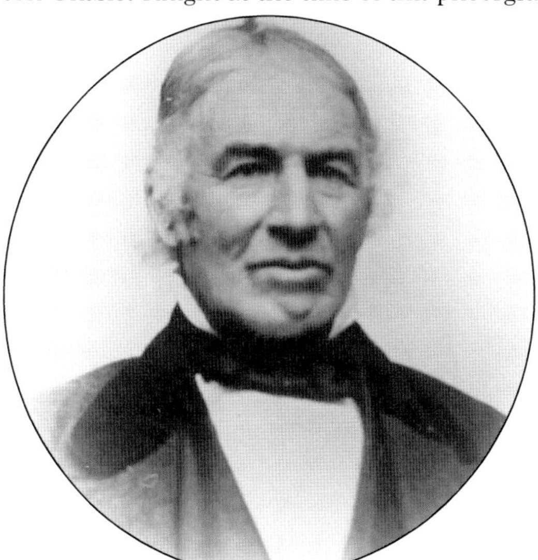

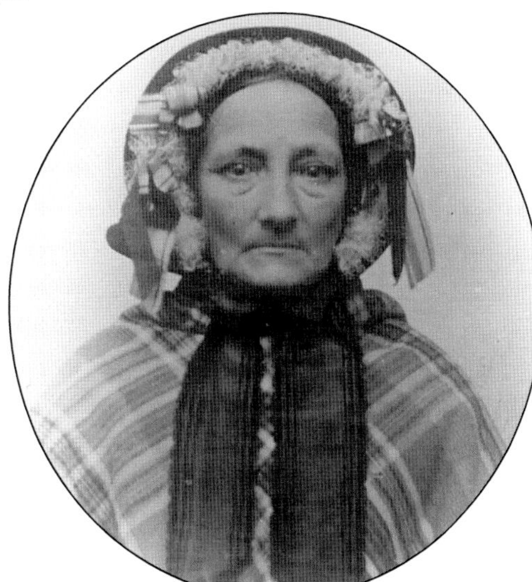

NATHAN CHURCH JR. AND MIRIAM CHUTE CHURCH, C. 1870. Nathan Church Jr., the son of Rev. Nathan Church, who settled in Bridgton in 1788 and served as pastor of the First Congregational Church for 34 years, married Miriam Chute of Naples in 1829. About ten years later, he later moved to Naples, where he ran the Elm House, one of Maine's first temperance hotels, until his death in 1873.

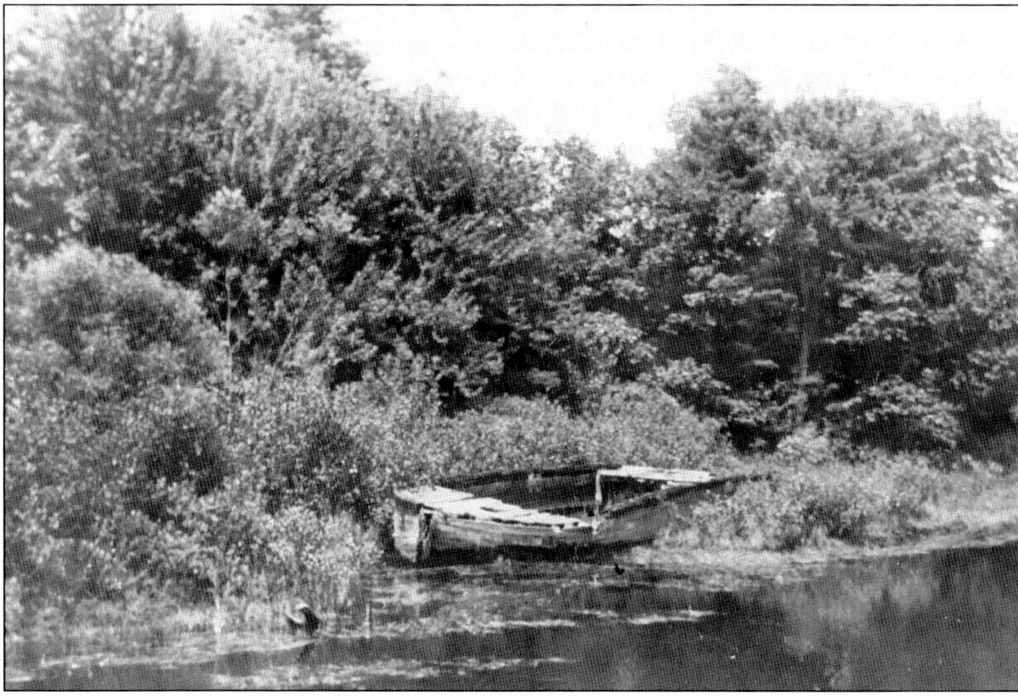

THE *HINKEY DINK*, C. 1930. The *Hinkey Dink*, very likely not the original name for this derelict canal boat wasting away on the bank of the Songo River, once plied the 50-mile water route to Portland, carrying freight and passengers. It was a standard canal boat: 60 feet long, with a 10-foot beam, a flat bottom, and two centerboards instead of a keel so that it could hug the mighty waves as it sailed, with a main and foresail set in jaws, down Sebago Lake to the Basin. A cabin in the stern served as a kitchen and sleeping quarters for the captain and crew of usually three.

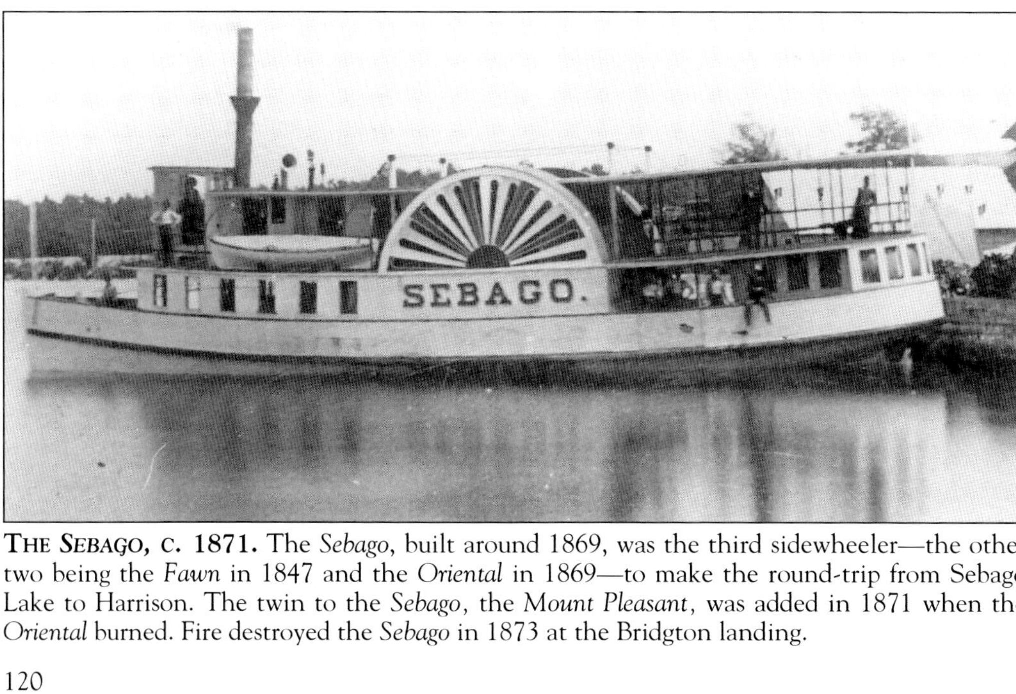

THE *SEBAGO*, C. 1871. The *Sebago*, built around 1869, was the third sidewheeler—the other two being the *Fawn* in 1847 and the *Oriental* in 1869—to make the round-trip from Sebago Lake to Harrison. The twin to the *Sebago*, the *Mount Pleasant*, was added in 1871 when the *Oriental* burned. Fire destroyed the *Sebago* in 1873 at the Bridgton landing.

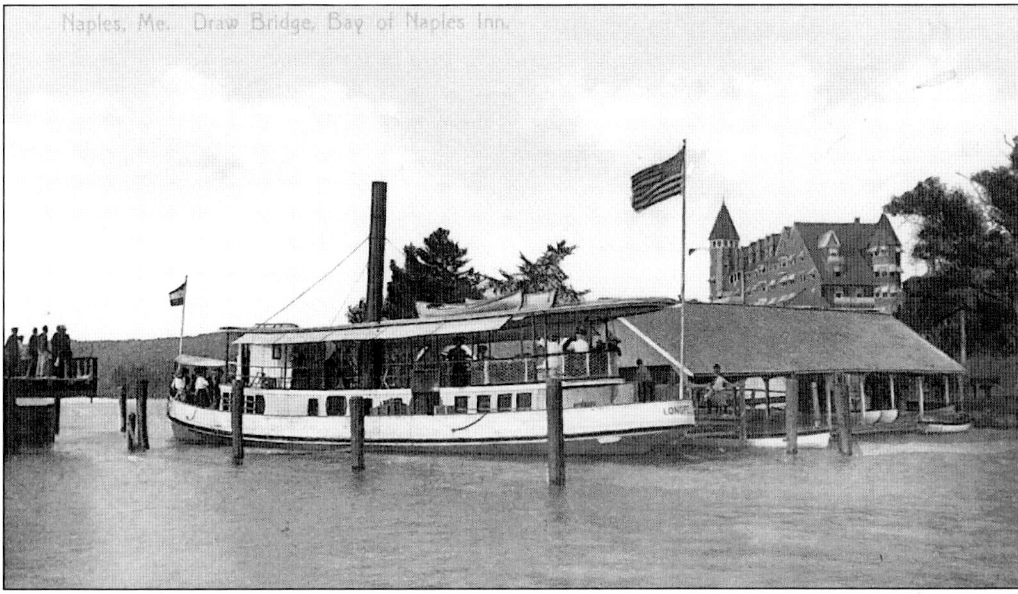

THE *LONGFELLOW*, C. 1905. The *Longfellow*, formerly the *Harriet*, was purchased in Portland c. 1880 and remodeled by Hon. Charles E. Gibbs of Bridgton, who owned and operated the line. Here, the *Longfellow* sails up Chute River from Brandy Pond and is about to pass through the swing bridge at the Causeway to dock at the Naples Hotel landing. The *Longfellow*, along with the *Hawthorne*, the *Minnehaha*, and the *Hiawatha*, were the first of the all-screw propeller boats to replace the side-wheelers.

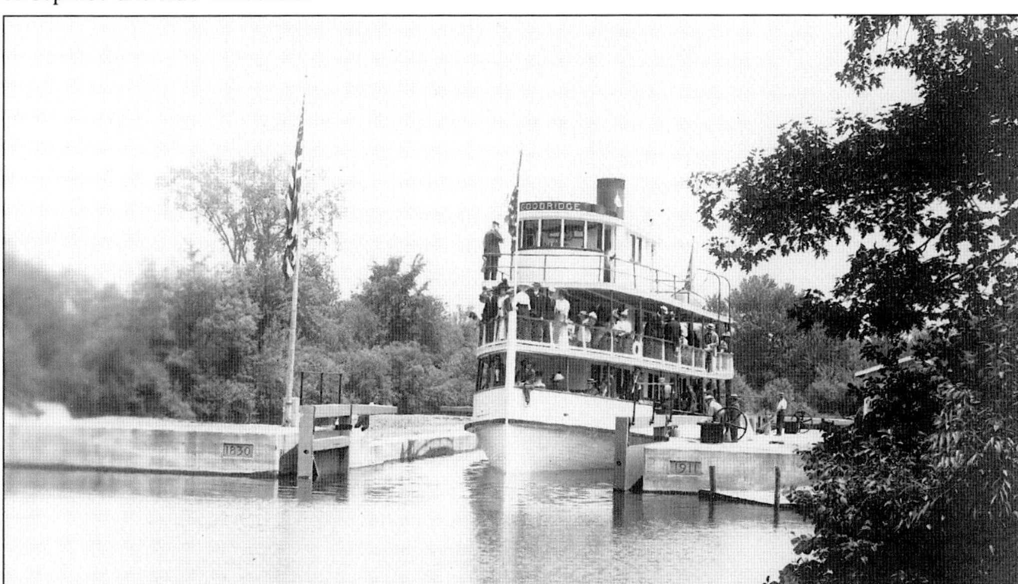

THE *GOODRIDGE* C. 1925. The *Goodridge*, named after Benjamin Goodridge, one of Naples's earliest settlers, departs from Songo Locks to continue up the Songo River to Naples. Capt. Charles L. Goodridge, Benjamin Goodridge's grandson, purchased the line shortly after Gibbs sold it to the S.D. Warren Company in 1892 and renamed it the Sebago Lake, Songo River, and Bay of Naples Line. The *Goodridge* was built at the Bath Iron Works and could carry up to 600 passengers.

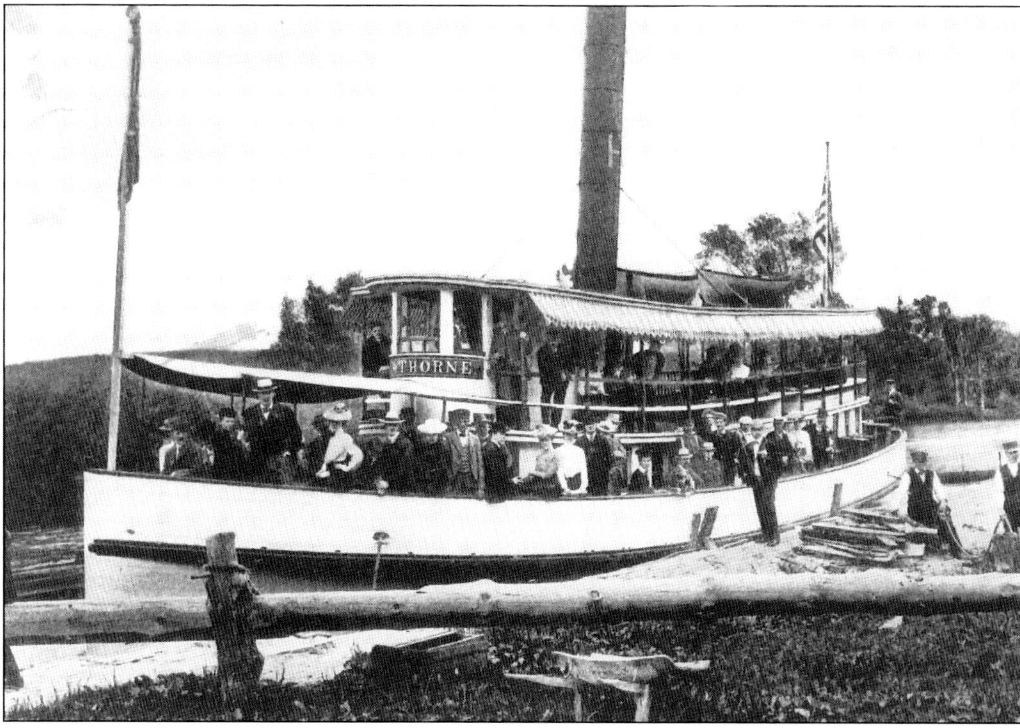

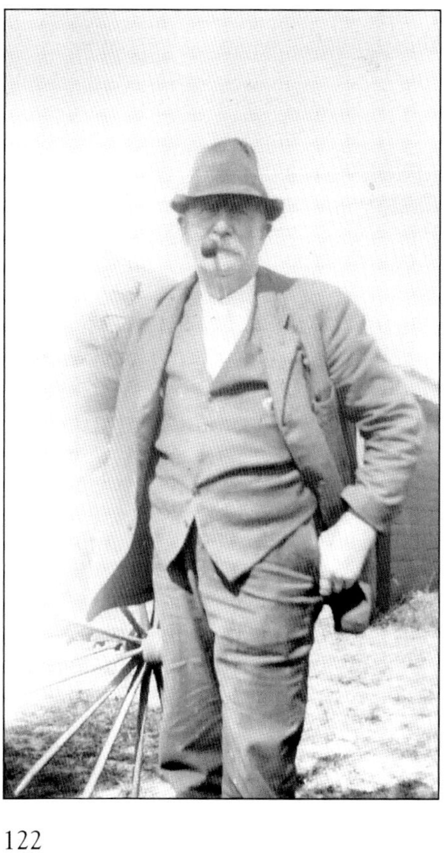

THE *HAWTHORNE*. In 1892, the *Hawthorne* was the only steamer still making the run from Sebago Lake Station to Harrison when the S.D. Warren Company purchased the line. Here it is entering the original Songo Locks—the only extant locks of the 28 locks, each about 10 feet high and slightly wider since the canal boats were 10 feet wide, that operated during the canal days—to be raised 5 feet to the upper level (272 feet above sea level) of the Songo River. S.D. Warren rebuilt and widened the lock in 1911. The *Longfellow* and the *Hawthorne* reflect the intimate connection these two literary giants and classmates at Bowdoin had to the Sebago Lake region.

CAPT. MEL BRACKETT, C. 1925. Capt. Mel Brackett, along with Lewis Knight, virtually dominated the freight traffic from Sebago Lake Station to Long Lake from 1913 to 1922 when they tied their freighter *Roosevelt* to the bank on Chute River in front of Knight's sawmill and later dismantled it. It is noteworthy that Minnie Brackett, a licensed steam engineer, kept the boiler of her husband's boat well stoked on each trip. Passenger service continued until the mysterious destruction by fire of the *Bay of Naples* in 1931 and the *Goodridge*, then owned by H.W. Robinson, the following year.

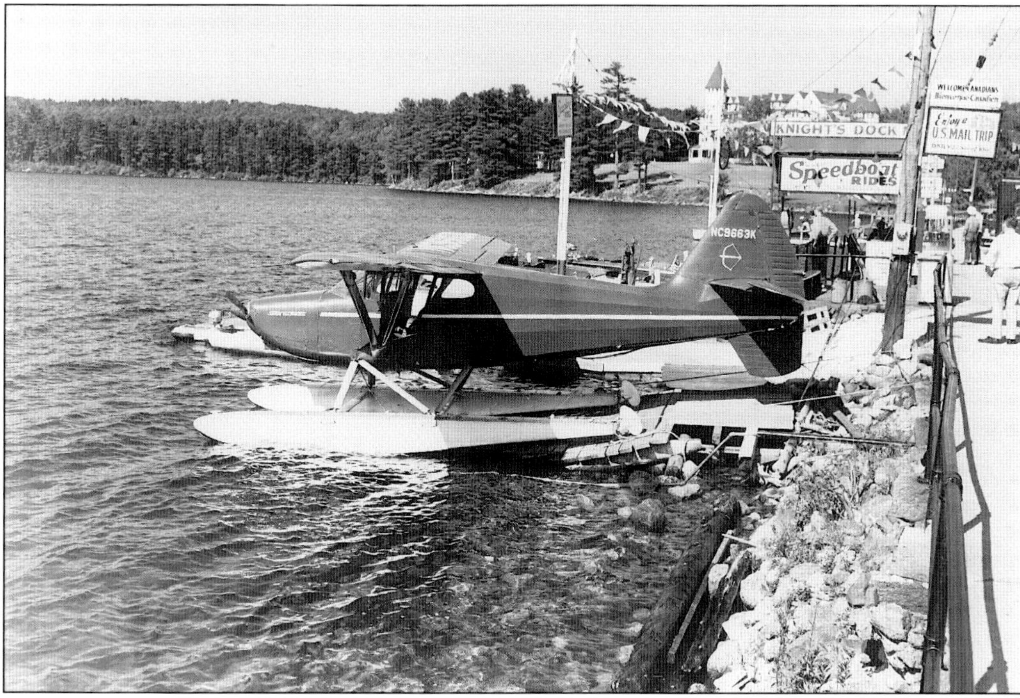

The Causeway, c. 1940. The Causeway bristles with activity from one end to the other from early morning until late at night. Young and old, summering or touring the Sebago Lake region flocked to Naples for a game of golf, a scenic seaplane ride, a fast twirl around lower Long Lake in a speedboat, a slow ride up the lake in the mail boat, and very likely a stop at Howard Johnson's. The old *Songo*, the last of Goodridge's "white fleet," had been renovated and was making excursions from Sebago Lake Station to Naples, and the Bay of Naples Hotel (Inn) was still prospering. World War II had yet to touch most Americans.

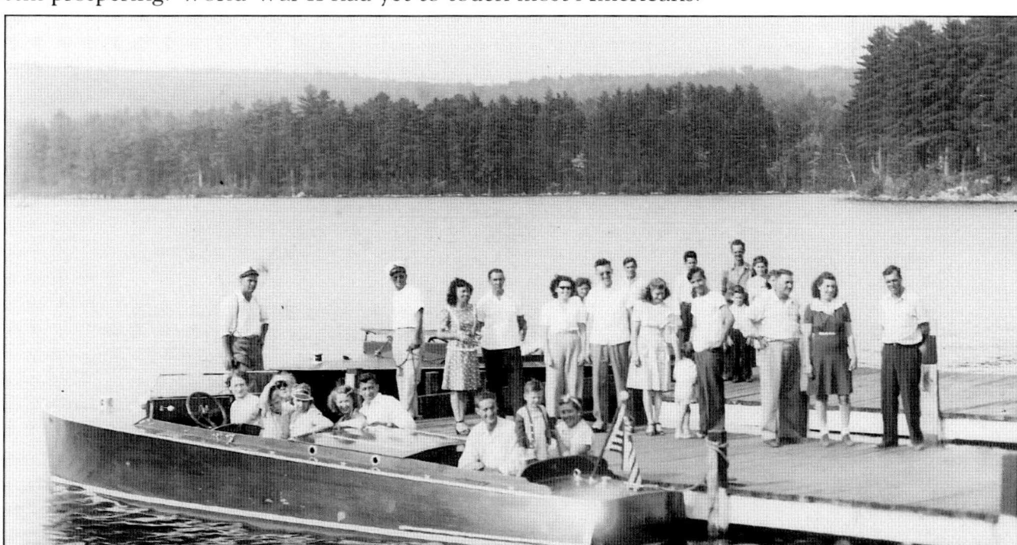

Don Paul's Famous Speedboat Rides, c. 1940. Don Paul's Famous Speedboat Rides on Long Lake were popular night and day during the summer months.

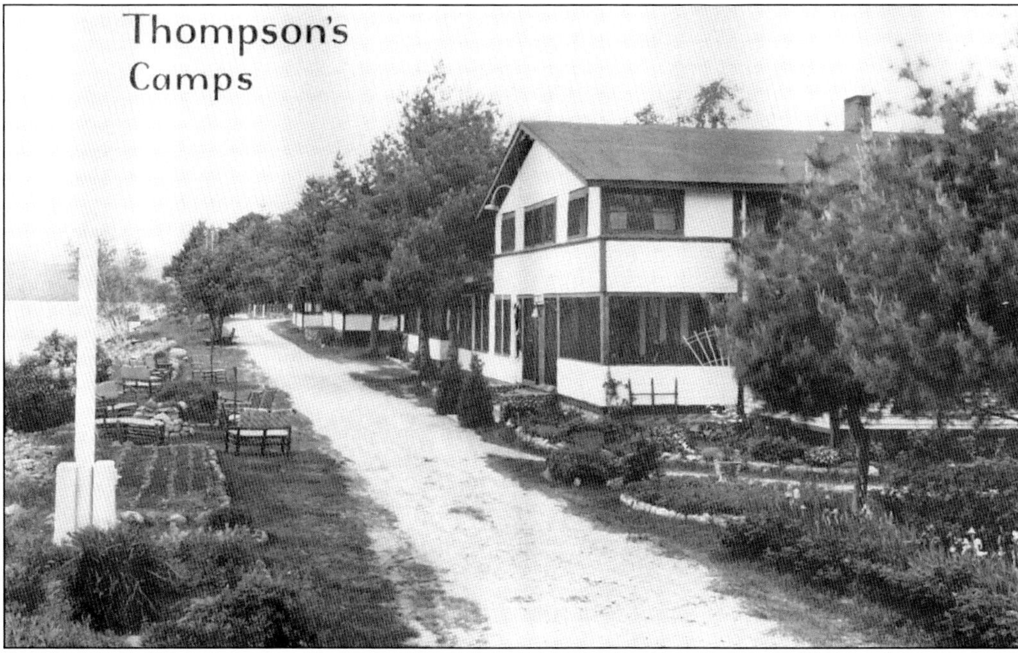

THOMPSON'S CAMPS, C. 1930. Thompson's Camps, located on the north end of Sebago Lake near the mouth of the Songo River, opened *c.* 1910. Roland Thompson, a wealthy shoe manufacturer, opened it as a rough camp to accommodate fishermen—mostly his friends—eager to catch some of Sebago Lake's famous landlocked salmon and savor superb food that he and his wife, Gertrude, served. By the early 1920s, he had purchased the entire point and was adding a number of more attractive camps along the shoreline. The camps opened on April 1, the opening day of the fishing season, or as soon as the ice was out, and they closed on October 1.

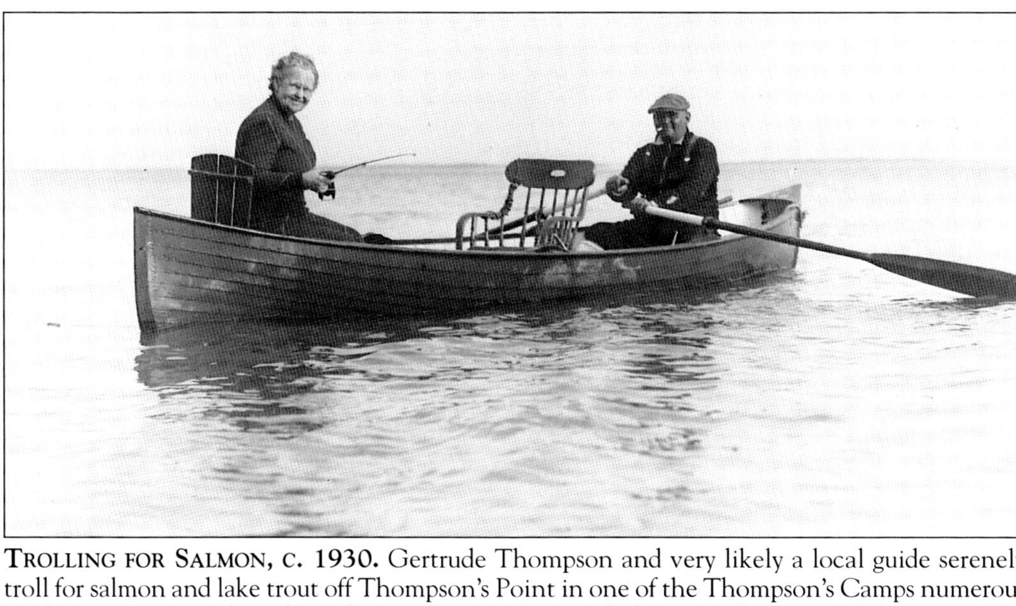

TROLLING FOR SALMON, C. 1930. Gertrude Thompson and very likely a local guide serenely troll for salmon and lake trout off Thompson's Point in one of the Thompson's Camps numerous rowboats at a time when the only sounds were the gentle lapping of waves and the occasional cry of a loon.

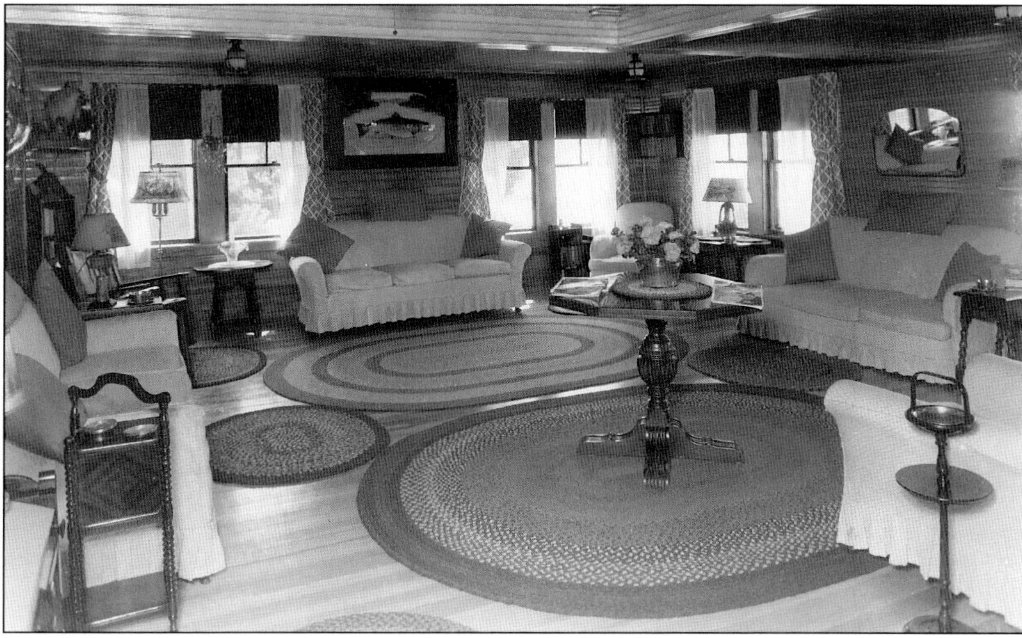

THE MAIN LODGE, C. 1950. The Main Lodge at Thompson's Camps featured this commodious lounge, a large dining room that seated over 100, and rooms for guests. In addition, there were 13 cabins and a variety of recreational facilities. In the early years most supplies were delivered by vendors in boats, and guests arrived either by horse and carriage or steamboat. Enormous quantities of ice, harvested from the lake and Muddy River, were stored in the icehouse each winter before the advent of the refrigerator. Roland Thompson died in 1931 and Gertrude Thompson, well-known for her enormous stein collection, continued to operate the camps until 1961 when they were sold to private owners.

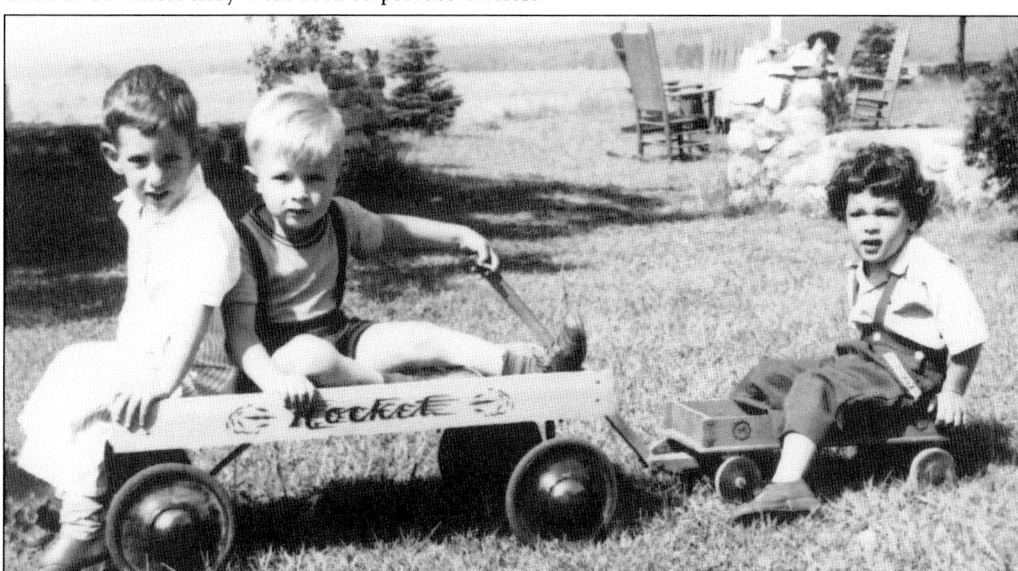

CHILDREN AT THOMPSON'S CAMPS, AUGUST 1945. Bill Weeks, center, of Portland, whose great-aunt operated the camps, enjoys the camaraderie of the children of summer guests.

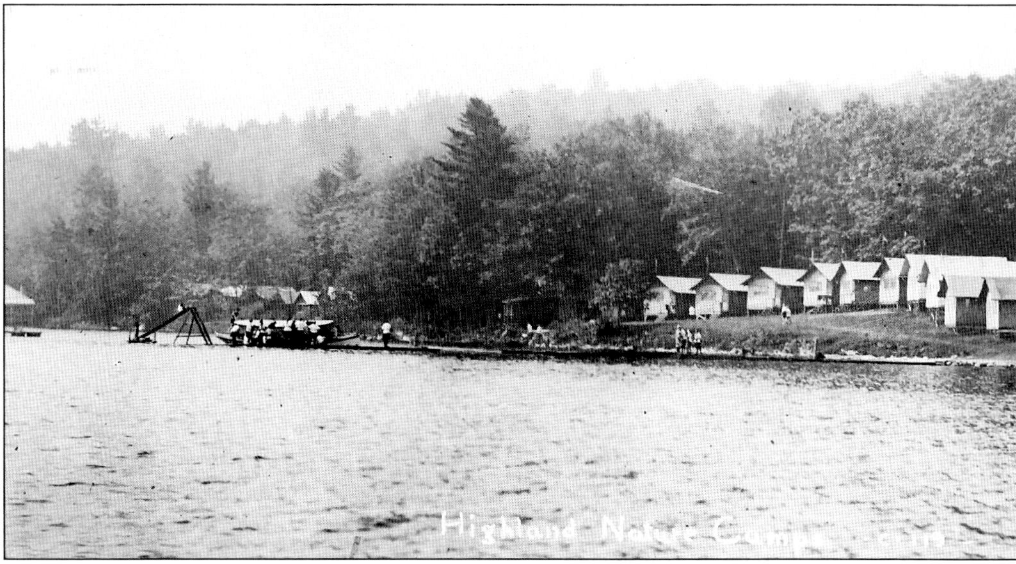

THE HIGHLAND NATURE CAMPS, C. 1935. The Highland Nature Camps, located in South Naples at the mouth of Muddy River on Sebago Lake, was the first girls' camp in Naples. It was founded by Dr. Eugene Lehman, America's first Rhodes scholar, who purchased the land c. 1913 from Lewis Knight. Lehman, who studied at Yale, Columbia, and the University of Berlin, was teaching at Yale when he arrived in winter by train at Mattocks, and hence to Naples via the mail stage, to look over the property. He was a founder and first president of the Maine Camp Director's Association. In the 1940s, the Highland Nature Camps became Camp Mataponi.

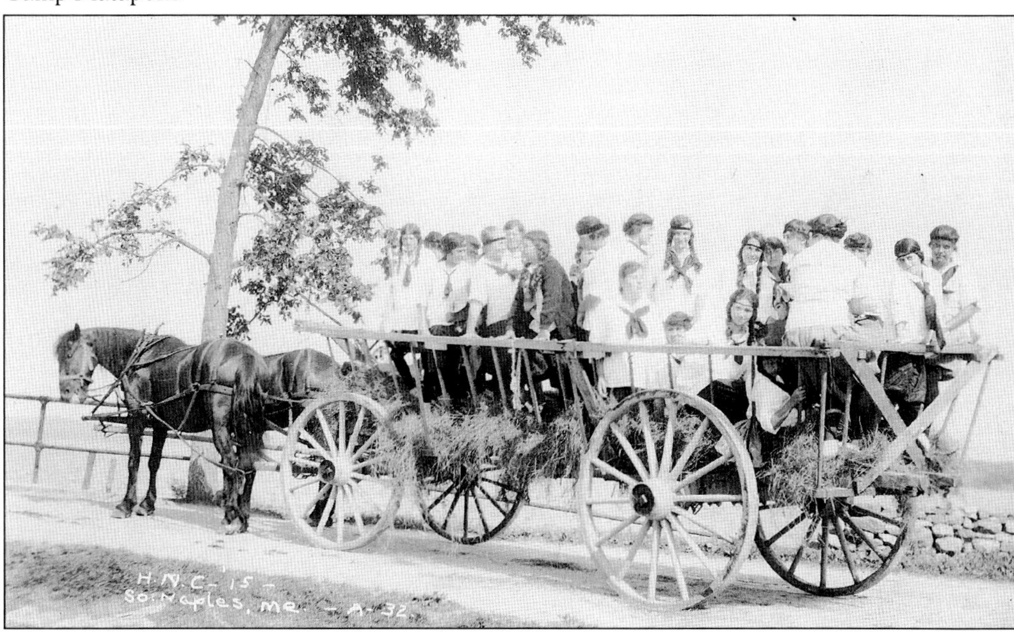

HIGHLAND NATURE CAMP GIRLS, C. 1925. The girls enjoy an outing in Harold Dearborn's horse-drawn hay wagon. In the early years, campers arrived by train at Sebago Lake Station and were conveyed up the lake, first in Lewis and Brackett's freight boat, the *Columbia*, and later by steamboat.

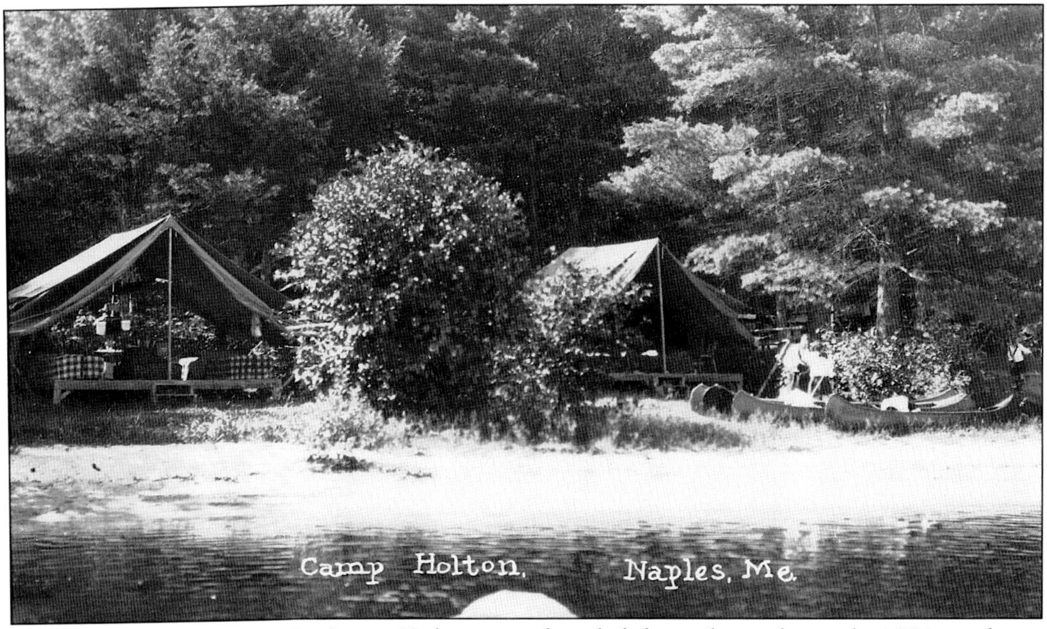

CAMP HOLTON, C. 1925. Camp Holton was founded for girls in the early 1920s and was located on Long Lake at Mast Cove. Like other boys' and girls' camps founded early in the 20th century in the area, campers and staff members slept in tents erected on wooden platforms. Canoeing was one of many activities featured, and each cabin group enjoyed at least one overnight or longer canoe trip along the scenic, extensive waterways. The sparsely populated shorelines and uninhabited islands, especially on Sebago Lake, were ideally suited for camping overnight.

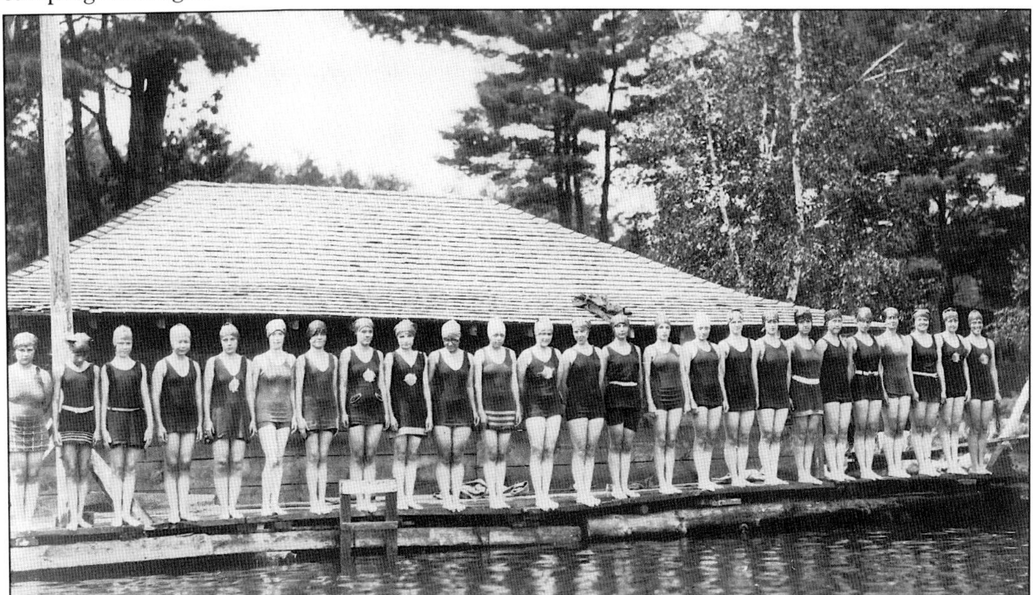

SENIOR CAMP HOLTON GIRLS, C. 1928. These girls lined up on the dock on the edge of Long Lake prepare to dive in unison into the swimming area. Swimming, diving, and lifesaving classes and all forms of competitive water sports were conducted here.

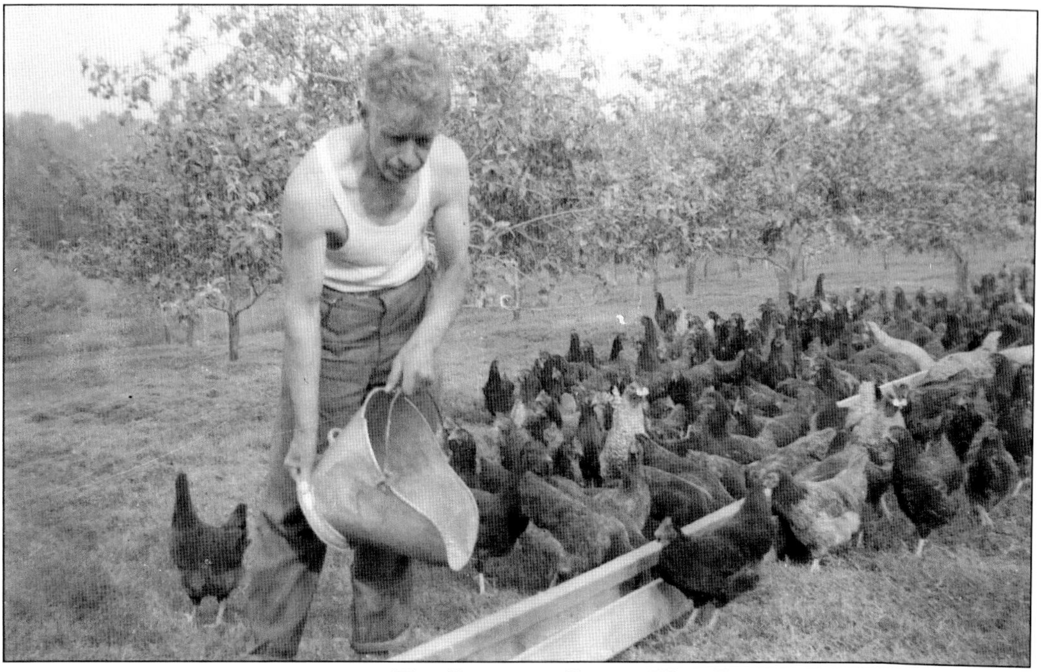

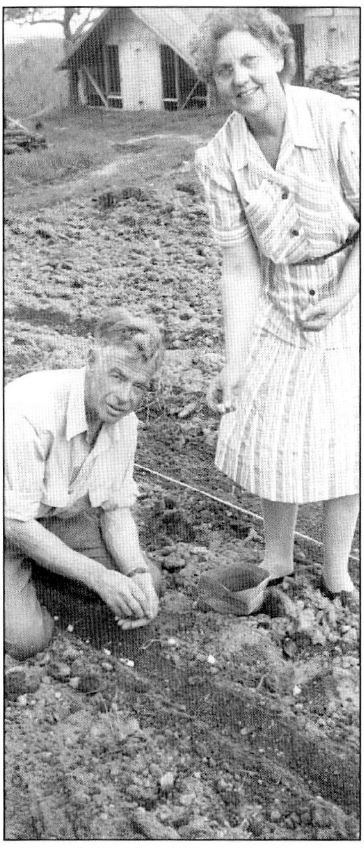

The Bucks of Rocky Hill Farm, c. 1939. At a time when agriculture in Naples and throughout Maine was on the rapid decline and many farms had been abandoned for decades, Dr. Charles Howe Buck and his wife, Eunice, made the momentous decision in 1929 to leave their home in Hartford, Connecticut. Buck, who had been practicing osteopathic medicine, chose to move with the two younger Buck children (the two older ones were in college) to the old Wight farm, which he had purchased at Kimballs Corner. Buck had earned a degree in osteopathy in 1924, graduated from Yale in 1929, married Eunice Barstow, and become a banker. For a few years after arriving in Naples, he combined farming with practicing medicine in Bridgton. However, after his office burned, he decided to devote full time to his woodland, one of the first in Maine to receive the title "tree farm," his apple orchard, and his 25,000 laying hens. In addition to being a mother and farmer's helper, Eunice Buck devoted much time and energy to various community services. For many years she was an itinerant pastor in churches in Sebago, Baldwin, and Limington. She was the founder and leader of the Sebago boys' 4-H Club and was active in the PTA, the Naples Library Association, and the Community Association in Naples. In 1958, she was named Maine State Outstanding Homemaker of the Year. From 1933 to 1936, a room at Rocky Hill Farm served as a classroom for their children Don and Mary and three other youngsters. The Bucks, like innumerable other folks who lived out their lives and made contributions to the four towns, deserve to be remembered.